EDUCATING
EMOTIONALLY DISTURBED CHILDREN

PSYCHOLOGY AND HUMAN DEVELOPMENT
IN EDUCATION
Nicholas Hobbs, *Consulting Editor*

Frandsen · Educational Psychology
Ginott · Group Psychotherapy with Children
Haring and Phillips · Educating Emotionally Disturbed Children
Van Dalen · Understanding Educational Research

EDUCATING EMOTIONALLY DISTURBED CHILDREN

NORRIS G. HARING, Ed.D., *1923-*

Associate Professor of Pediatrics and Education
Education Director, Children's Rehabilitation Unit
University of Kansas Medical Center

Former Associate Professor, University of Maryland
Former Coordinator, Services for Exceptional Children
Arlington, Virginia, and Consultant to Private Schools
Washington, D.C., Metropolitan Area

E. LAKIN PHILLIPS, Ph.D., *1915-*

Chief Psychologist, National Orthopedic and
Rehabilitation Hospital, Arlington, Virginia

Consultant to Public and Private Schools
Washington, D.C., Metropolitan Area
Co-Director, Psychological Testing Center
Washington, D.C., and Falls Church, Virginia

McGRAW-HILL BOOK COMPANY, INC.   1962

New York   San Francisco   Toronto   London

26420

EDUCATING EMOTIONALLY DISTURBED CHILDREN

FOREWORD

Probably no one group of exceptional children requires more understanding and greater diagnostic and educational skill by professional people than does that group of children with whom this volume is concerned. These are children who often present good mental ability, but who are unable to integrate their intellectual efforts and direct them toward realistic educational goals. These are children who have no visible pronounced motor disability, but whose neuromuscular coordination is so poor as to significantly interfere with learning. These are children who can see, but whose ability to translate what they perceive into meaningful action is impaired—who can hear, but whose ability to translate what they hear into acceptable social behavior is minimal. These are children who often would be welcomed into a social group, but whose behavior is so unpredictable, erratic, and uncontrolled that they are rejected by their peers. These are young people whom some call hyperactive, emotionally disturbed children.

The prevalence of these children in the American school is not known. Indeed it may never be known, for it appears that socioeconomic and cultural factors varying from community to

38237

community may be important in its incidence. On the other hand, as psychological and medical diagnostic techniques have developed, as knowledge of human growth and development has accrued, and as this knowledge has become a vital part of the profession of education, these children frequently have become identified as youngsters who for undetermined reasons fail to qualify as citizens in a child society.

Whether they have a central nervous system disorder or not is often not possible to determine. Yet whether or not their behavior is organically or functionally determined is of little practical concern to the teacher who must plan educationally for these children for long periods of time each school year. Teachers simply realize that something more than that which they can provide in the typical classroom is required to best meet the needs of these children.

For thirty years a small group of psychologists and educators have been concerned with educational and social planning for this group of children whose behavior appears to contradict that known to be typical of normative growth and development trends. Alfred A. Strauss, Heinz Werner, Newell Kephart, Laura Lehtinen, and others, who early worked together at the Wayne County Training School, comprise one important group of investigators—indeed, the first who attempted to implement theory and some experimentation with an educational program. Virginia Axline, Clark Moustakas, Daniel Prescott, Fritz Redl, Samuel Slavson, and many others have written extensively on somewhat similar problems. Axline and Redl, in particular, have attempted to translate theoretical positions into practical therapeutic experiments. Yet most of the writing which has been done in these thirty years has been theoretical and philosophical. Little definitive research has been done. Thus, while many school systems have moved to meet the problem of the hyperactive child, little is available to serve as a guide to courageous teachers and school administrators. This volume will help to fill this vacuum. It offers data on the problem of what happens to hyperactive, emotionally disturbed children in an ongoing public school program when they are provided with adequate diagnostic personnel and an educational program based on a realistic learning theory. When this study is placed alongside other studies which are presently under way and still others which are yet to be conceived and completed, the profession will have important guides basic to the realistic educational planning for yet another group of exceptional children.

William M. Cruickshank

PREFACE

This book is the result of several years of collaboration between us on a number of problems presented by emotionally
disturbed and other exceptional children in the public school
setting. Most of the preliminary work was done with individual
children who, although in psychotherapy, also needed help
with their educational problems in their normal school setting.
It became increasingly evident to us in the course of this work
that psychotherapy alone was of little value to the children's
educational progress; in fact, at times it could be an actual
hindrance! A good deal more than psychotherapy could offer
was called for, in the form of a more active program of work
with parents and school authorities.

In addition to the need for working directly with the school,
the parents of emotionally disturbed children revealed a need
for direct help with a number of problems presented them
by the children. These problems had to do with parental attitudes and actions related to the children's schoolwork, and
with equally important attitudes toward the children's household and family responsibilities. How the parents were to meet
temper and other emotional outbursts and how they were to

think and act in practical ways vis-à-vis the general behavioral disturbances presented by the children were also important problems on which help was needed.

The willingness to work directly with parents and teachers (who comprise the child's most significant adult relationships) forced us out of the older mode of "giving therapy to the child" and offered us a refreshing opportunity to weld a more functional and productive approach to all the educational and psychological problems the child presents. While we felt increasingly sure of the validity of our approach, it is often difficult to convince school personnel of the advisability of changing some of their theories and practices. We therefore began by asking ourselves and school personnel: "What can the school do, and what can the school help the parents to do, that will effectively aid the emotionally disturbed child's social, emotional and educational development?" Raising this type of very practical question helped us skirt some of the hoary preconceptions of school personnel and clinicians alike and got us off to a more solid start in providing answers which we felt to be workable.

Too often, we observe, the school has forced the problem of the emotionally disturbed child back on the parents and said: "We can't do anything; what are *you* going to do?" Perhaps most parents would be willing to do more to help if they had good guidance. Past methods of putting the whole responsibility of helping the emotionally disturbed child on the parents have netted poor returns. Where could the parents turn for help? To child guidance centers and residential institutions? Perhaps. But here they were faced with long waiting lists, a lack of concern for the child's educational welfare, a possible removal of the child from the home, and a lack of concerted effort at helping parents *and* school to unite in a solution to the problem.

What we are emphasizing in a broad way in this book has already been the practice to some extent in the education of other types of exceptional persons. Parents have formed groups for self-help and for educational guidance in the instances of the mentally retarded, the physically handicapped, the deaf, and the blind. Why could the school not do as much, at least in educational ways, to help the emotionally disturbed? We felt this to be a reasonable question, and we set out to see if it could be answered, at least in part, in ways that would be productive. We have not been unmindful of programs for the emotionally disturbed in some of the large city school systems, but we have felt that the clarity of purpose and procedure needed were not sufficiently evident in these programs.

We enlisted the help of parents and found them to be unusually cooperative. Their attitudes were shown in their willingness to report for group discussions, to keep in touch with the progress of the child in his daily classroom work, and to carry out suggestions for handling behavior problems offered during the parent discussion-group meetings. Since much of the success of our program depended upon the development of *continuity* between home and school attitudes and practices, it was essential that the parents participate fully in the program. This practice is distinctly different from practices in child treatment as observed in guidance clinics and among clinicians—psychologists, social workers, psychiatrists—in private practice. As one can tell from reading the protocols in Appendix A, our constant attention to educational progress was another step in a formerly neglected direction.

One of the most encouraging features of the program's success was its economy of operation and what this economy shows to be possible. Thus we came to believe sincerely that the average well-prepared teacher can be taught to handle small groups of emotionally disturbed children in the typical school setting. It becomes unnecessary to separate the child from his home environment (in the overwhelming number of instances) in order to help him with his emotional problems, just as it is unnecessary to neglect his educational progress in order to bring relief to his personality difficulties. Moreover, although some special attention and forbearance is needed, the over-all approach developed and utilized in this study lends itself to other special applications and to application in the regular classroom of more nearly normal children, and can be learned by interested and capable teachers.

This study serves as a small example of what we believe any well-intended school system can accomplish if it is willing to devote a reasonable amount of time, caution, and determination to the problem. In a day and age when 5 to 10 per cent of the general population is considered seriously enough emotionally disturbed to require special help (prolonged treatment, hospitalization), an intelligent approach to the problem in the natural home-school setting of the child seems mandatory.

ACKNOWLEDGMENTS

We would have been unable even to start on this venture without the cooperation and continuing support of many others. Fortunately, we were able to enlist the aid of a patient and energetic principal, Mrs. May Van Meter, in whose school the two special classes for emotionally disturbed children were placed, and whose counsel and support benefited us greatly throughout the period of time we were directly associated with the program. Our first two classroom teachers, Mrs. Jeannette Wright and Mrs. Kathryn Simpson (nee Miller), devoted much extra time and interest, especially in the early days of the project, to the understanding of the special problems they met daily. Their perseverance and skill made the program an initial success. Beginning with the second year of the project, two new teachers, Miss Rebecca Mauzy and Mr. William Wysong, came into the study to take the places of Mrs. Wright and Mrs. Simpson. The second pair of teachers carried on well with the work already started, and have stated their own views and practices in Appendix B of this report. Mrs. Wretha Peterson offered thoughtful critical evaluations of many of the ideas expressed herein. Drs. John William Asher and John de Jung served as research consultants on the study and gave valuable assistance on the research design and analysis of data. We are greatly indebted to Dr. William M. Cruickshank, who read the manuscript and offered theoretical support to much of our undertaking, by indirection, through his own research and writings. Dr. Herbert Goldstein also gave us a helpful review of the manuscript. We are indebted to the many members of the Arlington School System professional staff—visiting teachers, psychologists, principals, supervisors, and others—who ferreted out and referred to us the children making up the classes in this study, and who continued to support the program as an important part of the school's interest in developing better educational and psychological services. And last, but by no means least, our wives, Dorothy Haring and Gloria Phillips, who supported our work and helped us find the time and energy to produce this account of our undertaking.

Norris G. Haring
E. Lakin Phillips

CONTENTS

CONTENTS

1

INTRODUCTION

The education of children is a major responsibility of society. Indeed, a democratic society tries to educate all persons to the fullest extent. Yet society often falls far short of the ideal expressed in this laudable enough purpose. There are still large groups of people in our society who are certainly not educated to the fullest extent. Among these groups are the emotionally disturbed children about whom interest is now rapidly developing and expanding.

Many questions about these children come to the minds of teachers and other interested adults. "Who are these children? Are there some in *my* classroom? What can one do for them? How educable are they? What are their strengths and weaknesses? What is the best way to develop an educational environment for them?"

Emotionally disturbed children are children who have more or less serious problems with other people—peers and authority figures such as parents and teachers—or who are unhappy and unable to apply themselves in a manner commensurate with their abilities and interests. In general, one might say that an emotionally disturbed child is one who has a sizable "failure pattern" in living instead of a "success pattern."

Since emotional disturbance is no respecter of persons, this state of affairs may affect any child—an average child with low or high intelligence as well as a child with another type of handicap than emotional disturbance. The primary concerns in this volume are with emotional disturbances as a general category and with the education of these emotionally disturbed children regardless of other problems.

The thesis advanced here is that an emotionally disturbed child needs a particular kind of environment in which to recover normality. He needs a selected and regulated set of experiences in order to assume or reassume responsibilities, in order to learn more effectively, and in order to move toward and maintain general normality in living. Various efforts have been extended in the past to help the emotionally disturbed child return to a more satisfactory social and emotional state, but none of them have stressed the kind of solution proposed in this volume.

PAST AND PRESENT
RESOURCES AND THEIR GUIDING CONCEPTS

Child Guidance Clinics

The child guidance movement began in this country shortly after the turn of the century. In the five decades since their origin, hundreds of these clinics have developed throughout the United States [1, 3, 5, 6–8, 15, 19, 21, 22, 24–27, 43, 44, 50]. Almost every city or county of an appreciable size has some kind of mental health or child guidance clinic. In many metropolitan areas several such clinics exist. Also, there are adult mental hygiene clinics and family service organizations which administer help to parents and family members—help that may often lessen the plight of the emotionally disturbed child.

The general viewpoint of child guidance workers as to the nature of the child's emotional disturbances may be summarized in the words of Lippman:

Children in emotional conflict have been traumatized by their parents and by other adults whom the children have grown to distrust. They come to the therapist from homes filled with tension, hostility, misunderstanding, and confusion; from parents filled with guilt and self-blame for having failed in spite of great efforts to be good parents. [19, p. vi]

Lippman says further:

A child suffers emotional conflict whenever anything interferes with the satisfaction of his instinctual drives and his frustrations produce a state of tension [19, p. 3].

Child guidance clinics seek to bring emotional help to children, as individuals or in groups, through what is generally called *play therapy*. In this type of therapy the child "plays out" or exhibits his emotional problems, thus gaining emotional relief from the strain of not being able to understand or cope with his difficulties. Generally speaking, individual treatment of children, whether in child guidance clinics or in the private offices of psychologists, psychiatrists, and social workers, tends to take a fairly long period of time, ranging from a few months to several years. While many children are helped by the use of this resource, the child guidance clinic in most communities does not work closely with school personnel or with the classroom teacher, and little effort is extended toward helping the child with his *educational* problems. With child guidance center methods of treating children, the integral relationships between all facets of the child's life may not get the precise help needed.

Psychologists and educators today are placing more emphasis on helping the child in the context of his daily life, in his school environment, in relation to his learning tasks. Less emphasis is put on the negative aspects of the child's family life and his development and more emphasis on what to do about it, on what is good and wholesome and constructive in the child's make-up in his relations at home and elsewhere. A search is kept up for ways to intervene constructively.

Residential Treatment Centers

Residential treatment centers are of more recent origin than guidance clinics, and for the most part they are intended for the most seriously disturbed child. Not many of these centers exist—there are probably only a few dozen of them in the entire United States—because of expense of operation. Children who go to such centers are generally those who, it is felt, cannot live in their own homes for a variety of reasons and who are too disturbed to adjust to a typical school setting. In all the residential centers in the country there are probably only a few thousand children at most.

The greatest handicap of the residential center is its enormous expense. A few years ago Reid and Gagan's *Residential Treatment of Emotionally Disturbed Children* [46], a comprehensive publication on residential treatment centers, indicated costs to be from $4,000 to $5,000 per year per child. Not only is this cost so high that very few can afford it, but in addition the actual methods of the residential treatment center tend to stress permissiveness in child care and in education to the point that such practices would be highly impractical for the average school system to follow.

The theory of the child's difficulties, as indicated by the statement of Lippman above, stresses the *damage done to the child* by his interpersonal environment and emphasizes the need for "acting out," "releasing," and "uncovering" the emotional strains and experiences underlying the symptom complex that is observed in these children. As part of this permissive attitude, there is little emphasis on educational achievement. Children often may or may not go to school (or classes) as they themselves see fit; no ordering or arranging of the daily schedule is imposed upon the children, nor is any such ordering considered therapeutically beneficial. The total emphasis is in the opposite direction: almost total permissiveness.

Sometimes special schools exist which do emphasize education, but even in these schools permissiveness is the guide; structure and order and even any kind of usual expectation of them are underplayed or ignored, as these matters would be judged by the standards of most schools and by the standards of this volume.

Books such as those by Bettelheim [3], Devereux [6], Anna Freud [7, 8], Redl and associates [43–45], and others indicate the extent to which a permissive policy is followed. A recent book by the English author Neill, *Summerhill: A Radical Approach to Child Rearing* [24], gives an even fuller account of the general philosophy of allowing the child to do pretty much as he pleases in the educational setting and assumes that "in time" he will voluntarily want to take to learning and will develop self-motivation and self-direction.

While children may sometimes profit from the permissive setting in play therapy and in residential centers, this is far from demonstrating the basis for a permissive philosophy and practice as a total program for schools and agencies to adopt; and one of the greatest weaknesses of the work of both child guidance clinics and residential centers is the absence of control groups against which to compare results from these places. (Control groups might be composed of children who underwent contrasting therapies or children with disturbances who underwent no therapy at all for a given period of time.)

Thus, while most publications in the child guidance field and on child psychotherapy do foster a permissive philosophy, this is no guarantee of correctness, and it is certainly no reason to desist from developing new or different approaches. The situation today in our schools and in the homes of children with emotional difficulties is so demanding of better results from treatment that educators and psychologists cannot afford to assume that our present methods and techniques are even mildly adequate.

Guidance Services in the Schools

Guidance services in the schools exist for normal as well as for emotionally disturbed children. Most large school systems have some kind of psychological services where interviewing, testing, and parent consultation are carried on. Generally speaking, however, these services are more often diagnostic than therapeutic; they rarely perform psychotherapy or extended counseling or remedial services for the emotionally disturbed child.

In the junior and senior high schools, counseling and guidance departments may offer limited educational and vocational consultation along with psychological testing. This service reaches an extremely high percentage of the student body, but is not an intensive or individually directed program applicable to the emotionally disturbed child with more than passing complaints. As a screening device, however, the usual guidance and psychological facilities are excellent, and they can be relied upon to ferret out the more seriously disturbed child so that he can get the attention he needs.

Other services, such as are found in speech departments and in speech services for children with speech and hearing defects, are usually available to some extent to the emotionally disturbed child, especially where the child may have a speech disorder. Yet these services, like the other guidance services, are operated mainly on a screening or temporary-service basis, and do not extend into long-range educational programs for the emotionally disturbed child.

While all of these large categories of services to emotionally disturbed children are helpful, none of them—perhaps not all of them combined—do more than a small part of the total job required [1–3, 5–8, 15, 18–27, 41–45, 47, 48, 50, 51]. There is a growing realization that existing services leave much to be desired, and the great neglect heretofore of the emotionally disturbed child's educational needs is becoming more clearly perceived [2, 4, 9, 11–14, 16–18, 23, 29–42, 51].

Why is this true? Why has so major and so obvious a requirement as education been neglected? It has apparently not been neglected in helping brain-damaged, orthopedically handicapped, or slow-learning and mentally retarded children. But it is uncommon to find a both educationally and emotionally constructive environment for the emotionally disturbed child; very few plans for operating such programs exist in the public schools, and those in private settings are very expensive [3, 7, 8, 25–27, 43–46, 50]. Few or no models of how such a program could be carried on are available for study, and there exist few or no programs for training teachers to cope with the problems of the emotionally disturbed child [33].

POPULAR CONCEPTS REGARDING EMOTIONALLY DISTURBED CHILDREN

Parents naturally become concerned when they fully realize they have a seriously disturbed child. But when they turn to others for help, what do they find? Since understanding of the needs of the emotionally disturbed child is not fully developed, compared to the understanding of the conditions of other types of handicapped children, parents do not find available resources for helping their disturbed children. Of course, they do hear opinions, some of which may be summarized in the following list:

1. The child is just exaggerating his complaints or feelings; give him a few swats and send him on his way.

2. The child was "born that way" and will never be any different, no matter what you do for him. Don't waste your time, therefore, trying all kinds of efforts to help him; just admit he is a lost cause and go on from there.

3. If he won't adjust to home and family life, then put him in an institution. They know better how to care for such children, and they will make him behave better than you can.

4. Severe emotional disorder is due to a poorly understood

hereditary condition. Perhaps drugs will help, but little can be done in the child's environment that will help him.

5. The child has been rejected, repudiated, and unwanted from birth or shortly after, and feels this and is understandably resentful and withdrawn as a result.

6. The child is just going through a phase in development; he will "grow out of it" if you will just give him time.

As with most popular concepts dealing with complexities, there is a little bit of truth in each of these but not enough truth to form a solid basis for treatment and for educational programs. What is called for is not an "end-all, be-all" explanation, searched for because of the feeling that if one does just the *right* thing and avoids just the *wrong* thing all will be well. What is called for is, rather, a broad-based, scientific, concerted, consistent type of program designed to cover as many facets of the child's life as possible. This appears to be the case even when a program emanates primarily from the school environment and has its main applicability in the school setting, as the program presented here does.

RATIONALE FOR THE PRESENT APPROACH

Criticism is most useful when it can point to reasonable alternatives, and this rule is the basis of the advice to school personnel in this book: Find out what is wrong in a child's behavior and achievement, then set out to correct the ills. Go beyond criticizing what is wrong with previous methods; offer alternatives that can solve the common problems better than did previously used methods.

But what, beyond this basic general advice, is the rationale for the present approach? In a word, it is the central concept of *structure*. This means the setting up of ordered educational and social-emotional experiences within the confines of the school, so that the child's emotional difficulties and related educational problems receive a joint consideration.

Following are some of the meanings given this central con-

cept of structure in this book, stated as changes in general outlook, or general philosophy, that had either to precede or accompany the experiment in educating emotionally disturbed
children which will be discussed:

1. Emphasis was shifted from trying to determine what
caused the disturbance in the first place (etiology) to *what could
be done about something that already existed* to overcome or
ameliorate the situation. This point of view led to considering
and discussing how conditions could be *controlled* and modified
rather than how they might have arisen from a historical standpoint.

2. An emphasis naturally fell on examining the *present status*
of a child and his family, including their readiness for a program explicitly designed to control and correct the emotional
problems and their correlated educational problems.

3. The school and the teachers were especially prepared to
receive these children into the school, in that a definite purpose
and a reasonably planned but not rigid program were adhered
to. These children were not put in a small class simply with a
vague hope that they would progress if given more individual
attention. The *kind* of attention—a definite program with
specific limits and requirements—was the important thing.

4. Nearly all previous programs, educational and otherwise,
for the treatment of emotionally disturbed children emphasize
a permissive and unstructured (nondirective) social or classroom atmosphere. In the study reported on in this volume, a
structured classroom atmosphere was utilized as a basis for the
study.

5. Broadly speaking, structure refers to the clarification of
the relationship between behavior and its consequences. More
specifically, the term refers to the following procedures: setting
up a definite and dependable classroom routine; giving at first
very specific and limited tasks, which can later be extended and
embellished as the child increases in emotional self-control and
educational application; having the teacher remain consistent
in giving and following through on requirements to the child

until they are reasonably fulfilled; forwarding the impression that the children are at school for work, with recreational activities coming after acceptable work has been completed; having the child repeat or redo careless or incomplete work; fostering a persistent pattern of returning to work at hand after an emotional blowup or after other distractions; fostering in the child a strong and healthy respect for the requirements set by the teacher; and fostering in the teacher an equally strong respect for the child's efforts and achievements. In the structured classroom reported on here, a large number of particular applications of these procedures were made—applications about which this entire book is concerned.

6. A permissive attitude characterized by "I'll do the work if I feel like it" was not accepted.[1] In time, the children began to respect the firmness and clarity of requirements; they learned that the routine was secure and dependable and that it was fair and reasonable.

7. A distinct emphasis was put on reasonable effort and achievement. No attempt was made to separate the child's emotional condition from his social relations or from his achievement. A human being gains in mental health and stability and self-respect by doing the jobs he has to do; conversely, not to meet his daily obligations results in loss of respect for self and job and in a generally deteriorated emotional condition.

8. The main hypothesis advanced in this study was that children suffer from emotional disturbance because they lack order or structure or definiteness in their daily living at home and at school, and that within the confines of the school program, it would be desirable and constructive to rectify past excesses in habits, attitudes, and achievement.

9. The parents were directly involved. Later the reader will

[1] A permissive and unstructured environment may fail to promote order with respect to achievement and with respect to disciplined ways of behaving in a social situation. A permissive environment may promote one kind of order, but not so useful or broad-based a kind as is found under a structured condition.

observe that one criterion for accepting a child into a special class was to require parental cooperation, part of which involved coming to group discussion meetings periodically. This was insisted upon because of the importance attached to continuity and consistency between the school's outlook on the problems and the parental outlook.

10. Program leaders held periodic consultations with the teachers and made visits to the classroom in order to observe the manner in which these ideas were implemented and to serve as a bulwark of advice and help to the classroom teacher in the face of crises that arose.

A large number of other details might be listed, but the reader will grasp these as they unfold in the reading of this report. The precise manner in which the structuring practices were discussed and embellished can be found, in part, by reading the verbatim protocols from the parent group sessions in Appendix A, which make clear, for example, that parent-teacher consistency was a vital and far-reaching factor.

DEVELOPMENT OF THE EXPERIMENT

Professionals as well as laymen tend to offer services to the needy regardless of the known value of the services rendered. Perhaps this is the way our knowledge grows: necessity makes it possible to offer services, and experience over time tells if the services are satisfactory. On the basis of inching along, year by year, trying new methods and techniques, knowledge is gradually built up which is both reliable and serviceable. Yet one limitation of previous methods of treating emotionally disturbed children has been the continuing absence of reasonable evidence that the methods used have been profitable ones.

This is where the effort discussed in this volume comes into bolder relief. Knowledge that every school system has a number of children with social and emotional problems, but not clear and efficient resources for dealing with them, and growing realization that these children needed help that was unattainable either in the school system or in the community led the authors to develop *and test* the program reported upon here.

One major hypothesis was that a lack of structure or order in the daily life of the emotionally disturbed child is the reason for the difficulty and also a reason for the perpetuation of the difficulty, that is, for the fact that the child does not improve with the passage of time. This hypothesis was put to test by developing two classroom atmospheres of a structured nature. Control groups were not subjected to any specific type of treatment but were left to the devices of the teachers in the regular classroom; and another control group was in a small class but in a more permissive environment.

Another major hypothesis was that educational achievement will improve along with social and emotional behavior. In most previous studies, as has already been indicated, the social-emotional changes were sought in their own right, without references to the educational progress of the child. In fact, in many if not in most cases, the educational problems of the child had to be left alone or actually screened out in order for the social and emotional problems to clear up, it was felt. In this study, the ordering or structuring process was intended to cover all facets of the child's psychological development, not just the emotional sides. To insure that this aspect of the broad study would be kept under control, parents were involved in the manner stated above; and greater assurance was had, than is apparently true of previous studies, that the parental cooperation would be consonant with the school program. This was in preference to the usual method of more or less random counseling of parents or not considering them at all in any systematic manner.

PRACTICAL CONSIDERATIONS

Aside from the research aspects of the study reported here, several practical considerations need to be kept in mind in evaluating the outcomes of the study.

1. The cost of operating the type of program discussed is far less than with conventional methods. A reduction of the usual class size of about thirty children to not more than eight or ten constitutes the major expense. But any program that is worth its effort, regardless of the methods used, will need to reduce class size; hence the necessity of the smaller classes employed in the demonstration of the structured approach presented here is no unusual or unexpected factor.

2. Fewer personnel are required. Other than teachers for the smaller-ratio classes, no additional personnel are *necessary,* although some additional personnel may be desirable in some instances. In a contrasting research program in a residential center for emotionally disturbed children, the ratio of professional and semiprofessional personnel to the number of children was about six to one; in the program considered here, the ratio was about one professional to eight children, so that this program was about one-fiftieth as expensive. Research staff aside, the professional staff needed for the type of program reported on here could easily be only 2 to 5 per cent as expensive as in existing programs outside the school system.

3. This type of program exists within the school system and preserves the general purposes and outlook of the school system. The child stays essentially within his normal orbit of home and school living. Greater flexibility therefore exists in treating any special problems associated with physical health, with moving a child from one school or class to another, or with making normal or near normal progress from grade to grade. Curriculum problems and their eventual relationship to future vocational preparation are therefore minimized and can be kept in clearer perspective.

4. No aspect of the child's general well-being is neglected. Living at home and working out problems with parents, siblings, and peers are to the betterment of the child's development. Add to these the opportunity to develop educationally, and a valuable combination is achieved.

CONTROVERSY: ESSENTIAL AND PROFITABLE

Many other controversial topics could be raised concerning the method used in this study in contrast to older ones. Not all available data are presented in this report, and not all of the assets and liabilities of older methods can be reviewed here. As in all scientific undertakings, controversies are healthy, and they often give rise to new questions and new perspectives. Rather than worry over many small points of difference between older and newer methods of handling emotionally disturbed children, attention should be drawn to the types of questions which can settle controversial issues and give rise at the same time to more effective methods of treatment and instruction.

Such questions might include, among others, the following:

What is needed for the emotionally disturbed child to progress?

What freedom of action does the classroom teacher have at his disposal? What additional freedom of action might he have if he were more resourceful?

What are the individual behavioral and learning characteristics of the emotionally disturbed child?

What presentation and follow-through are needed for the child to learn more effectively and to behave with better self-control?

How can the classroom teacher avoid complicating the life of the emotionally disturbed child and, better yet, contribute to his social and emotional maturing?

As an attempt is made to answer these and many related questions, stress is placed over and over again on the importance of structure in the classroom. The purposes of this book are to develop points related to structure as fully as possible, given the present state of knowledge of those responsible for the program's design and execution.

SUMMARY

In the last decade, society has begun to realize that it has neglected the problem of educating the emotionally disturbed child. Emotionally disturbed children are defined as those who have more or less serious problems with other people (peers and such authority figures as parents and teachers) or who are unhappy and unable to apply themselves in a manner commensurate with their abilities and interests. These children have to be taught and directed in special ways, and a wholesome and constructive environment has to be developed for this purpose.

There are many existing resources for emotionally disturbed children; but none of them stress education, and none of them attempt to weld together the educational and social-emotional considerations. Child guidance clinics, residential treatment centers, and the treatment of children with psychotherapy in the offices of psychologists, psychiatrists, and social workers do not supply the needed help to educational problems. The guidance services in the public schools act as a screening and limited-help program, but do not offer sustained help in the manner needed.

In this chapter the subject of the book was introduced with a brief description of how a *structured* program in the classroom can be implemented to meet the requirements of the emotionally disturbed child. The concept of structure puts an emphasis on the present home and school environments of the child and on what can be done to bring about growth-producing changes in educational achievement, as well as social-emotional changes. Structure also refers to an especially prepared daily program of educational tasks and behavioral limits and to a definite over-all routine.

The values associated with a structured program include economy of operation, a minimal use of extra professional help, an increase in educational achievement along with emotional growth, and a set of methods and techniques that can be implemented in the typical school system by the well-intended and mature teacher.

In the operation of the structured program, the child and his home are included in the school-centered management of the difficulties; the child is not removed from his natural orbit of home, school, and neighborhood living. The way is kept open for the child to return to normal classes, to maintain educational continuity throughout his school career, and to prepare for future educational and vocational requirements.

2

SELECTED REVIEW OF
EDUCATIONAL PRACTICES

The major portion of the literature which will be reviewed
here deals more with causes, behavior symptoms, and methods
of treatment than with methods and curricula for teaching. It
is widely believed that the education of the emotionally disturbed child should be secondary to the treatment of his emotional illness. It has been said that the emotionally disturbed
child is ill and should be under medical care, with education as
well as other aspects of treatment prescribed by the supervising
psychiatrist. As a result of this subordinate function of education in the treatment, very little attention has been given to
the development of teaching methods. Educational practices
which have been reported, chiefly by Bettelheim [3] and Redl
and associates [43–45], have been based largely upon the expressed interests of the child, with stress on projects as units of
activity.[1] Many of the units have been planned without partic-

[1] Classes for emotionally disturbed children have appeared in some
places—Baltimore, Chicago, Cincinnati, Dade County, Los Angeles, New
York City, Philadelphia, Rochester, N.Y., Seattle, and in Montgomery
County, Md.—but they generally have gotten less publicity and less
explicit support than the more formal programs mentioned in this
chapter.

17

ular attention to the child's competence or level of achievement in academic-tool subjects. In fact, attention to these necessary tools in the school program has been spasmodic and unplanned.

Previous approaches in teaching emotionally disturbed children also have been permissive ones. Where educational tasks have been assigned, the children have not been held to the assignment until completed. They have been permitted to select only what they want to do. Education as a treatment tool seems to take on different meanings depending upon the theory of personality being used. As an example, when the treatment orientation is psychoanalytic, schoolwork is supposed to be used as a medium to assist the child in bringing into the conscious his unconscious conflicts. If the nondirective approach is used, the educational structure is one which will permit the youngster to release his negative feelings, rather than one designed to assist or promote achievement.

Only a few studies report the use of the academic subjects as a medium for working with disturbed children. Goldberg [10] has reported a study in which remedial reading was used as a method of psychotherapy for schizophrenic children. Jacobson and Faegre [18] discovered that certain reading materials stimulated disturbing responses from the hyperactive, aggressive boys with whom they were working at the National Institute of Mental Health. Hay [12] has referred to the school as a fertile place for children to work out their conflicts. He stressed nonacademic units of experience to help the child develop self-confidence. He recommended the use of activities such as music, ceramics, carpentry, block building, housekeeping, and playing store. In the Detroit public school program [13] academic subjects have been used to some extent with socially maladjusted children enrolled in special classes.

The value of education in the treatment of disturbed children has been stressed by Hirshberg [15]. He believes that academic tasks offer excellent potential for building ego, developing skill and mastery, developing self-esteem, and offering gratification at varying levels of ability. Hirshberg states that education can utilize to the greatest advantage the developmental stages of growth in designing the training sequence for the child. In addition, education offers group participation and group identification which meet the child's need for social development and also provide contact with reality.

A more detailed report of the education of children with emotional disturbances will be offered in the following pages. Although this is not a complete review of the literature, an attempt has been made to represent the major ideologies forming the bases for developing educational programs used with these children. For the sake of categorizing, these educational approaches have been organized into four groups. These are the psychoanalytic approach, the nondirective-permissive approach, the child study approach, and the structured approach. The first three approaches will be considered in this chapter, the structured approach in Chapter 3.

THE PSYCHOANALYTIC APPROACH

Contributions of Bruno Bettelheim

Bruno Bettelheim's work with emotionally disturbed children, carried on at the Sonia Shankman Orthogenic School at the University of Chicago, was among the first research projects designed to study a school program for these children [3]. Even though it is difficult to discern in the report of the project any systematic approach to the education of the emotionally disturbed children at the school, the philosophy and pattern of treatment are quite evident. Bettelheim follows the orthodox psychoanalytic procedures in the treatment of the school children. Very little structure is set. In general, the approach centers around encouraging free expressions of emotion, with an attempt to interpret the meaning of the avenues of release and thus gain a better understanding of the children's disturbances. School activities may be used as a resource for the expression of feelings of fear, hostility, and anxiety.

Bettelheim believes that in many children anxiety about learning is associated with a broader fear of learning more about the world. The children are thought to believe they may discover something through the newly acquired knowledge that will be devastating to their personal integrity. He believes that reading is the most likely of the tool subjects to bring out these fears of more intensive investigation or learning. In many cases, Bettelheim states, exploring nature can be successful in reducing the fear of learning (particularly of reading). He cites a teacher who, to get one boy to study arithmetic, promised to go fishing with the lad if he would do his work in the subject.

Bettelheim believes that the classroom environment can be reassuring for children if they are given an opportunity to act out some of their primitive pleasures in the classroom. He says that teachers using his approach do not go as far as to allow children to bring baby bottles to school to suck milk from, but that a boy was encouraged, as a science lesson, to rig up a complicated siphoning system. The boy made the assembly work by sucking on a rubber tube, thus simulating sucking from a bottle. By taking advantage of his "needs for sucking," the boy was able to act out a basic need and conduct a scientific experiment at the same time. Through this he gained confidence and courage enough to approach his reading assignment, the discussion indicates.

According to Bettelheim's report of his study, no educational plan was too elaborate to follow if it was consistent with the interpretation of a child's need, fear, anxieties, or hostilities. All cues for program planning came from the child, and only minimal or absolutely necessary outside structure was established. An essential theme throughout the program was providing the avenues for children to bring into consciousness their unconscious repressions.

The adaptations of this plan to a regular or special day-school program would seem highly impractical. Although day-school programs can be modified extensively through special classes, the differences between the basic ideology of Bettelheim and his colleagues and that of many educators would make it extremely difficult to conduct such a program in any typical school environment. In addition, educators in general would demand more scientific evidence to support use of the methods and techniques prescribed by Bettelheim. Most of the evidence reported was subjective. Objectively, it is not possible to be sure of the gain that these children made. One would question whether they could go back into a typical school program and be successful. In the situation reported here, some behavior improvements would be expected just from the fact that almost all conflicts and problems were reduced for the children. The environment was specifically adapted to them. They had few conflicting situations or demands to come to grips with and solve. Before making any concluding statement about the practicality of this program, one would have to know whether or not these children are now better able to cope with their conflicts in a typical school setting.

Contributions of Gerald Pearson

Gerald Pearson, author of *Psychoanalysis and the Education of the Child* [27] and *Emotional Disorders of Children* [26], discusses the contribution of psychoanalytic research to better understanding of the learning process, the development of ego functions, the relation of the ego to reality, and the development of the superego. Pearson's basic ideology is consistent with Bettelheim in that both stress the importance of bringing unconscious material into consciousness in the treatment and education of children. Pearson, however, would probably not support Bettelheim's permissiveness in allowing children free rein in their expression of primitive needs [27].

Pearson is particularly lucid in expressing his opinion of some of Freud's followers and their interpretation of Freud's ideas concerning more permissiveness in sex education. According to Pearson: Psychoanalytically based sex education is not satisfactory. A large number of the children who received this approach to sex education later developed disturbances and behavior disorders. These children, compared to children educated according to convention, showed a lesser variety of interests and talents. Children reared in the more permissive psychoanalytic environment showed greater perseverance on tasks but also retained infantile behavior patterns and habits. They were more emotionally impulsive and showed less control over body functions, including bowel and bladder control. These children had more difficulty adjusting to a regular school situation and were a greater strain on the teacher. Even in a progressive-school environment they revealed less spontaneity and creativity. They were less able to respect the rights of others and were intolerant of the demands of adults. Routine demands related to meals, manners, hygienic measures, and schedules were extremely conflictful issues with these children. They could not adjust to society's demands and restrictions.

Pearson believes that the results of psychoanalytic sex education were not caused by misapplication of Freud's principles but by failure to complete the application. He feels that educators have also formed an erroneous interpretation of Freud's writings by granting more permissiveness in educational structure, curriculum, and methods of teaching. Progressive education, he believes, neglects the academic tools and places emphasis on the contemporary world at the sacrifice of the past. The children are dissatisfied with their school experience because they do not learn more. Traditional schools which modify certain parts of the curricula to use progressive concepts risk doing a poor job of accomplishing purposes set forth by both philosophies, Pearson feels. He states that they may not be doing an adequate job of teaching either the academic subjects or the knowledge of the world, how it functions, and how they can most successfully fit into the whole scheme.

With reference to learning problems encountered in children, Pearson says that psychologists and educators should refer children with such problems to psychoanalysts who specialize in the treatment of children. He believes the vast amount of research which has been conducted through the use of the psychoanalytic approach should be brought together and used more extensively with children who have learning problems.

In his coverage of disturbances in the learning process, Pearson divides learning disorders into two types: those that do not involve neurotic conflict and those that do. The learning disorders that do not involve neurotic conflict are summarized as follows:

Intellectual differences. Children who are intellectually retarded are naturally slower in the maturational process, including that which is necessary for learning to read, write, and do arithmetic. The readiness of these children for learning the academic subjects is somewhat in proportion to their retardation. A child with retardation or maturation lag may be handicapped by a secondary cause, such as the presentation of learning materials for which the child is not yet ready or the lack of acceptance by parents and others of the child's retardation.

Defects resulting from illnesses and organic brain injury. A second classification of children with nonneurotic learning disorders includes those with chronic fatigue, chronic illnesses, and vision and hearing impairments. This group also includes children whose ability to learn is affected by physiological disturbance in the central nervous system, such as certain cortical or subcortical lesions.

Pearson gives the following as causes of learning disorder resulting from conflicts in the ego:

Improper or unpleasant conditioning experiences. Disturbances in learning may be caused by the child's association of learning with an extremely unpleasant or traumatic experience he has had.

Disturbed current object relations. If there is disturbance in relationships between the child and the adults with whom he identifies, e.g., if the child fears or hates his teacher or displaces to the teacher feelings of fear or hatred for his parents, learning difficulties may arise.

Pearson states that all learning is a function of the ego.

(Instincts are the basis for the energy which is used by the ego and the superego.) Learning difficulties may arise when the learning process becomes involved in intrapsychic conflicts between the three parts of the personality: id, ego, and superego. Deflection of attention; feelings of guilt, shame, and embarrassment; worries; fears; threats to security; daydreams; and instinctual desires are all intrapsychic conflicts that disturb the learning process. These neurotic conflicts may result either in inability to receive the stimuli from the material to be learned or in inability to make meaningful associations and assimilate the material learned. Disorders in the learning process which are involved with neurotic conflict are as follows:

Diminished capacity to learn because of a disturbance in the relation to reality. Children whose reality picture of themselves and their environment is disturbed and children who resort to fantasy may have learning disorders resulting from conflicts thus engendered. Reality distortion and/or marked discrepancy between reality and the perception of what is real may occur.

Diminished capacity to learn because the child has not learned tolerance for anxiety from drives. Because of the permissive child rearing practices used by parents over the past ten to fifteen years, children have not had to deal with conflicts arising from not being able to have their instinctual demands met. This has resulted in the lack of tolerance for anxiety; therefore, the development of the ego defenses of repression, reaction formation, change of aim, and sublimation is greatly retarded. These children have little energy and little interest or curiosity to learn. They have a need only to have their instinctual demands met, not to meet demands encountered in typical learning experiences.

They will begin to learn only when they are subjected to the slow educational process of being compelled to postpone immediate gratification of instinctual drives and to begin to tolerate the anxiety which necessarily must arise during this educational procedure [27, p. 54].

Contributions of Fritz Redl

Fritz Redl has done a considerable amount of experimentation in residential treatment centers with delinquent boys. He founded the Detroit Group Project in 1948, directed and conducted a "group therapy home" in Detroit called Pioneer House, and directed the Child Research Branch of the National Institute of Mental Health. Redl's outstanding contribution has been made through his intensive study of the emotions of delinquent boys, which has increased our understanding of the reason for hate, anger, and fear in these boys, and through his description of the process of treatment by ego development. His contribution to education is most noteworthy, particularly his publications on mental health in education. His book with William Wattenberg, *Mental Hygiene in Teaching* [43], has received acceptance by educators throughout the country. Redl was among the first to stress the relationship between mental health and education and show specific ways in which the learning process assisted mental health [44, 45].

Listed below are some of the ways Redl believes learning contributes to emotional development:

1. Learning builds and supports the child's feeling of self-worth.

2. Learning can help to satisfy the need for belonging.

3. Learning builds confidence, which will in turn increase the drive for further learning.

4. Achievement in learning helps the child set realistic goals for himself.

In the treatment and education of emotionally disturbed children, Redl utilizes the basic concepts of psychoanalysis, with emphasis upon ego development. The basis of treatment is gained through an understanding of various functions and disturbances in the ego and superego. He believes that it is necessary to study intensively the various ways in which the child's control and functioning break down.

Through understanding more about the child's behavior control and defense mechanisms, the necessary steps for reconstruction can be determined, Redl feels. He believes in structure and limits but says that the child should be given considerable freedom of choices of behavioral responses within the limits. It is through the relatively free atmosphere that the disturbed behavior is studied and classified. As a result of his observations, he has described twenty-two different functions of the ego.

Redl has not yet published his report on the treatment methods used with the "acting-out" boy, the subject of an experimental project at the National Institute of Mental Health. But as a result of several visits to the project at the National Institute of Mental Health, it has been tentatively concluded by the authors that the diagnostic and treatment methods used there were an elaboration of the design used at Pioneer House.

Contributions of Ruth Newman

While at the National Institute of Mental Health, working under the direction of Redl, Ruth Newman [25] conducted and published observations on the characteristics, methods of treatment, and educational adjustments of acting-out boys, aged nine to thirteen years. The boys who were selected for study had severe behavior and learning disorders. Their behavior was characterized by the lack of ability to control impulses, by physical and verbal aggressiveness, and by inability to foresee consequences. The research was designed to study three areas in the lives of the boys selected: a total living situation, individual therapy, and the educational situation.

Newman states that the teacher who becomes involved with instructing these hyperactive, aggressive boys must alter significantly his expectations of the children. He should have extra training in techniques and materials. He needs the ability to plan ahead and then discard his plans and develop new plans on the spot. Newman believes that allowing the children to act out is an essential part of the treatment—that the goal in studying and treating pathological behavior is to create a permissive atmosphere that seeks to examine rather than suppress or control the behavior.

Newman believes that because of affectional deprivation in the past, these boys crave a one-to-one relationship, on one hand, but fear the closeness of such a relationship, on the other hand. In the Newman study an opportunity was made available for each child to have a one-to-one relationship each week. This provision for undivided tutoring was believed to be important because of the assumption that children must learn to relate in such a close personal relationship. In addition, each of the boys differed so greatly in academic achievement, learning characteristics, and motivations, that individual attention was necessary.

Educational needs. Newman summarizes the educational needs of these children as follows:

1. The emotionally disturbed boy needs opportunity to work with various kinds of material in a group. When he is given a permissive atmosphere, he regresses to a three- or four-year-old level in his need to play and in the use of materials. This is regarded as necessary before he can progress up the educational scale.

2. Once he is accepted at his functioning level and has learned to form a relationship with an adult, the youngster becomes more receptive to academic learning.

3. The environment for the emotionally disturbed, hyper-aggressive child must be radically modified so that he may unlearn old learning patterns and learn new ones.

4. The teacher must begin at the academic level on which the child is able to function. The teacher must be accepting, dependable, and consistent.

5. The disturbed child's program should provide opportunities for infantile gratification and easy, fast success.

6. He should be offered a surplus of food, care, and affection. This change in environment conditions will cause the child to give up old defenses. The teacher at first must accept the unac-

ceptable symptom, later tolerate but not accept, and finally, when the symptom is no longer necessary, set a limit to the behavior.

The teacher of hyperactive, aggressive children, Newman states, should have certain definable characteristics:

1. The teacher must be stable, flexible, accepting, dependable, and consistent.

2. The teacher should have competences with a variety of educational methods, materials, and subject matter from preschool to high school.

3. The teacher must feel secure and confident within his own right and not need the accomplishments of his pupils for support and confidence.

4. The teacher must be able to respond to a variety of behavior from his pupils without being threatened; he must be able to take a child back into the classroom even after a personal attack, and in the face of all of this, he must be able to maintain warmth toward the child.

Methods of teaching. Newman feels that certain rather specific methods should be used in teaching emotionally disturbed children. These methods, although first used with hyperactive, brain-injured children by Strauss and Lehtinen, seem to have similar effectiveness when used with hyperactive, emotionally disturbed children without perceptible brain damage. Specialized methods used with these children are listed as follows:

1. Directions for all activity, academic or recreational, should be clear, lucid, and simple, requiring only one step at a time.

2. The time required for any assigned task must be limited, yet enough time must be allowed to complete the task.

3. Stimulation, particularly in the beginning, should be very limited. Excessive stimulation increases activity.

4. Materials to be learned should be presented in part rather than whole, and should be concrete rather than abstract or verbal.

5. Materials and subject matter should be carefully chosen.

Stories should be short and neutral, with science or nature as content.

6. Group activities for these children should be delayed and gradually introduced, beginning with two and then three children in a group.

That unlearning occurs before relearning takes place is a major hypothesis of Redl and his group. Newman states that the reeducational process is a long, complicated, tedious procedure which requires understanding, great competences, skill, and organized planning and effort.

The methods listed by Newman represent a considerable change from the original teaching-and-treatment approach reported by Redl. If these techniques were developed as a result of the study at the National Institute of Mental Health, an obvious trend from the relatively unstructured, permissive approach to a definitely structured one has apparently resulted. Redl's report on this study has not yet been published. We shall have to await the release of his report to learn of the modification in his original hypothesis, if any, which may have resulted from this study.

Contributions of Samuel Slavson

Another writer who has contributed greatly to concepts of group therapy and education of emotionally disturbed children is Samuel Slavson [50]. Slavson states that emotionally disturbed children are incapable of memorizing dates, places, and other unrelated facts and events because of their short attention spans, anxiety, and hostility. He believes that the emotional problems must be reduced before learning, at least of an academic nature, can take place. Slavson is specific about steps he considers necessary to improve learning conditions for these children. He does not place a great deal of importance on the academic-tool subjects. He does believe that orderliness and routine are an important aspect of the school environment of these children.

The aim of Slavson's plan for the education of emotionally

disturbed children is to reduce the emotional problems of these youths through broadening their interests and by giving them more ways of expression through doing. This aim is achieved by providing more learning activities which are consistent with the interests of the youth, by reducing the abstract phases of learning, and by increasing the motor or activity aspect through actual experiences in life situations.

According to Slavson, the ordinary school curriculum must be modified. He believes that the academic-tool subjects can remain in the curriculum but that these subjects should be incorporated into everyday-life experiences. He stresses, as a great aid to the aims he describes, the discontinuation of the formal academic curriculum and the establishment of a program free from a rigid, restrictive school environment.

THE NONDIRECTIVE APPROACH

Contributions of Carl Rogers

Carl Rogers [47, 48] is found among the authors dealing with the treatment and education of the child with emotional disturbance. He works with what is known as the nondirective or client-centered approach.

The basic assumption underlying Rogers's position is that treatment occurs when, within defined limits, a completely permissive relationship exists for self-expression and activity of the child. Through the complete freedom of expression the child gains an understanding of himself which he can use to make better solutions to his problems and conflicts. This point of view stresses the right of every individual to be psychologically independent and holds that when given the opportunity within a permissive environment, the individual can achieve an adequate solution to his problem.

Rogers feels that the school environment is far too punitive to provide an adequate setting for therapy. He does believe that the school can work in conjunction with treatment agencies by employing the following suggestions for methods and curricula:

1. The tasks given the child should be satisfying and challenging.

2. The work should be within the child's capacity, so that a sense of accomplishment can be experienced.

3. Tasks that are in keeping with the child's interests should be planned.

4. The child should have the proper educational placement.

5. The curriculum should be adjusted to suit the child.

6. The special abilities and talents of the child should be utilized.

7. Children with learning problems should be given remedial teaching.

8. The teacher must feel that every child needs success and must find opportunities for the child to accomplish and to get recognition for it.

9. The child's needs for attention can be granted by rewarding his positive behavior. The teacher should provide extra privileges and responsibilities in order to be able to give the child attention.

10. The teachers should be informal, personal, and confidential with the child. In some circumstances the teacher may provide the lack of parental love.

11. Children who have difficulty with social relationships should be drawn into social situations on their own level. Appropriate social settings should be planned within the classroom as a part of the schoolwork, if possible.

12. In dealing with children who escape from reality through daydreaming, opportunities should be given them to express the dreams. The teacher should give the child opportunities to follow his interest and give expression to it in every way possible.

13. When the rebellious emotionally disturbed child is defiant, it is most unwise to be punitive. Defiance should be ignored and a reasonable explanation made to the child, giving him a choice of action.

The above suggestions for adjusting the techniques of teaching emotionally disturbed children offered by Rogers [48] place a great deal of emphasis upon rearranging the social situation to fit the child. Thus, the curriculum should be planned to meet the child's interests, the teachers should not command the disturbed child, and he is told to avoid punitive responses to the child's defiant behavior. In addition, Rogers recommends that any achievement that the child makes be amply rewarded and that his failures and rebellious behavior be ignored if possible.

Contributions of Virginia Axline

Strong in her support of and belief in the nondirective approach to therapy and education, Virginia Axline [1] has specific recommendations for use of this technique in education. She states that providing permissiveness, understanding, acceptance, recognition of feelings, and clarification of feelings results in growth and change within the child as he gains insight into his own conflicts. She feels that the implications of this process for education are tremendous. Axline believes that the most important single factor in establishing sound mental health is the relationship that is developed between teacher and child.

The following ideas are proposed by Axline for the consideration of educators in the teaching of children, with particular relevance to those with emotional problems:

1. The teacher should reflect friendliness and warmth in her relationship with the child.

2. An atmosphere of permissiveness should be established, so that the child can feel free to express his feelings and be himself.

3. The teacher should recognize the feelings that the child expresses and reflect those feelings back to the child in order for him to gain insights into his behavior.

4. The setting of limits is necessary. When it is necessary to correct a child, it should be done in such a way that the child's feeling is reflected back.

5. Choices of action should be given in cases of misbehavior.

One choice is conforming to the prescribed limit; the other is appropriate consequences.

6. The teacher, through respecting the dignity of the child, is developing the child's ability to become a responsible, independent person.

7. Emotional growth is a gradual process which cannot be hurried.

8. The teacher should meet the real needs of the child, not just material needs such as reading, writing, and arithmetic.

Axline places a great deal of value on the idea that the teacher should accept the behavior of the child and reflect it back to him. Through this process, she believes, growth in the child's capacity to form insight and modify his own behavior is made possible. She believes the teacher can play the role of a "teacher-therapist" and provide a therapeutic school environment. Therefore the school setting should offer as much opportunity for free expression as possible. The release of feeling in a permissive environment is the key to understanding the child better and to the child's subsequent self-understanding.

The nondirective approach to the psychological and educational development of children has been one of the strong therapeutic influences on education in the past two decades. The technique offers a great deal to educators because of its direct and uncomplicated framework. It does not involve intricate, preconceived ideas about personality development. But it does require a genuine belief in the growth potential of the individual and conviction that this growth occurs normally unless unnatural environmental conditions impair it. To use this technique successfully, a person must believe that the only way to understand the individual is through understanding the individual's perception of himself and of his reality. The basis for the child's growth, according to this philosophy, is the child leading the way toward a better understanding of himself in an empathically reflecting environment.

Contributions of Clark Moustakas

Probably the most influential contribution to teachers in relation to the nondirective ideology has been that of Clark Moustakas [21, 22]. He has taken over where Axline left off in his consideration for the teacher as a genuinely effective therapist. Moustakas earnestly feels that teachers can and do in many instances provide a therapeutic school environment for children with emotional problems.

Moustakas believes that the emotionally disturbed child differs from the well-adjusted child because the emotional growth of the disturbed child has been impaired during some stage of development. The disturbed child's attitude toward himself and others is distrust; his response to his environment is predominantly negative; he is generally hostile and overtly expresses hostility to others. It is believed that the source of hostility is anxiety. Negative feeling and anxiety are a result of disturbances in interpersonal relationships between the child and parents during early childhood. The child may get the idea from his parents that he is not worthy. This may set off a chain reaction within the child and affect attitudes toward himself and others. As he expresses this feeling of hostility, he feels even more guilty. This reinforces his opinion of himself which, in turn, increases the hostility. Under these circumstances the apparent circular behavior will continue and impair the child's growth unless or until it is interrupted in some way.

Moustakas feels that play therapy offers many opportunities for the disturbed child to grow through exploring and expressing his problems at various emotional levels starting from infancy. It is through providing an atmosphere in which the child can feel free in expressing his most hateful feeling without condemnation that real growth can be caused to occur. Expressing his feelings in the presence of a sensitive, accepting therapist breaks the impasse and provides the necessary nurture for emotional growth.

According to Moustakas, the above ideas can be applied to the classroom successfully. The teacher can plan a time in which a relationship with the children can be established in an atmosphere of acceptance and warmth. When a relationship like this exists, the children can express themselves freely and release the anxiety and hostility.

Contributions of Katherine D'Evelyn

In her book *Meeting Children's Emotional Needs* [5] Katherine D'Evelyn presents ways in which the teacher and the school can provide an environment conducive to healthy emotional development. D'Evelyn states that the dependency needs of young children must be met by the significant adults in their lives. The child looks toward his parents for support before he enters school. After he begins school, he seeks approval and confidence from his teacher. To make certain that these needs are met is an important role of the teacher. During his early school experiences, the teacher's acceptance and support become essential to the child as a guide toward becoming more independent and self-controlled. At this stage of development successful achievement in the school task is vital to the youngster in his attainment of self-confidence. Important in conjunction with fostering successful school achievement is providing an opportunity for the child to develop his creative abilities. Sound mental health is fostered through creative expression and productivity.

D'Evelyn lists and discusses the following as symptoms of unsatisfactory emotional development:

1. Stealing
2. Aggressive behavior
3. Excessively withdrawn behavior
4. Fear of going to school
5. Disabilities in academic learning
6. Truancy
7. Speech problems
8. Tantrums
9. Enuresis and nervousness

D'Evelyn feels that aggressive behavior results from feelings of fear and lack of self-worth and confidence. When the meaning of behavior is recognized, steps can be taken by parents and teachers to help. The aggressive child can be helped by their improving the child's feelings of self-worth and confidence. Withdrawn behavior also results from the child's poor concept of himself. He feels unworthy of attention; in fact, he may actually draw back further when attention is directed toward him. Again the importance of understanding the cause of behavior and the cooperative working relation of teacher and parents are stressed.

Anxiousness and fear, besides causing aggressive behavior, can be the cause of so-called school phobia, D'Evelyn says. The fear of going to school, probably a form of withdrawn behavior, is a strong indication of anxiety in the child. Children who experience this fear should be kept in school if possible, and steps should be taken to reduce the anxiety.

Children with normal intelligence who have severe learning disabilities are emotionally disturbed, according to D'Evelyn. She says the learning disabilities are caused by the following conditions:

1. Lack of motivation for school learning in the home
2. Presentation of material to the child and expectation of its completion before he has reached adequate academic readiness
3. Refusing to learn as a manifestation of not wanting to grow up
4. Lacks in affection and attention from parents
5. Fear of learning forbidden things originally or often connected with sex

D'Evelyn states that punishment, extra study, and remedial reading do not help significantly in decreasing the child's learning disability. She feels that in cases where remedial work has seemed to help, the additional attention the child gets from a new person coming into his life is more responsible for the gains he may show than the remedial help. If a remedial reading teacher is warm and accepting, therapeutic value can sometimes come from the approach this person uses.

D'Evelyn believes the teacher should have the benefit of a complete psychological study of the child with learning disability. Working cooperatively with the school psychologist, the teacher can get help in determining the educational approach to use with the child. The teacher can help the child with learning problems by giving him encouragement and support through personal attention and warmth. Such an approach may require a great deal of personal involvement.

CHILD STUDY APPROACH

Contributions of James Hymes

James Hymes uses a child development frame of reference in approaching the education of children with emotional problems [16, 17]. The first principle proposed by Hymes as basic to child development approach is that the children must like the teacher. In addition, the following specific procedures are proposed for teachers:

1. Observe the children with poor academic records.

2. Watch the children who are rejected, picked on, or made fun of.

3. Observe particularly children who are exceptional, physically or mentally.

4. Get to know children better. Visit the home.

5. Provide some way for the child who usually comes in last to find success.

6. Make certain that children with high intellectual ability are challenged.

7. Readiness is a result of growth combined with general life experiences. Make sure the expectations are not ahead of the child's readiness.

8. Make the educational program as individualized as possible.

9. Avoid, whenever possible, situations which will embarrass or belittle the child.

10. Avoid labeling children.

11. Give careful attention to children who are quiet and withdrawn.

Hymes lists the following needs as important for children with emotional problems, which he says should be understood by the teacher in approaching the educational program: (a) physical needs, (b) emotional needs, (c) social needs.

His specific suggestions to teachers for teaching these children are the following:

1. Have limits, but at the same time be friendly and sympathetic.

2. Stop misbehavior for the protection of the class and the educational program.

3. Lead the child toward good discipline through firmness, sympathy, warmth, and understanding.

4. Build a relationship, or kinship, with the child; this must exist before the teacher can discipline the child.

5. Understand the child: understanding is the first step in discipline.

6. Use the classroom program to provide love, achievement, belonging, praise, acceptance, and independence.

7. Find more constructive and acceptable ways for the child to gain satisfaction.

8. Allow enough time for a change in behavior among children.

9. Expect the process to be slow. Do not be disappointed by setbacks in the child's progress.

Contributions of Daniel Prescott

Daniel Prescott [41, 42], pioneer and leader in the utilization of the child study process for understanding the development of children, has based his assumptions upon religious, philosophical, and ethical values. These assumptions are:

1. Every human being is valuable, regardless of his age, sex, race, creed, cultural background, social status, capacities, knowledge, or state of emotional adjustment. An individual's value lies in the fact that he is a living human being with potentialities to be realized.

2. Every human being has the right to strive for those conditions of living, learning and action, for those relationships with other human beings, and for those experiences which are necessary and appropriate to the achievement of his optimum development as a person; and to his optimum usefulness within society, providing always that these conditions, relationships and experiences are at the same time consistent with the welfare and optimum development of other human beings. It is the proper function of all social institutions and of every individual to assist each person to achieve optimum development and usefulness.

3. Whatever promotes wholesome development is moral; whatever blocks or prevents optimum development is evil.

4. Every human being has the right to be treated at all times in ways that show respect for his dignity and permit him to retain respect for himself as a person. This is an essential condition to optimum development.

5. The Golden Rule is the soundest ethical principle against which to evaluate the behavior of individuals, the programs of social institutions and the politics of nations. [42, p. 28]

Of major concern here are the scientific assumptions which are made by Prescott. The assumptions listed below form the scientific basis for the child study approach.

1. Behavior is caused and is meaningful. It is the result of the tensions set up by a series of forces operating within and upon the individual. The behavior of the child usually makes sense when viewed through the eyes of the behaver.

2. The causes which underlie behavior are always multiple. Some of them are physical—within the body or acting upon the body. Some are relationships of love or hatred, of friendship or antagonism, with other individuals. Some are cultural, depending upon ideas, habits, and attitudes taken in from

the family and the community or pressed upon the individual by the operation of various social institutions. Some grow out of participation in group activities with persons of the same maturity level. Still others grow out of the individual's own interpretations of his accumulative experiences as he defines them, as he strives toward goals, and works out defenses against frustrations and limiting circumstances.

3. Each individual is an indivisible unit. The forces that shape him do not merely accumulate to produce a human being. Rather they interact. Consequently, one cannot take the individual apart, figuratively speaking, and deal with only one aspect of his dynamic make-up at a time. The whole child will participate in and be influenced by all educative experiences.

4. The human individual develops. No child or youth was born as he is or is necessarily destined to become what he is. As the body grows and becomes more elaborate, new capacities for experiences accumulate and more and more meanings and feelings are differentiated.

5. Every human individual is a dynamic energy system, not just a machine acted upon from without. This dynamic organization of energy is potentially a self-actualizing unity. It emerges from the interaction of organism with world and society. But it always has the potentiality of going on from where it is to participate in shaping its own future destiny together with that of the society of which it is a part, and even that of mankind.

6. Dynamic self-actualization is made possible to an individual by the existence of an organizing core of meanings (values) at the center of the personality. These meanings or values govern the interaction between the individual and the successions of situations in which he finds himself.

7. Each individual is different from every other. The same basic forces and processes operate to shape all human beings and are available to all for self-realization. But these forces and processes vary both qualitatively and quantitatively from person to person. Consequently, an individual can be understood and intelligently assisted in his self-actualization only if one has very explicit information about him. The information

needed concerns his circumstances and experiences in life and the meanings and accompanying feelings that these experiences have engendered in him. These meanings and feelings are often discernible from systematic accumulations of objective descriptions of his behavior. [42, pp. 29–31]

Prescott stresses the value of teachers using the clinical approach in understanding children better. Decisions which affect the child in the process of his education should be based upon as much objective information as can be collected. He believes that educational planning will be greatly improved when teachers approach this planning for each child based upon an adequate knowledge of the child's total developmental status and the physical, social, and emotional factors which influence his performance.

In addition to the teacher's adequate scientific knowledge of the child, Prescott feels that teachers need to study philosophy and religion. He believes that the clinical approach to children requires certain attitudes and values.

The following value constructs, he believes, should be included in the attitude structure of teachers:

1. Active and sincere valuing of each child at all times.

2. Genuine expectation and acceptance of the fact that every child is unique.

3. Genuine expectation and acceptance of multiple or complex motivation behind behavior.

4. Acceptance of the necessity for trying many different approaches, in sequence or in combination, in order to evoke needed changes in behavior and the learning necessary to further development.

5. Genuine faith that, when enough causal factors favor it for a sufficiently long time, the necessary learning and behavioral changes will occur.

6. Ability to discriminate between acceptable and unacceptable patterns of behavior and to help the child to discriminate, without rejecting or blaming the child as a person, yet refusing to accept his actions.

7. Willingness to allow plenty of time for a child to learn,

to change his patterns of behavior, his attitudes, or his goals.

8. Refusal to feel frustrated, inadequate, a failure, or otherwise threatened, during the period before the child has begun to show improvement.

9. Scrupulous observance of a comprehensive and rigid code of professional ethics; ability to keep confidential all personal information about each child and his family in order to safeguard him from humiliation and loss of reputation or self-respect. [42, pp. 83–86]

In returning to the clinical approach to understanding children, Prescott uses a well-organized set of procedures based upon scientific methods of studying children. This elaborate approach includes:

1. Obtaining extensive information through
   a. Observing systematically the child behaving in a variety of settings and making objective recording of this behavior
   b. Studying cumulative records
   c. Visiting the child's home and conferring with the parents
   d. Studying as many influencing factors as possible in the life of the child
   e. Meeting with other teachers and collecting facts from them about the child's behavior in other circumstances
   f. Collecting samples of the child's work
   g. Talking with the child informally
2. Organizing the information which has been collected in a framework including the following areas of data:
   a. Physical factors and processes
   b. Love relationships and related processes
   c. Cultural background and socialization processes
   d. Peer-group status and processes
   e. Self-developmental factors and processes
   f. Self-adjustive factors and processes
3. Developing hypotheses which seem reasonable when based on information and experience

4. Checking the hypotheses against data
5. Accepting and rejecting hypotheses on the basis of supportive data
6. Restating hypotheses in terms of supportive evidence
7. Drawing conclusions based upon accepted hypotheses

Prescott's child study approach and the basic assumptions underlying it are, of course, proposed for the study of all children, exceptional and nonexceptional alike. The unique value of the approach to the understanding and education of emotionally disturbed children seems clear. The systematic collection and analysis of data will substantially increase the number of appropriate decisions the teacher may make concerning steps to take in teaching an emotionally disturbed child.

Contributions of Cruickshank et al.

Several years ago the supervisor of special education in Montgomery County, Maryland, began exploration of different classroom settings, teaching methods, and materials in search of an appropriate educational environment for children with central nervous system disorders [4]. Being dissatisfied with traditional educational methods and results, the supervisor, aided by William Cruickshank and other Montgomery County educators, hoped to develop a rationale and practice suitable to all types of hyperactive and aggressive children.

A marked similarity in learning and behavior problems had been previously observed among children with neurological disorders and those with emotional problems. As a result of this observation, the supervisor of special education placed a small group of emotionally disturbed children in a highly structured classroom environment with brain-injured children. For the first time in their educational experiences, the emotionally disturbed children began to show academic gains and to adjust to the classroom situation. The controls imposed by the carefully controlled structure, the steady routine, and the specialized techniques of teaching made it possible for the children to gradually develop greater adaptability within the classroom setting and also to improve upon their educational status.

Experimental design. Because of these apparently satisfactory and encouraging gains, a study was planned to investigate the effectiveness with hyperactive, aggressive children of teaching methods and materials which had originally been tailored to the needs of brain-injured children. The study was financed by the combined efforts of the Cooperative Research Project, U.S. Office of Education; Syracuse University; and the Montgomery County Board of Education.

Two experimental and two control groups were placed in three public elementary schools in Montgomery County. Forty children were selected through pediatric, neurological, psychiatric, psychological, and educational evaluations. Five children with a diagnostic classification of brain-injured and five children diagnostically classified as emotionally disturbed were placed in each of four classes.

Educational program. The following modifications in teaching methods, materials, and classroom environments were accomplished for the two experimental classes:

1. Reduction of environmental stimuli
2. Reduction in available space
3. A structured school program and planned routine
4. An increase in the amount of stimulus value contained within the teaching materials

In addition to the above modifications, the teaching methods and materials were designed to employ to a fuller extent than usual the auditory, kinesthetic, and tactile sensory processes in learning. The school schedule was firmly planned with respect to time and activity. Academic tasks were assigned and followed through with all children without significant deviation from the planned program.

In the control classes, no basic modifications were made in the classroom as to controlling stimuli or space. The teachers in the control classes did, however, use screens and makeshift objects to help isolate children at times in an effort to temporarily reduce undue stimulation. The teachers of the control groups were given special instructions similar to the teachers in the experimental (structured) classrooms, but were not required to use such methods.

Results indicate that the children in the experimental, structured groups made significant gains in achievement, visual perception, and social behavior, as measured by pre- and post-testing. Although the data were not analyzed so as to reveal whether or not there were differences between the brain-injured and the hyperactive, emotionally disturbed children, an inspection of the data indicates that no significant differences could be expected between these two groups in the dimensions studied.

From these data it would be reasonable to conclude that the hyperactive, emotionally disturbed children can respond quite successfully to the highly structured, planned routine of the classroom that has proved so useful in the education of brain-injured children.

EVALUATIONAL TECHNIQUES; PRESENT TRENDS

What can be said about these approaches to the emotionally disturbed child? First, they are clinically, not educationally oriented (except for the Cruickshank study). Secondly, the emotional rehabilitation of the disturbed child has been placed mainly in the hands of clinicians—clinical psychologists, psychiatrists, and social workers—and the educator has played a minor role. Thirdly, as a result of the first two characteristics of the approaches, the education of the emotionally disturbed child has been largely neglected; indeed, it has not been generally recognized as an important problem in its own right.

With school population increases, and with increases in the number of problems in learning among children, methods have to be developed which are both more flexible and more widely applicable than the methods of the past. The possibilities of wider and more precise interrelationships between treatment of emotional problems and attention to the daily educational tasks and opportunities of the child are now being more clearly recognized. The older methods of treating first or only the emotional state of the child are not so much wrong as they are narrow and inapplicable to the present vast educational arena where newer and more serviceable methods are needed.

In small and encouraging ways newer methods are coming to the forefront, many of them designed and carried out with research intentions but in the setting of the classroom. The emotional problems of the child are not being neglected; rather, they are being handled and combined in over-all–treatment and psychoeducational setting. The educational and emotional problems of the disturbed child, which are in reality part and parcel of the same problem, have to be exposed to the same rehabilitative processes in the same setting if either is to be solved [29, 30, 32–36, 38–40].

SUMMARY

Since the belief has been that education should be secondary to the treatment of the emotional illness of disturbed children, most of the literature deals with causes of illness, behavior symptoms, and methods of treatment. There is a dearth of writing on methods of teaching and curricula for emotionally disturbed children, but in general, previous approaches in teaching emotionally disturbed children have been relatively permissive.

Education as a treatment tool seems to take on different meanings depending on the personality theory being used. However, there are few studies which have utilized academic subjects as a medium. Among these are those of Goldberg and of Jacobson and Faegre. Hirshberg stresses the value of academic tasks for building ego, developing self-esteem, social development. The Detroit public school program has made some use of academic subjects with socially maladjusted children in special classes. But it is more common for authors in this area to recommend nonacademic activities such as music, ceramics, etc., as school activities for these children.

The representative review in this chapter of major ideologies forming the bases for developing educational programs used with these children included the following: (a) the psychoanalytic approach, (b) the nondirective-permissive approach, (c) the child study approach, and (d) the structured approach.

The Psychoanalytic Approach

Bruno Bettelheim's study of emotionally disturbed children, carried on at the Sonia Shankman Orthogenic School, University of Chicago, was among the first research projects on a school program for these children. The orthodox psychoanalytic approach was followed; this allows for a relatively loosely structured setting. According to Bettelheim's report of this study, no educational plan was too elaborate to follow if it was consistent with the interpretation of the child's need, fear, anxieties, or hostilities. In this program all cues for planning came from the child. Only minimal or absolutely necessary outside structure was established. An essential theme throughout the program was providing the avenues for children to bring into consciousness their unconscious repressions.

This plan is not practical to incorporate into regular school programs. Although some behavioral improvements were reported, such improvements would be expected just from the fact that almost all conflicts and problems were reduced for the children.

Gerald Pearson, like Bettelheim, stresses the importance of bringing unconscious material into consciousness in the treatment and education of children. However, he does not support an attitude of permissiveness. He believes in the extensive use of the psychoanalytic approach with children who have learning problems. He states that deflection of attention; feelings of guilt, shame, and embarrassment; worries; fears; threats to security; daydreams; and instinctual desires are all intrapsychic conflicts that disturb the learning process, and that learning is a function of ego.

Fritz Redl's contribution is mainly in the area of residential treatment with delinquent boys. He stresses the relationship between mental health and education. He lists the following ways that learning assists emotional development:

1. Learning builds and supports the child's feeling of self-worth.

2. Learning can help to satisfy the need for belonging.

3. Learning builds confidence, which will in turn increase the drive for further learning.

4. Achievement in learning helps the child set realistic goals for himself.

Ruth Newman believes in a permissive atmosphere which will allow the child to act out. This, in Newman's opinion, gives the therapist an opportunity to examine the pathology as it is displayed. Newman also lists educational needs of emotionally disturbed children, certain definable characteristics for the teacher of these children, and methods of teaching.

Newman states that the reeducation process is a long, complicated, tedious procedure which requires understanding, great competences, skill, and organized planning and effort.

In Newman's study there is an obvious trend from the unstructured, permissive approach to a definitely structured one.

Samuel Slavson believes in the modification of the ordinary school curriculum. He suggests a program free of rigid, restrictive school environment.

The Nondirective Approach

Carl Rogers believes that treatment occurs when, within defined limits, a completely permissive relationship exists for self-expression and activity of the child. He finds the school environment far too punitive to provide an adequate setting for therapy and believes that the school can work in conjunction with treatment agencies by employing certain suggestions that he lists. These suggestions place a great deal of emphasis upon rearranging the social situation to fit the child. Rogers further believes in ignoring the failures and greatly rewarding the successes of the child.

Virginia Axline sees the relationship between teacher and child as the most important factor in establishing sound mental health. She does allow permissiveness only to the extent that it enables the child to express his feelings freely. The teacher, according to Axline, should provide a therapeutic school environment for the child by meeting the real needs of the child as well as his educational needs. Axline's approach requires the person to believe that the only way to understand the individual is through the understanding of the individual's perception of himself and of his reality.

Clark Moustakas has been most influential in considering the teacher as a genuinely effective therapist. He sees the cause of the child's emotional disturbance as disturbed child-parent relationship during early developmental stages. Moustakas is much in favor of play therapy and believes that an atmosphere of acceptance and warmth can be established in the classroom at a planned time.

Katherine D'Evelyn also believes that teacher and school can provide an environment for healthy emotional development. She believes it is necessary to meet the child's dependency needs and allow him to experience acceptance and support to become more independent and self-controlled. She discusses nine symptoms of emotional disturbance, including stealing, aggressive behavior, learning disabilities, etc. She points out the importance of psychological study of the child and working cooperatively with the school psychologist in dealing more effectively with the child and his problems.

Child Study Approach

James Hymes believes that the crucial factor is to have children like the teacher. He proposes for teachers close and careful observation of the children to know academic and/or interpersonal difficulties and exceptionalities that exist. He believes that the teacher should understand the child's physical, emotional, and social needs in order to establish a satisfactory and successful program. He lists specific suggestions for the teachers of these children.

Daniel Prescott bases understanding the development of children upon religious, philosophical, and ethical values. He emphasizes the value of every individual regardless of his age, sex, race, or social, emotional, and educational state and adjustment. Respect for one's dignity is essential to optimum development. Whatever prevents such development, he believes, is evil. He believes that each kind of behavior is meaningful and has more than one cause. He believes in holistic approach, that is, that we should study and help the child as one unit—not consider only one aspect of his development. Although he states that the basic forces and processes that shape all human beings are the same, he believes strongly in individual differences and the different interactions of these forces. Therefore he believes that educational planning can be greatly improved if based on adequate knowledge and understanding of the needs and development of the individual children. He finds a clinical approach useful for this, but says that certain attitudes and values are necessary for the teacher using this approach.

William Cruickshank has long been in search of an appropriate educational environment for children with organic disorders. He observed similar learning and behavior problems in children with such disorders and emotionally disturbed children and placed a small group of the latter in a highly structured educational environment with brain-injured children. Obvious and marked academic gain and social adjustment were noted. This encouraged a research project involving effective application with emotionally disturbed children of teaching methods and materials which had originally been designed to meet the needs of brain-injured children. The experiment was carried on with two experimental and two control groups placed in three public elementary schools in Montgomery

County, Maryland. In all four groups there were both emotionally disturbed and brain-injured children.

Results indicated that the hyperactive, emotionally disturbed children can respond quite successfully to the highly structured, planned routine of the classroom that has proved so useful in the education of brain-injured children.

3

RECENT DEVELOPMENTS IN
STRUCTURING CLASSROOM LEARNING

Evidence is pointing more and more to the value of a structured classroom environment, as against the traditional setting for working with emotionally disturbed children. The more structured setting is particularly applicable to educational problems; and it is increasingly apparent that what is good for educational progress is also good for social and emotional development.

Many will say that the pendulum is swinging again. Before the present era of permissiveness an attitude of harshness and authoritarianism prevailed in education and child rearing. Just how harsh and authoritarian was the past no one can say with scientific authority because studies of classroom atmosphere and of child rearing techniques were nonexistent. But whatever swing the pendulum may be displaying, there is clear evidence that much scientific support, as well as sophisticated opinion, is available today to bolster up and give credence to an argument for the firm structuring of the classroom environment as a way to promote effective learning.

As any educator or psychologist knows, effective learning is important for obvious scholastic reasons. That effective learning is also important for classroom management of behavior problems, attitudes, and emotional well-being has not been as clearly recognized. A brief review of some current developments will give independent support to the methods utilized in the present book, as well as acquaint the reader with broader considerations involved in the education of all types of exceptional children.

TEACHER CHARACTERISTICS
AND CLASSROOM CLIMATE

A recent highly provocative report on the characteristics of teacher behavior and the resultant educational progress of children has been made by Heil, Powell, and Feifer [14]. They, along with many others, emphasize the importance of evaluating teacher efficiency indirectly, that is, in terms of student growth, but recognize the difficulties inherent in accurate and reliable measures of student progress.

In their attack on this problem several questions were raised and studied:

> What kinds of children's achievement are found in classes taught by different teachers? For what kind of children is such achievement shown? What does the teacher do (teacher behavior patterns) which is related to the various kinds of achievement demonstrated by children in various kinds of teaching situations and environments? What kinds of teacher experiences and personality factors are directly related to the kind and quality of teacher behavior and activity revealed in relation to the children? [14, p. 3]

Without going into the details of methods and procedures in the study of Heil *et al.*, suffice it to say that three kinds of teachers were delineated. Type A was characterized as "turbulent both in feelings and thought" [14, p. 14]. Type-B teacher showed the modal characteristics of "self control and the need to have things run smoothly" [14, p. 16]. And type-C teacher showed his central characteristic to be one of "fearfulness"

[14, p. 18]. Fifty-five teachers, male and female, were studied by a variety of standard techniques, resulting in these modal descriptive characteristics.

The personality characteristics of the children were also subdivided into several categories: Group A, conformers (N = 203); Group B, opposers (N = 109); Group C, waverers (N = 75); Group D, strivers (N = 133). These classifications were based on a variety of standard psychological tests.

The results from the study point up the currently increasing interest in the importance of structure in teaching and in the classroom management of children.

Heil and his coworkers report on the average performance in various subject-matter fields of the children in each category taught by the teachers from the various personality subgroups. Results show, that is, average performance indicates, that all types of children do better under type-B teacher in reading, spelling, and language. In arithmetic, social studies, and science, the other two types of teachers (types A and C) fare slightly better than the type-B teacher, although the average achievement of the children in these subject-matter fields does not favor one type of teacher as much as the language-spelling-reading areas do. Incidentally, some attempt is made by Heil *et al.* to relate the kinds of achievement (language, science, etc.) to the major interest areas of the teacher, so that the results from the achievement profiles are not wholly a function of teacher personality and/or method.

Some quotations from the authors will help fill out the picture and enable the reader to draw conclusions related to the stressing of structure in the classroom management of emotionally disturbed children:

> This kind of teacher [type B] focuses on structure, order and planning. This focus is also accompanied by high work-orientation. There is likely to be a sensitivity to children's feelings and a warmth toward children, which is an integral part of this personality-type's character and which is not, therefore, predicated upon a need to feed upon the children's

offering her affection. This teacher is also likely to emphasize interpersonal relationships in the classroom. [14, p. 70]

Many educators and psychologists have felt that firmness was contraindicated in the case of the hyperactive, rebellious, and defiant child. These authors observe an effect of the firm teacher which throws doubt on such a feeling.

> Interestingly enough, opposing children with the B-type teacher tend to perceive authority as more controlling, but, at the same time, there is a clear-cut increase in their perception of authority as effective. It would appear, therefore, that these children are likely to be more threatened by and rebellious towards authority figures whom they regard as ineffectual, because of lack of structure and order, than towards authority figures who may be directly hostile to them. [14, p. 71]

In short, in the hands of the B-type teacher authority becomes effective. On the other hand, the very weakness of the C-type teacher is exposed by authority; this type of teacher tends to lack the strength and personal conviction to carry out disciplinary and task requirements, thus permitting anxiety in children to mount and educational efforts to sag. The authors report in this connection that the C-type teacher is essentially ineffectual with all types of children except the strivers.

Two summary statements from Heil *et al.* epitomize their findings regarding the effectiveness of the B-type teacher:

> It appears quite clear from the data . . . that the structuring and ordering characteristics of the B-type teacher (which includes emphasis on work and detail) plus the warmth in interpersonal contacts (with the former bearing more weight) account for the major part of her superiority in obtaining achievement with all personality-type children [14, p. 74].

And,

> Just as the personality of the children showed little alteration with the B-type teacher, so does the B-type teacher show little personality change with the various type children. She apparently moves slightly higher on leadership with opposing and wavering children which appears to be directly responsive

to their needs, is higher in orderliness with them and is even less prone to aggressiveness with opposing children than with any of the others. This is in direct contradistinction to both the A-type and the C-type teacher, both of which types react with *more* aggressiveness when dealing with opposing children. [14, p. 75]

As a result of these findings the authors call for a complete rethinking of the value of permissiveness. They state:

The significance of structure and order as important conditions for achievement in the elementary grades suggests a rethinking of the meaning of structure and the clarification of and abuses of the concept of permissiveness. . . . The confusion of structure and order with irrational authority, as expressed by Fromm, carrying with it all the connotations of autocratic, antidemocratic and limiting, has tended to cause the baby to be thrown out with the bath water. . . . If articulation is poor and structure is not demarcated, the efforts of the learner are dissipated in attempting to create order so that learning can proceed. This is not to say that the contention of those who see as one of the valuable outcomes of learning the development of the capacity to see relationships and evolve principles is not important. This ability, however, must be nurtured. One has to have experience with order, with principles, with structure before one can create this structure on his own. The one must grow from the other just as independence cannot develop before original dependency needs are satisfied. Relevant to this are the misconceptions concerning permissiveness that have filtered down through home and school alike. One concerns the failure to differentiate between emotional and behavioral aspects. A tendency has developed to interpret permissiveness as accepting the child's behavior instead of accepting his feelings and guiding his behavior. . . . [14, p. 77]

Although this study was primarily concerned with normal children, the implications of the findings would appear to support the practice of firming up the classroom structure in the case of the emotionally disturbed child.

Medley and Mitzel [20] studied the classroom effectiveness of forty-nine teachers. Effectiveness was judged in terms of achievement of the students and the self-ratings of the teachers, among other variables. Achievement was not found to be correlated with classroom behavior of teachers or students, but the teachers who rated themselves as most effective tended to allow less autonomous student work and to supervise or control student participation more. While this study does not clearly favor structure as important in the classroom, the self-ratings of the teachers point to the importance the teachers laid to their own structuring of the work situation.

The current change in thinking about classroom atmosphere suggested here appears to be affecting the role of the teacher, according to Beilin [2]. In 1927, when the now famous Wickman study was done, teachers tended to be quite different from mental health experts in their attitudes toward behavior problems of children. Subsequently, with the advent of emphasis on general mental health considerations and with the emphasis permissiveness has received over the past several decades, teachers moved closer toward the attitudes of clinicians, and began to perceive their teaching roles more in clinical than in educational terms. But there is a limit to how far teachers and mental health experts can coincide in their roles and attitudes, according to Beilin, who points out that the teacher's orientation is basically a task orientation, while the clinician is basically concerned with adjustment.

The similarities and differences in teaching and clinical roles pointed out by Beilin are precisely the region where much of the thinking in this book comes into focus. It is intended in this work to illustrate that an overlapping between the clinician's role and that of the teacher can be achieved, at least in the classroom, by concentrating on the achievement and mental health aspects of a structured classroom. The clinician's role and the teacher's role can become complementary and supplementary. The teacher need not repudiate or ignore the adjustment orientation of the clinician, and the clinician need not consider the more task-oriented and practical considerations of the teacher to be of only secondary importance. They are both needed, and they need not perform contradictory roles. Moreover, this complementary role taking of teacher and clinician would appear to have its most fruitful application in a structured classroom.

In the study that is the main subject of this volume it became apparent that consultation with the teachers could help ameliorate many serious behavior and achievement problems and preclude the development of less serious problems. A kind of "arsenal" of special education, psychology, and mental health considerations was found to be of much value to the classroom teacher in coping with particularly refractory problems. The emphasis put on the teacher's coping with classroom problems was somewhat different in this study from that reported by Nass in his work [23], but the intentions and goals of the two approaches were the same.

Nass reported on a one-year period of meeting with beginning teachers to discuss teacher adjustment and student progress. The content of the sessions with the psychologist was left up to the teachers, but fell into four categories: authority relationships, expectations of self as teacher, relationships to colleagues, and relationships to students. The area of his work which will be briefly reported on here is that of student-teacher interactions.

Nass observed that the teachers tended to read feeling and meaning into the children's reactions to such a thing as cleaning up after activity periods. It was apparent that the teachers, wishing to be liked and accepted by the students, tended to have difficulty in setting limits on tasks and on conduct. It may be one of the most difficult things for the beginning teacher to realize that limits have to be set and that difficult or even disagreeable tasks have to be performed. Nass remarks:

> On a more general level it was clear that the group initially felt that it was essential to be liked by the pupils. Interpretation of this attitude by them brought about the realization

that they experienced difficulty in setting limits for the class. They feared that setting limits would complicate their relationships with the children. It has become increasingly apparent to them, however, that their position reflected both their needs and their distortions of the problem and did not represent the needs of their youngsters in the classroom setting. [23, p. 566]

Teachers, like the rest of us, operate on the basis of a variety of assumptions, and, like the rest of us, they have to revise these assumptions from time to time. It may well be that the teacher's assumption that strong friendships must be made with the children is unwarranted and unnecessary for the sake of both educational and mental health requirements. A more structured and task-oriented attitude on the teacher's part may be the best foundation for any classroom activity. When, in the study of the present authors, it became apparent that the teacher was not handling some disciplinary or educational matters as well as possible, the reason was almost always that the teacher was presuming too much about the child's behavior. Such presumptions (or assumptions) included: "He won't do it again." "He *knows* what he's supposed to do, and can therefore be left entirely on his own to do as he should." "His intentions are good, so this should be enough to see him through his responsibility." It was apparent that the teacher who made such assumptions had a more difficult time with classroom achievement and discipline as a result, and had to back up and realign himself with new assumptions about the children and their behavior. Nass's first-year teachers were evidently finding out the same thing.

AUTOMATIC TEACHING

In recent years there has been a rapid growth in what is called *automatic teaching,* in which the instructor places greatest emphasis on *programming* an amount of subject matter. This programming consists in a number of important instructional details which include, among others, proper presentation of materials to be learned, clear directions, immediate reinforcement of the student's correct efforts, reprogramming in order to make up for failure, and so on through various levels of efficiency.

The volume on automatic teaching by Galanter [9] goes into the subject more extensively and intensively than can be done here. Suffice it to say that the entire matter of programming instruction appears to dovetail well with the current emphasis on structure. Programming is a way of structuring the whole presentation of an amount of subject matter, whether it is a daily lesson in spelling or a whole course in elementary algebra. Careful programming becomes, in a phrase, a theory of learning.

The reader will have grasped by now that the effort in this book also is, in effect, to present a theory of learning—a theory applicable to the classroom instruction of emotionally disturbed children. It is a theory that might apply as well, with specific modifications, to any instructional situation with any kind of child. The additional emphasis in this volume, however, is that the kind of programming or instructing described is not only of great advantage in learning academic work, but also of equal advantage to the disturbed child in learning the ordinary lessons of everyday adjustment and living. When the two aspects —educational and mental health—can be combined in general practice in a single program for the disturbed child, the results may be expected to be even more worthwhile.

USE OF STRUCTURE
WITH BRAIN-INJURED CHILDREN

Before moving ahead to present the empirical findings of the present authors' study, attention will be turned momentarily to the work of Strauss and others in their studies on brain-injured children, in order to fill in the picture of recent developments in promoting a structured classroom setting for dealing with the problems of the exceptional child.

The similarity in behavior of brain-injured children who display hyperactivity and children classified as emotionally disturbed has been noted [4]. It has also been suggested that the behavioral symptom complex found in both brain-injured and emotionally disturbed children may offer more helpful cues for the psychological and educational treatment of these children than is offered by study of the etiology of these disorders.

In the middle 1940s, Strauss and Lehtinen [51] and their colleagues were developing a neurologically based viewpoint to guide the treatment and reeducation of children who met certain diagnostic criteria for disordered behavior. Although justified criticism has been levied against his criteria [49], Strauss pioneered a structured educational approach for brain-damaged children which has also widely influenced current thinking about educating emotionally disturbed children.

Strauss observed perceptual, thinking, and behavior disorders in brain-damaged children. These children displayed a variety of perceptual and conceptual disturbances, as well as emotional instability, distractibility, and hyperactivity. Based largely on the observations of these psychological characteristics, the children were diagnosed by Strauss as being brain-injured.

Strauss and Lehtinen worked out a general educational approach for these children which took into account the effects of the above-named psychological and behavioral characteristics; in addition, they designed a curriculum appropriate to the requirements of these children. Besides the needed change in educational requirements from what would be used with normals, the physical environment of the classroom was modified to provide less stimulation and less distraction. The classroom, then, became an appropriate setting not only for the education of brain-injured children but for the achievement of better social development and better emotional control.

The hyperactivity displayed by the children was a result of

brain injury, according to Strauss. These children were observed to be abnormally responsive to ongoing visual and auditory stimuli. This susceptibility to stimuli created a chain of disturbing behavior responses, so that instruction in the ordinary sense of the term became almost impossible to achieve. The teacher needed to constantly remind the child to sit still, to pay attention, to finish work, so that more time was spent in monitoring the child than in getting real achievement.

Strauss considered how the learning environment could be modified to counteract the hyperactivity and distractibility displayed by brain-injured children. Several modifications were proposed. The pupil-teacher ratio was greatly reduced. Each child was seated a greater distance from his neighbor than would be the case in a classroom of normal children. Distracting physical objects—bulletin boards, art work, etc.—were removed from sight so as to minimize the basis for distractibility. The lower quarters of outside windows were even frosted to remove the temptation to look outside. The walls were painted a light, neutral shade. The most distractible children were placed in a corner facing the wall to reduce their almost uncontrolled response to stimuli.

In support of the reduction of physical stimuli, auditory and visual, the material to be learned was also stripped of all extraneous distractions, and the specific words to be read or numbers to be computed were set off in one way or another from their background. Lessons were planned to include controlled motor activity so as to further reduce the children's tendency to respond indiscriminately to stimuli. Such activities as manipulating the abacus, sorting, tracing, cutting, and using pegboards played an important role in the lesson planning.

Another consideration in the treatment program for the brain-injured children was control of their perceptual disturbance. According to Strauss, these children showed figure-ground disturbances and distortions, an inability to integrate visual form and space correctly, and distortion in auditory reception. When certain of the children displayed perceptual disorders associated with foreground-and-background relationships, with size and shape, color was used to aid the correct perception of size and shape. Various educational materials were also used to concretize and dramatize discriminatory processes. In general, a wide variety of ingenious and practical devices were fashioned to structure, order, and control the behavior of the brain-injured child.

Education considerations of importance in controlling the hyperactivity and distractibility of children like those studied by Strauss might be summed up in the following suggestions:

1. Reduce all extraneous stimuli.

2. Reduce excessive physical activity during study periods.

3. Detail methods and add order to the materials to be learned.

4. Increase the stimulus value of materials to be learned.

5. Follow step-by-step sequences in presenting complex materials.

6. Insist upon accuracy of work.

7. Prevent unnecessary or careless failures to do work acceptably.

But if a stimulus-reduced environment is an effective climate for the education of the brain-injured child, may it not apply equally well to the problems of the emotionally disturbed child? Are not the hyperactivity, the restlessness, the easy distractibility of the emotionally disturbed child related, at least at an educational level, to the "same" behavior in the brain-injured child? It is unimportant and speculative at best to argue about the possible physiological basis for the similarity in symptoms in the two groups; the organic etiology is not the important issue in the educational setting.

ADAPTATIONS FOR
EMOTIONALLY DISTURBED CHILDREN

Close in conception and importance to the Strauss studies is that of Cruickshank and associates [4] which was discussed in more detail in Chapter 2, pages 43 to 45. Cruickshank noted that children with hyperactivity and visuoperceptual disturbances—with or without demonstrated brain pathology—responded as well to the ordered educational setting as did the known brain-injured children. In his study about one-half the children were considered as brain-injured and the other half as primarily emotionally disturbed. Although the research design did not separate the effect of the learning environment on these two categories of disturbance, both groups appeared to progress educationally in the type of classroom structure studied.

Cruickshank's assumptions as to etiology paralleled those of the present study, in that the traditional psychiatric viewpoint that learning was impaired by fear and anxiety was not adhered to. Cruickshank states:

> The teacher works with children in terms of enlisting the support of the ego in acquiring mastery of the learning skills. The existence and resolution of psychopathological aspects of the personality is secondary to the instructional goal, and the success of the teaching situation is gauged in relation to the degree to which children achieve academic progress. [2, p. 624]

Little attention was given to the psychological disturbance per se in the Cruickshank study. The regulated school environment, the ordered time schedule, carefully planned task assignments, and constant follow-through on work expected were the keynotes to the classroom program. The academic framework provided the bases for the general rehabilitation of these youngsters.

The remainder of this book will present the findings of the present authors' two-year study of emotionally disturbed children in a public school setting. The emphasis on structure will predominate throughout. The reader is asked to share the reasoning behind the structured approach; conclusions as to the adequacy of the present approach are the reader's own choice, although the implications seem clear to all who are interested in improving education for all children as well as for the emotionally disturbed.

SUMMARY

An examination of several recent investigations supports classroom procedures based upon structure involving consistent, realistic expectations. The importance of effective learning both in maintaining classroom control and in managing behavior problems, attitudes, and emotional organization has been demonstrated. The teacher who, in addition to working in the structured classroom environment, carefully plans and organizes the presentation of materials with an attitude of high work orientation fares better in terms of the behavior and academic progress of normal children.

Educational procedures used with brain-injured children appear to offer equal advantages to hyperactive, emotionally disturbed children. Apparently principles such as controlled extraneous stimuli, reduced social activity, and ordered presentation of the materials to be learned are basic to successful classroom experiences of emotionally disturbed children.

4

AN EXPERIMENT IN EDUCATING
EMOTIONALLY DISTURBED CHILDREN

One of the strongest considerations of practical school administrators is whether or not the cost of special classes and programs for the education of emotionally disturbed children should be the responsibility of the school. The cause for concern has been real. In many instances the special classes have proved expensive. This has been true even in cases where little improvement has been seen in the child's behavior and academic achievement. It is believed, however, that school administrators could accept special programs if the cost were within reason and if the program could demonstrate its worthwhileness in educational rehabilitation. If educators of exceptional children are to renew their assertions that public school systems can and should assume the responsibility of the education of these children, they must demonstrate that children in these classes can make substantial educational and behavioral gains.

The education methods described in this book were subjected to experimentation for the purpose of objectively testing their effect upon children with disordered emotional development. This chapter is a report of this study, which was initiated four years ago in Arlington County, Virginia, near Washington, D.C.

EXPERIMENTAL PROCEDURE

The experiment was conducted in nine elementary schools in the Arlington County Public Schools.[1] The children in the study were moderately to severely emotionally disturbed and had reflected their disturbance in a wide range of behavior symptoms. These children had provoked frequent hours of case conferences, involving ten to fifteen highly paid professionals, with little improvement resulting in the children. They were children who were selected—by the aid of the files and personal knowledge of the coordinator of special education, principals, supervisors, teachers, visiting teachers, and school psychologists —as children who had presented serious and protracted problems.

The Arlington County Public Schools assumed the obligations of developing ways to cope with the classroom behavior of these children and of providing an educational program suitable to their needs. The administration and the board of education of the school system had a sincere interest in seeking more practical and effective ways of educating these children and offered their full cooperation. In the effort to study the problems, three different methods of teaching and three grouping situations were utilized.

SELECTION CRITERIA

All of the children were referred on the bases of their behavior and educational performance as observed by teachers, school psychologists, and supervisors. The general diagnosis of emotional disturbance was required before final selection was made. This diagnosis was made by the diagnostic staff, consisting of the coordinator of special education, the school physician,

[1] John W. Asher of the School of Education, University of Pittsburgh, and John de Jung, Bureau of Child Research, University of Kansas, served as statistical consultants.

the chief psychologist, the director of speech and hearing, the chief school social worker, and each child's teacher. Each child considered by the diagnostic staff had had complete neurological, speech, hearing, pediatric, and psychological evaluations. The teachers' observations and the psychologist's report were important influences in the final selection of the children. Although the neurological evaluations of the children did not reveal positive signs, the possibility that some of the children in this experiment had organic brain pathology cannot be entirely precluded.

Specifically, the following four criteria were used for selection of the children:

1. Hyperactive, distractible, attention-getting behavior; withdrawn, uncooperative behavior; or tendencies to both

2. Average or near average intelligence (with the recognition, however, that tested intelligence might be an underestimate owing to the emotional disturbance)

3. Presence in the school at least one year (preferably two) before the referral, with educational retardation of one year (preferably two)

4. The likelihood that the parents could and would cooperate, attend parent group meetings, and generally support the school's efforts

Since the study was done with elementary-age children, grade levels 2 to 5, an implicit criterion was that the referred child be in the research study at least one year, preferably two, before going on to junior high, in order that time for follow-up would be available before the child moved from the elementary school level.

TEACHING METHODS AND
SETTINGS FOR THE THREE GROUPS

Description of Group I (structured)

There were three groups of emotionally disturbed children with, for the first year, fifteen children in each group. The children in Group I were placed in two special classes. One was a primary class (aged seven to nine), the other an intermediate class (aged nine to eleven). These classes provided a highly structured, stimuli-reduced educational setting. The teachers closely followed the general aim of increasing order and structure as described throughout this book. Preliminary conferences with the teachers were held by the psychologist, and weekly conferences with the teachers and observations of the classroom climates were carried on by the coordination of special education and the project psychologist throughout the first year. As the teachers became acquainted with the structured methods and were settled into the routine, less supervision of their techniques was necessary. The following are some of the educational procedures used with Group I.

Assignments and skill limits of each child. Assignments were determined initially on the basis of intellectual and achievement tests and on the basis of information in each child's personal file. Modifications of assignments were necessary in cases where, for example, a child disliked arithmetic or was especially poor in spelling. The children often tried to postpone work on disliked subjects or acted as if they did not understand directions sufficiently well to proceed on their own. To remedy these conditions, assignments were made very brief and clear; a close, consistent follow-through was then maintained by the teacher. As the teacher got the feel of each child's attitudes and work skills, she gradually gave the child more independence in his work. Piece by piece, day by day, these tolerances and limits were extended.

Seating and movement limits. In addition to regular seats in the classroom, there were two small work tables, about 2½ by 5 feet, and five "offices," or booths. The booths were used to enable the children to work under a minimum of distracting conditions, to increase the tolerance for independent work, and to handle restless, hyperactive, and socially disturbed behavior. The booths, which lined one wall of the classroom, were about 3½ by 3½ feet with a movable chair and fixed table-level desk across the back of each. Sometimes children stored supplies in the booths as well as in the assigned desk each had in the center of the classroom.

Play and recreational limits. Children were held to the completion of assigned work before play or recreational opportunities were available. Most of the academic work was done in the morning; physical education, art, music, and free play periods came in the afternoon *provided* a child's work was up to par. Brief periods allowing for free play with art materials or clay were sometimes sandwiched in during the morning work periods if the child had completed work assigned to him. Care was exercised not to allow the recreational pursuits to crowd out assigned work, and assigned work had a constant, first-order priority at the beginning of each school day.

Free moving privileges. Free moving privileges included access to the rest rooms, moving about in the classroom, moving from group to individual desk work, occasional errands to the school office, and getting in line for lunch. Children asked permission to leave the room. Tasks and errands were distributed weekly among the children, so that all got a chance to carry on "official business" with the school office. The children were free to move from desk to booth to work bench provided a move was closely related to the assigned work. Free roaming about, or movement in lieu of doing work, was kept to a minimum. To preclude the development of fatigue, the group would be taken at appointed times for a walk and thus be allowed a "seventh-inning stretch" during the morning work period. Water in the classroom sink was kept off; art materials were kept under cover so as to minimize distraction. The children knew these materials were available after they qualified to use them, and it did not take long to establish these elementary limits concerning the use of supplies.

Social-emotional conduct limits. Some of the children provoked others unrelentingly, especially at first. Others often came to school "in a bad mood" and hypersensitively interpreted classroom problems personally. They displayed attitudes characterized by refusal to work, to communicate, to participate. In these situations, which were difficult to control effectively and constructively, several guidelines helped. The teachers did early what they would normally be required to do later in the way of setting behavior limits; they did not participate with a child who was upset, i.e., become involved in his upset, but instead gave him time to calm down first, gave one warning, and then acted; isolation was normally the preferred and most effective technique when a child's behavioral disturbance adversely affected others; and a specific emphasis was always placed by the teacher on solution or resolution of a problem in preference to queries as to why the child behaved as he did.

In the conferences each week with the coordinator of special education and the project psychologist, the teachers would discuss accumulated instances of problems they had handled well and those they felt they had not coped with successfully. It was helpful to have contrasting success-failure instances for discussion; in time, this procedure cut down on the failure instances and increased the confidence of the teachers that they could deal with most problems that might be presented. It was simply a matter of successive approximations to more desirable and constructive solutions to problems, both academic and social-emotional. The general guidelines to increasing or firming up structure were held to. The specific solutions to problems fell under this general aim, but it was often necessary to shift and maneuver, to roll with the punches, in order to keep the structure both firm and flexible.

Parent discussion groups. The parents of children in Group I were invited to meet with the teacher and psychologist on an average of once a month for the first year of the study. Only four parent meetings were held in the second year, and only four in the third year. The nature of the parent group is explained fully in Chapter 9. The specific content of these group discussions can be seen in Appendix A.

Description of Group II (regular grades)

The children of Group II were in regular classrooms in six elementary schools in the county. The teachers used methods of teaching emotionally disturbed children generally employed in a regular class setting. The parents were brought into the situation by the teacher as incidents of a child's behavior became disturbing. Nearly all known techniques for coping with behavior problems in a classroom were used from time to time. All school personnel regularly appointed for the responsibility of helping the school with learning and behavior disorders, such as the psychologist, visiting teacher, school physician, nurse, helping teacher, elementary supervisor, and remedial reading teacher, were available for helping the teachers. In addition, regular monthly school staff conferences were held with all school personnel involved in these cases. It was not unusual to have ten to fifteen highly paid professional staff members involved in hours of conference over one child.

Teaching methods and materials. To the extent that was possible, the children assigned to the regular classes were given the regular curriculum used in grades 1 to 5. With this range as a reference base, the teachers made every effort to understand the emotional problems of the children and made all the modifications in their classes which could be permitted. The following considerations were uppermost in the practices of the teachers of the children in Group II:

1. All assigned work was well within the child's ability.

2. Wherever possible, the school work was modified to suit the child's interest.

3. The child was given experiences in which he could find success.

4. The child was given opportunities to find accomplishments and recognition.

5. Extra privileges and responsibilities were provided in order to give the child attention.

6. Punitive responses to the child's aggressive, rebellious behavior were avoided by the teachers.

Description of Group III (permissive)

The fifteen children in Group III were assigned to a special class. The children in this class, like the children in the regular classes, had available the services of the psychologist, physician, visiting teacher, nurse, helping teacher, elementary supervisor, and remedial reading teacher. The teacher of Group III had some experience in and educational background for teaching children with emotional disorders.

The following teaching methods, curriculum, and classroom environment comprised the educational setting for this group:

1. The curriculum was modified to suit the interests of the children.

2. The teacher reflected friendliness and warmth with the children.

3. An atmosphere of relative permissiveness was established, so that the children felt free to express their feelings and anxiety.

4. The teacher recognized the children's feelings and reflected these feelings back to them.

5. When limits were set, the teacher still made sure that the children's feelings were accepted and reflected back.

6. The teacher believed in the importance of meeting the real emotional needs of the child, not only the material, academic needs.

To repeat briefly, Group I was in a highly structured special class environment with a prepared sequence of academic tasks. The tasks were assigned and completed. The structure was relaxed gradually to permit the development of more individual initiative, but a generally firm and nonpermissive structure was held to throughout the period reported on herein. Children in Group II were in fifteen regular classrooms; the necessary modifications were made for teaching these children within that context, but the curriculum and methods were similar to those used with undisturbed children. Group III had a comparatively nonstructured, permissive special class setting. The more conventional educational methods for emotionally disturbed children were utilized. The idea that children must act out their "unconscious conflicts" was prevalent. Thirty emotionally disturbed children were assigned to Groups I and II randomly. The chronological age of the children in these two groups ranged from seven to twelve years. It was not possible to assign the children to Group II completely at random because of the location of the special class. The children in Group III ranged in age from ten to twelve years.

RESULTS SHOWN BY TESTING IN FIRST YEAR

Before-and-after tests of academic achievement and behavior were administered to the three groups in the first year of the program. A testing design involving repeated measurements of the same subjects was employed in comparing the three groups in terms of both achievement scores and behavior ratings. A comparison of the three groups with regard to academic achievement, as measured by the California Achievement Test, will be considered first.

The grade levels reported for the children were assessed at the beginning and at the end of the school year on the CAT. Data on the three groups from this analysis are presented in Table 1.

Both the CAT and the Behavior Rating Scale (BRS) were administered the first week in November and again the first week in May (approximately six months later). The BRS (see Appendix C) was developed by the authors to measure change in overt behavior. The 5-point rating scale consisted of twenty-seven items. The judge rated each child from 1 to 5 on each item of tested behavior. Four teachers were used as judges. The judge observed and rated the children (A) in the classroom, (B) on the playground with supervision, and (C) in play activities without supervision. The ratings in the above three settings were pooled for each item.

Analysis of Academic Achievement

In examining the data, our principal focus was upon gain scores. For academic achievement, gain scores were computed simply by subtracting each pupil's beginning CAT score from the score he earned the following spring. The three behavior ratings (A, B, and C) were combined into a total behavior score for both the initial and final testings. The behavioral gain score for each pupil was the difference between his initial and final composite behavioral scores. Moderately low negative correlations between initial and gain scores were found for both the CAT and behavior rating data; correlations of $-.18$ and $-.35$, respectively.

Our interest was in comparing the effectiveness of the methods used in each group. The mean differences between each pair of groups in gain scores for the academic (CAT) and for the behavioral (ratings) measures were tested for significance by means of t ratios. The significance of differences between the variances of the gain distributions for each pair of groups was examined in terms of F ratios. These analyses are summarized in Tables 1 and 2.

TABLE 1

Summary Data for Tests of Mean Differences and Homogeneity of Variance for CAT Gain Scores Made by Emotionally Disturbed Public School Children in Three Different Instructional Settings.

Group	N	$\overline{D}$	σD	$\sigma \overline{D}_1 - \overline{D}_2$	t	F
I	15	1.973	1.198	.381	2.50*	2.40
II	15	1.020	.773			
I	15	1.973	1.198	.348	3.68†	9.21†
III	14	.693	.394			
II	15	1.020	.773	.239	1.37	3.84*
III	14	.693	.394			

* Significant at the .05 level of confidence.
† Significant at the .01 level of confidence.

As is evident in Table 1, Group I pupils achieved the greatest gain scores in CAT over the six-month initial-final testing period. The mean gain score for Group I is significantly higher at the .05 and .01 levels of confidence than are scores for either Groups II or III, respectively. The differences between the mean gain scores of Groups II and III do not differ significantly at the .05 level of confidence. The average gain score of 1.973 for Group I compares very favorably with expected gain scores for normal school children of comparable ages.

The F values in the right column of Table 1 are derived from differences in the variabilities of the gain scores within groups for each of the three comparisons made. There is greater variability of the CAT gain scores among the pupils in Group I than there is among pupils in either of the other groups. Gain scores of pupils in Group III vary the least, significantly less (at the .01 and .05 levels of confidence, respectively) than those for pupils in Groups I or II. Apparently the Group I treatment is more differentially supportive, i.e., though all the pupils made some gain, some made much more than others, resulting in a much larger variance for that group.

The relative gains of the three groups of emotionally disturbed children may be seen graphically in Figure 1. The youngest child in Group III was ten years, two months; in Group I, six years, nine months; and in Group II, seven years. The initial difference in grade level on the CAT between Groups I and III was approximately 3 years and two months. This difference was reduced in six months to just less than two years. The gain in Group II was a year, which is reasonably good considering the lack of modifications and individual attention available in the regular classroom.

The summary data for the analysis of the BRS scores for the three groups of emotionally disturbed children are presented in Table 2. As was the case for the CAT scores, Group I children again exhibited the greatest gains in the six-month interval. The t ratios based on the comparisons of the mean gains in behavioral rating scores of this group with those of Groups II

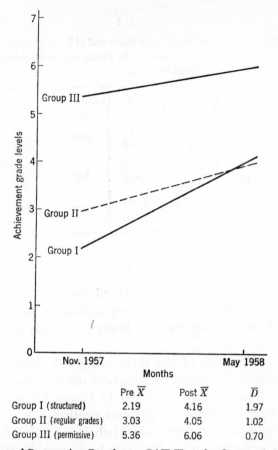

	Pre $\overline{X}$	Post $\overline{X}$	$\overline{D}$
Group I (structured)	2.19	4.16	1.97
Group II (regular grades)	3.03	4.05	1.02
Group III (permissive)	5.36	6.06	0.70

Fig. 1. Pre- and Post-testing Results on CAT Tests by Groups I, II, and III.

and III were significant in both instances at the .01 level of confidence. The Group II mean behavior rating remained practically constant over the six-month observational period. The mean gain in Group III ratings, somewhat less than half of the gain for Group I, was significantly greater than that for Group II (at the .05 level of confidence).

None of the F tests for homogeneity of variance were found to be significant at the .05 level of confidence. Apparently there is approximately the same variability in individual pupil be-

TABLE 2

Summary Data for Tests of Mean Differences and of Homogeneity of Variance
for BRS Gain Scores Made by Emotionally Disturbed Public School Children
in Three Different Instructional Settings.

Group	N	$\overline{D}$	σD	$\sigma \overline{D}_1 - \overline{D}_2$	t	F
I	15	5.607	2.717	.985	5.42†	1.19
II	15	.273	2.489			
I	15	5.607	2.717	.888	3.59†	2.37
III	14	2.421	1.760			
II	15	.273	2.489	.835	2.57*	1.99
III	14	2.421	1.760			

* Significant at .05 level of confidence.
† Significant at .01 level of confidence.

havioral rating gains within each of the groups. Group II
showed a negligible mean gain; approximately one-half of the
children in this group received lower behavioral ratings after
six months.

The relative gains of the three groups of emotionally disturbed children are graphically represented in Figure 2. It is to
be remembered that the children in Group III are approximately two years older on the average than the children in
Groups I and II. The mean initial behavioral rating for Group
I was 4.00 rating points less than that for Group III. Six months
later the difference in mean behavioral ratings between these
two groups was less than one rating point. As is further apparent
from Figure 2, the mean behavioral rating for Group II remained practically constant over the six-month period.

SUMMARY AND DISCUSSION

From a practical standpoint, the children who were placed in
the structured, academically programmed special class showed
an increase in academic achievement and behavior adjustment.

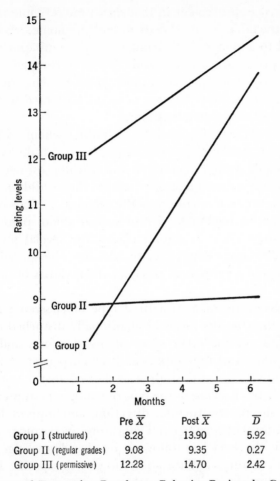

	Pre $\overline{X}$	Post $\overline{X}$	$\overline{D}$
Group I (structured)	8.28	13.90	5.92
Group II (regular grades)	9.08	9.35	0.27
Group III (permissive)	12.28	14.70	2.42

Fig. 2. Pre- and Post-testing Results on Behavior Ratings by Groups I, II, and III.

It can be argued that these are only overt changes and that the child still has within him the same disturbing feelings, fears, and anxieties, which must be brought out and resolved in order to effect real changes in the child's adjustment. It is not possible to say whether this assertion is true or not. It can be said, however, that the children who were placed in the experimental

class showed improvement in that they were (*a*) more constructive and tractable in the classroom and the home, (*b*) eager to
learn and to accomplish academic tasks, (*c*) significantly higher
in school progress as a whole, and (*d*) able to complete assigned
chores in the home. In general their system of behavior became
better organized. They became more goal-oriented with much
less meaningless, random behavior.

This experiment demonstrates to public school administrators first that special classes can be productive in the education
of emotionally disturbed children and that the cost need not be
out of proportion with that of educating these children in regular classes. When one considers the amount of time normally
required of the high-salaried professional school personnel by
these children when in regular classes, the special program is
not markedly more expensive. In addition, the special class is
not considered a permanent place for the majority of these children.

The advantages of a structured type of classroom environment for meeting the needs of emotionally disturbed children
exceed those of the other types discussed above, and exceed
the expectations of the authors and school personnel involved
in this study. Thus, the study also showed that a teacher can
successfully teach a class of the type of youngsters studied herein
provided she has instruction, direction, and support from experienced psychologists, special educators, and principals. Good
teaching is the model to follow; it involves knowledge of each
child's potentialities and the ability to give the specific direction
necessary for the child's growth and progress. A structured
classroom is one in which clear direction, firm expectations, and
consistent follow-through are paramount; this is presumably
a healthy state of affairs for normal children, as well as necessary for optimal growth of emotionally disturbed children.

RESULTS DEMONSTRATED IN SECOND YEAR

The results in the second year of the study are necessarily more qualitatively than quantitatively demonstrable. Owing to the turnover in teachers and normal changes in class composition —some children moving on to regular classes and new children coming into the group—it was impossible to gain the same meaning from before-and-after testing and to make the same comparisons made during the first year of the study.

On the basis of tests given when new children entered the group and at the end of the school year, some qualitative findings may be reported. These are briefly summarized below.

First, the five new children who entered at the beginning of the second year and the sixth new child who entered after the start of the fall term appeared to be similar to the children originally composing the experimental (structured class) group. That is, the new children had IQs in the 90 to 110 range and were about two to two and one-half grades below grade level on achievement in arithmetic, reading, spelling, and the fundamentals of grammar.

Second, of the original fifteen in the experimental group, three returned to their regular classes by the beginning of the second year and two moved out of the community. With five children moving out and six moving in, the new N for the experimental group, after a few weeks of the second year, was raised to 16.

Third, the three children who moved back to their regular classes continued to adjust and achieve normally and had, by the end of the second year, reintegrated themselves into regular classes.

Fourth, the new composition of the experimental (structured class) group shortly after the beginning of the second year, with sixteen children, continued to progress well as a group in all academic subjects. For example, over-all achievement for this group of sixteen on the CAT was 1.17 grade levels, probably indicating that the pace of the structured class was not much below that of the first year of the experiment and commensurate with that expected of average or normal children in regular classes.

Fifth, the second-year group made additional gains in social adjustment as rated by the two teachers early and late in the second year. The second-year teachers, being new, did not know or observe the emotionally disturbed children during the first year of the special class; hence the second-year ratings of social adjustment represented the net change observed during that period of time.

Sixth, during the second year there was a large reduction in serious overt classroom and playground disturbances (fights, temper outbursts, refusals to work, etc.). This is presumably attributable to the fact that the ten carry-over students from the first year were a well-settled group by the beginning of the second year and exerted a calming influence on the new students who arrived the second year. By the end of the first year it was evident that a structured classroom had some fairly definite limits and expectations. First-year students were often heard to remark to the new students: "You can't get by with that stuff in here. You really have to work in this class."

Seventh, the second year saw the beginning of a more enriched academic program with the introduction of social science, science, and related materials (see Teachers' Observations and Comments, Appendix B). The students began to work more on their own and for longer periods of time on the basis of preliminary instructions. The outcome of a structured and clearcut milieu is not that of making the child dependent upon others but, rather, of increasing his self-discipline and his ability to work independently. The real aim of a structured setting is to place a model before the child showing what the consequences of his actions will be—an aim which leads to the interiorization of this model rather than to increased dependence on outside forces.

Ideally, from a research standpoint, one ought to be able to accumulate applicants for special class placement up to the point where a whole new class could be activated. Then each new class and teacher could be treated as a unit to be compared in a variety of ways with other experimental and control classes. In a service setting, however, the methodological considerations had to give way to practical considerations; hence the new children were fed into the special classes whenever the administrative machinery required and permitted such an action. It is for this reason that the new children admitted into the structured classes beginning with the second year just dribbled in as opportunities permitted. From the second year onward, the whole program became more of a demonstration project than a research project.

The second year and later years (the project at the time of publication of this book is in its fifth year) proved easier not only in the actual management of the classes, but in the work with parents. Parental participation settled into a fairly structured groove with good attendance at meetings and with a pattern established as to how the children's conduct and educational problems were to be evaluated and improved upon. There was less despair on the part of parents about their children, and they were encouraged about the probable effectiveness of the special classes. The feeling became general that the structured classroom program and the parent discussion meetings had real merit and needed only proper and consistent implementation.

It was not possible to follow the permissive special class group into the second year. This class was abandoned and the children scattered into regular classes, but no record was kept of where each child was reassigned or how well each did in a regular class.

Attention is turned in the following chapters to the practical management aspects of carrying out a program for emotionally disturbed children. It should be clearly understood that the procedures reported here are suggested as a flexible pattern which might be followed by interested schools and departments of special education. Whatever procedures one may use, the real test is made by observing the results of the special classes, rather than by setting up rigid procedures in advance.

5

ESTABLISHMENT OF CLASSES; REFERRAL AND CLASSROOM ORGANIZATION

ADMINISTRATIVE ORGANIZATION

Special classes for emotionally disturbed children should be part of the special education program of a school system and fall under the administration of the special education coordinator, director, or supervisor, as the case may be. It is desirable for the administrator of special education to be in such a position that he can coordinate the psychological, health, and visiting teacher services as they are applied to children being considered for special classes. School systems in which the role of the special educator includes the coordination of all services for exceptional children, as well as administration of the special education programs, have a built-in advantage because here cooperation from the above vital services is a normal and assumed practice.

The special education administrator who has had experiences with initiating classes for exceptional children will know of the many problems and perplexities that can accompany this job. Even when great care is taken, conflicts will arise. This is to be expected because schools and special education personnel are still finding their way in these complex educational areas.

There are common considerations in establishing any special education class that also apply to classes for the emotionally disturbed. Some of these considerations are the following:

Where should the classes be placed? One of the first considerations is the question of the best location for the class. Generally speaking, special classes are placed in one of the existing facilities. The construction of new classrooms for the emotionally disturbed is not necessary in most cases.

Since it is advisable to start a program of this type with children in the primary and intermediate grades, it is highly desirable that these classes be placed in a regular elementary school. Even though in some cases there is a special building for exceptional children, classes for the emotionally disturbed do not belong there. Later in the program gradual reintegration of these children in the regular classroom can become an essential part of the plan. Disturbed children should have readily available opportunities to return to regular classes in the same school, and location in a typical school setting will facilitate this move.

The elementary school principal. Once it has been agreed that these classes should be an integral part of a regular elementary school program, the next most important consideration is the principal. The success or the failure of any special class program can rest in his or her hands. For the principal to be interested, understanding, and supportive of the program and all of the ideas upon which it is based is a real advantage. If he does not understand or accept the program, it has virtually no chance of being a success. A study conducted by Haring, Stern, and Cruickshank [11] pointed up the importance of acceptance and understanding on the part of principals and regular classroom teachers to the success of programs for exceptional children in special and regular classrooms. This consideration is almost axiomatic, and must be clearly met when activating a special class.

The classroom size and facilities. The classroom need not be larger than or different from a regular classroom. Too much space as well as too little can create unnecessary problems. Large unoccupied space is an invitation for restless physical activity. All space should be accounted for and used for instructional purposes.

Faucets at the sink or wash basin should be turned off and kept off. Equipment for noninstructional and recreational purposes should be removed from sight when not in use.

Classroom wall cabinets and space to store all materials and equipment which is not in use at any given time are essential. Any item in excess of what is immediately needed for instructional purposes is an unnecessary additional source of stimuli. Since it is just as simple to control as it is to ignore this phase of the learning environment, it should be controlled.

Color of classroom. The colors used in the room should not be drab. On the other hand, colors which are too bright may be distracting and overstimulating. Experimental evidence regarding the effect of color on emotional expression is conflicting. In general, color as a variable is not a major concern. There is no point in going out of the way to invite a color consultant and modify the whole color scheme of the walls and woodwork until such a time as someone demonstrates its importance for emotionally disturbed children. Light, neutral shades of color which are bright but nondistracting would seem to be the most practical.

The value of cubicles. Cubicles, or small study booths, have been used for instructional purposes for many years. Traditional educational systems advised the use of isolation for children who did not concentrate on their work. During previous decades educators did not use terms like "hyperactivity" or "distractible," but the behavior to which they referred was the same as that to which these terms refer. Isolation was considered punishment. The child took his place in the corner or out in the hall beside the door because he would not settle down. Now it is better recognized that a few children find the distraction of a classroom much too overstimulating. Even though they cannot tell the teacher directly that the excessive stimuli are the source of inattentiveness and distraction, teachers who will take the time to watch these children carefully will see much evidence to support the observation that these children have great difficulty in cutting out extraneous stimulation.

Thus the purpose in using cubicles or isolation corners is not a punitive one. To provide a place that is quiet, "private," and relatively free of visual stimulation is an important way to respond to the learning needs of children with emotional problems. When the use of these private areas for study does not carry with it the stigma of punishment, the child with an emotionally based kind of learning problem will often express a desire to have a less distracting place to do his work.

In the beginning the most hyperactive children should use these areas the major portion of the day. They can be brought out gradually as there is reason to believe that they can work in the classroom at tables or desks or in a small group. Usually from four to six booths will provide enough space for the children who will need them.

The rest of the furnishings in the room can be conventional. Movable table-desks with separate chairs are advisable because they provide for a flexible grouping arrangement. There is an advantage in having one large round or rectangular-shaped table for small-group and individual instruction. Sometimes the children's desks can also be moved to provide for this.

Number of children. Setting the limit on the number of children to admit to a special class for emotionally disturbed children is done more on the basis of empirical than experimental evidence. The teacher-pupil ratio for these children is still set by rule of thumb.

In the Arlington County, Virginia, study described in the preceding chapter, no more than eight children were placed in each class; and certainly the over-all social and behavior dynamics would have to be carefully considered before admitting more than eight to ten children. Because of the individual nature of the instruction and the ordered sequence of presenting material, the work and time involved in preparing these materials can be overwhelming for the teacher if the class is larger than eight to ten students.

Teacher assistants. A substantial amount of the preparation of teaching materials can be done by a teacher assistant. Teacher assistants can prove their worth manifold by doing the time-consuming routine duties involved in running a classroom of this nature. The additional salary of the assistant can be justified, mainly through the increased quality of instruction made possible by having more teaching materials especially prepared for the children. With such assistance, it may be possible to have up to ten children in the class. One teacher assistant can serve two or three classroom teachers at different times during the day.

Age of children. Cruickshank has said many times that in organizing new programs for exceptional children it is unfortunate but necessary to cross off one generation. By and large, when beginning a special class for the first time in any area of exceptionality, it is wise to begin with the youngest children. In the case of emotionally disturbed children, the earlier a child can be given attention, the more amenable he is to change and the less time is lost in educational growth.

In the most severe cases it is usually possible to make a positive diagnosis of emotional disturbance sometime during the child's first school year; frequently the less severely disturbed child will show moderate disturbance later. The first year at school calls upon the child to make some fairly major adjustments which may take him a few months to accomplish with confidence. After the initial demands to adjust have been met, he can often get through the rest of the year with less difficulty. From the group of emotionally immature children, a small number may have a relatively unstable and difficult time throughout the first year or two and then begin to show progress. The child who "grows out of it" after the second grade is an infrequent case, however. Thus, if the first three grades are carefully watched for signs of immaturity that is gross or severe, a good start can be made in coping with a troubled child's problems early in his school career.

Careful selection of children for a special class can certainly take place as early as grade 1 or 2. If the ages of children selected for study are from six to eleven, the range is wide enough to necessitate two classes, primary and intermediate. Establishment of a junior high class can be held off at least two years before it will be necessary to include a few of the older group. If all goes well, possibly the older children (intermediate grades) can be ready for reintegration in the regular seventh grade after a year or more in a special class.

Bringing children into the class. It is very wise to activate a class for emotionally disturbed children with less than the total complement expected, say, to begin with five or six students, then increase class size to eight or ten when the teacher is ready. To start all the children at one time is asking for unnecessary trouble. It is advisable to bring children into the class one at a time, with at least a week or two elapsing between each child's entrance. This gives the teacher and each new child an opportunity to get to know each other and to begin the new child's program before another addition occurs.

Scheduling. Scheduling in this type of program can play a far greater role than would be expected. For example, certain advantages can accrue from a shortened day, although it is not necessary. A school day lasting from 9:00 A.M. to 1:30 or 2:00 P.M. can provide a full day's activity for the children as well as offer the teachers some after-class time for organizing instructional material for the following day.

The morning should be used predominantly for working with the academic-tool subjects. The academic-task periods can be broken up with short, controlled, recreational activity once or twice during the morning. Caution should be taken not to try to sandwich in physical activities during the morning. Active physical games interrupt academic-work sessions and make it difficult for children to return to the relative quiet of work.

Other nonacademic programs such as music and art should be scheduled for the afternoon session. Arrangements should be made for the children who did not finish assigned academic tasks in the morning to continue afternoon work while the other children engage in the nonacademic activities. Withholding the more recreational and less demanding activities from children who are reluctant in finishing their academic work can have real motivational value for the children by helping to bring about constructive attitude changes toward schoolwork.

IDENTIFYING AND REFERRING CHILDREN NEEDING HELP

The first question an educator has to ask when considering classes for the emotionally disturbed is: "What children should be selected?" The second question is: "What criteria should be used?"

Since emotional disturbance seems largely unrelated (in a causal sense) to such other factors as age, sex, intelligence, and school achievement, where does one begin? Care should be taken not to have a motley assortment of cases, a "grab-bag," or "catchall," class into which any child can be dumped regardless of the amount or type of his disturbance. Care should be taken not to put in children who would be better off in a class concerned with poor sight, retardation, or physical handicaps. Children are desired who are primarily emotionally (or socially) disturbed, who need special handling in the classroom, and who are not so delinquent or "acting-out" as to disrupt the special classes so much that the class loses its proposed benefits.

Even though emotional disturbance is not closely related to age or sex or intelligence, these variables may still be needed to help with the establishment of favorable conditions for the initiation of such classes. For example, it is better to have children close in age in such classes owing to the older, larger child's frequent tendency to "lord it over" the smaller, younger ones. One should avoid any unnecessary handicaps in the establishment of such classes since there are enough handicaps to cope with under the most desirable circumstances. At the outset, conditions ought to be as favorable as possible since the actual handling of the children, educationally and socially, is itself enough of a task to occupy the full attention and skill of a professional staff.

When word goes out to principals from the appropriate administrative office that a class or classes for emotionally disturbed children are to be activated, the following guidelines are suggested in choosing the class members. In particular school settings, these guidelines may need to be altered in several ways.

Intellectual considerations. Since mental retardation is, in a sense, a fairly separate educational consideration, it is best to eliminate naturally retarded children. Admission of the low-IQ child tends to change the general educational objectives of a class for the emotionally disturbed, and changes the social-emotional character of the group, making the class into something other than what it started out to be.

A consideration to be kept in mind when doing psychological testing stems from the fact that seriously disturbed children often function poorly on tests. Even tests, like the Stanford-Binet and the Wechsler Intelligence Scale for Children, often underrate the emotionally disturbed child's *potential* level of intellectual functioning. However, a dividing line has to be established for practical purposes. Since an IQ of 80 to 89 is still within the "dull-normal" limits, the children falling within this range can be included unless for other reasons the class is to include only "above-average" (IQ 110 and above) children. By studying the test protocol the school psychologist or special education expert can determine whether a child whose score indicates an IQ of, say, 81 or 82 is potentially capable of performance at the 90-to-100 (or higher) IQ level with the improvement of his emotional condition.

Also, if children are likely to be referred who have high IQs —that is, above 130—care should be taken not to have too wide a range in ability. The relative ease with which a high IQ youngster learns to read and handle other fundamentals—when he is emotionally receptive and has proper skills—is so great in comparison to, say, a child with an IQ of 85, that to put them constantly together may work in a debilitating way for both youngsters. However, the extent to which individual instruction can be maintained in this type of class is also the extent to which discrepancies in ability can be modified and constructively handled.

Age and sex. As has been noted, the age range ought to be kept narrow, certainly not greater than the three-year range ordinarily found in the normal classroom. If enough children are referred to special classes, subdivisions can be made to allow for greater control of individual differences in age.

There is no a priori reason why the sexes have to be segregated. In most schools, behavior problems occur three or four times as often among boys, which makes classes for boys more likely. Even in highly emotionally disturbed populations of children, e.g., those found in residential treatment centers, the boys outnumber the girls perhaps as high as three or four to one. But there seems to be no reason, in terms of the *psychology* of the sexes or their *development,* for forcing them into separate classes for the emotionally disturbed any more than for separating them in normal classrooms. One or two girls in a class of six to ten boys should have no adverse affect; in fact, it could be argued that their presence there preserves a kind of typicality or normality in terms of everyday school life.

School achievement. Since many emotionally disturbed children display part of their disturbance in terms of poor achievement, this is a logical criterion for inclusion. Even at the fourth-grade level, the lack of achievement may put a child behind as much as two or three years. It is surprising how little achievement the emotionally disturbed child may sometimes display. This may be due, in part, to a lack of cooperation on tests and to lack of motivation to do well. However, even in daily class work, these children often show a similar failure pattern. After awhile the pattern of not working, not caring, becomes fairly standard and may therefore go on for years until or unless some constructive intervention is possible.

When the failure pattern has gone on for months or years, the child becomes actually *deficient* in fundamental skills as well as in his approach to learning. A fourth grader who reads on the first- or second-grade level is confronted all day long with failures: failure to keep up, failure to understand what is required, failure in his feelings of adequacy and ability to participate in classroom learning. When such a child is tested, the psychologist may say: "No wonder he cannot do fourth-grade work; he can read only on the first-grade level. He is so lacking in skills and knowledge that he is always behind."

How much achievement loss is required as a criterion? This can be answered only in reference to the composition of the class that is to be activated. If one has many referrals for classes for the emotionally disturbed, three or three-and-a-half years of educational (not to be confused with intellectual) retardation can be required for inclusion. If one is beginning on a preliminary basis and wishes to increase the achievement of less educationally deficient youngsters, a criterion of one to two years below proper grade level can be used.

Administrators and supervisors often ask about IQ level as a base line, rather than or in addition to grade level. For example, a child in the fourth grade with an IQ of 130 ought to be achieving at one grade level (or more) above his grade placement. If the child is actually functioning on the third-grade level, is he one year or two years behind? This depends upon which criterion—IQ or grade placement—is considered. There is no single *right* answer to this question. Equal justification can be had for either standard, and the final choice of children will depend more upon the number of children referred, the proposed size of the classes, and so on, than on the IQ or grade-level consideration alone.

Some children are emotionally disturbed in a variety of ways but show no achievement problems. Should they be included in such a class? The answer to this depends upon what one wishes to achieve in such classes. If there are not enough children who are both underachievers and emotionally disturbed, then the inclusion of emotionally disturbed children who have no noticeable achievement problems will certainly not work a handicap on such a child or on his peers in the special class. Sometimes a child like this who "has problems" but who, fortunately, can do his school work fairly well, can be a model and a motivator to the child who wants to do better but lacks perseverance, skill, and sufficient willingness.

Classroom and playground behavior. Emotionally disturbed children come in many patterns, sizes, and shapes. The disturbance may not show itself in all settings; it may be more blatantly present at school than at home, or vice versa. It may show itself more in free play situations on the playground or during relaxation or recreation periods in the classroom. Some emotionally disturbed children control themselves fairly well in class but "go to pieces," run away, pick fights, sulk, and become uncooperative on the playground. Each child has, so to speak, his preferred ways of stating his disturbance. Some social and play situations exacerbate emotional problems. Until a person knows the child well, he may not understand the how and why of such behavioral aberrations. He may not know just how to handle them until some approach like the special class is attempted and results are observed.

It might be sufficient to say that regardless of how and where the child shows his emotional disturbance, if the disturbance is judged great enough, then the placing of the child in a constructive classroom environment is likely to be salutary.

In summary of the above criteria, it is apparent that no fixed or final demarcation lines can be drawn. While considerations of age, sex, intelligence, and achievement are useful criteria, judgments in final analysis also have to be made on administrative, psychological, space, and other grounds. The discussion of outer limits, so to speak, on intelligence and achievement, is meant to serve as a set of suggestions, not to serve as a rigid criterion which all special classes for emotionally disturbed children should meet. As long as such a class is meeting the needs and requirements of both child and school, it can be a very constructive experience, almost regardless of the limits placed on intelligence and achievement.

Case Study

Billy was an emotionally disturbed youngster in the fifth grade. He was prone to picking fights in class and on the playground. He had been "talked to" by teachers and principals almost every week of his four-and-one-half years of school. He always resolved to do better but never seemed to keep his word for more than a week or two. Consultation with parents, although the parents tried to be helpful, seemed to lead nowhere.

Billy had been tested several times by individual and group intelligence tests, personality tests, and routine achievement tests with his class at the end of the second and fourth grades. On the IQ tests his scores ranged from 110 to 122, the lower scores being obtained on a group test. On personality tests, Billy tended to appear overly hostile and critical and to show clear signs of lack of confidence in himself. He seemed to be in social and emotional turmoil in one way or another a large part of each of his four-and-one-half school years.

Achievement test results showed him at grade levels 1.8 in arithmetic, 1.5 in spelling, 1.8 in language, and 2.0 in reading at the end of the second grade. If he had been up to par, his score should have been at around grade level 2.9 at this time. Two years later, Billy had gained only 0.5 to 1.0 grade levels in the same courses. Thus, after four years of schooling he was about two or two-and-one-half years educationally underachieving.

When Billy's characteristics were discussed by the principal, his classroom teacher, the school psychologist, and the special education director, it was unanimously agreed that he should be put in a special class for emotionally disturbed children. These recommendations were checked with Billy's parents and with Billy, and complete agreement was obtained. Billy said, in agreement with his usual attitude of promising to do better after a blowup, "I'd like to do better, and I think I can in a smaller class where I can get more help when I need it."

Consonant with the principles of handling children in a special class, which are to be laid down in subsequent chapters, Billy entered a special class at the beginning of the second semester of his fifth year in school. By the end of the school year, he had gained an average of one full year of achievement in each of the subject-matter fields measured above—about four times his typical gain and twice the normal gain—and wanted to go on to summer school in order to catch up completely with his regular class. He said that he wanted to return to his regular class as soon as he had caught up with their level of work. The teacher and principal agreed with Billy in this objective but added that he had to learn to control himself and settle his problems more constructively before he could return.

An additional year found Billy under excellent control socially and emotionally, up to his class level or ahead in all subjects. He was ready to go back to his regular school and class and take his rightful place among his peers in a renewed and mature manner.

In the special classes Billy experienced a more detailed, structured set of requirements. He knew *what* he was supposed to do, *how* to do his work, and he learned of the *consequences* of doing or not doing his work. He was respected, and he learned to respect himself and others more fully. He gained in the manner that it is predicted children will gain, both in achievement and in social-emotional living, when the opportunity is presented in small, regulated, structured classroom settings where fairness, firmness, consistency, and respect are the uppermost considerations.

CLASSROOM ORGANIZATION

The energy used by emotionally disturbed children in making their various assertions and adjustments is generally not being used for constructive learning activities; and this redundant pattern of behavior saps from these children a vast amount of energy which could just as well be used for constructive learning activities. It is our responsibility to order the learning environment so that it can provide academically and socially successful experiences.

To begin with, the full day is so well planned that the child becomes a part of the daily routine without choice of doing otherwise. If he attempts to pull out, he is gently but firmly pulled back into the job at hand. There can be no choices of activities in the first phases. The tasks are preplanned and prearranged. Later, as the child becomes capable of making choices, he may be allowed to choose between two acceptable courses of action. Care should be exercised in introducing this matter of choices. We must be certain that the two choices of action are clearly presented and that he understands that he must make a choice between only the two alternatives. If it is evident that he is not ready to participate in decision making, choices should be kept withdrawn for a while longer. To be able to make a simple two-choice decision is a sign of progress.

What are some of the ways in which the child can be helped to respond within this program? This aspect of the program will be considered in greater detail in Chapter 8; but perhaps the following basic suggestions should be brought out now:

1. Keep verbal directions to an absolute minimum.

2. *Show* the child what is expected of him whenever possible.

3. Assume that the child wants to do his best but must have a firm supporting hand.

4. Avoid head-on clashes whenever possible. If your assignment is reasonable, however, and he refuses, hold to your assignment regardless.

5. Clearly define all imposed limits. But do not go into long, drawn-out explanations of the limits.

6. Make sure he understands what is expected of him. Sometimes with the child who can read, it is helpful to write out a list of the accomplishments expected for each day, which he can check off as he completes them.

Curriculum Considerations[1]

Many of the children in the primary grades, even though they may have had one, two, or three years in school, will still be functioning on or below academic readiness. Do not be deceived by the fact that they have been exposed to the pre-primers and the primer; they may still need a readiness program. There may be a lag in both gross and fine motor coordination, in eye-hand coordination, in perception, and in laterality. It is vitally important to determine each child's level of development in each of these areas because this information is the basis of the program that is developed for him.

The following activities in each area might serve as a guide to assist the teacher in determining the child's level of development:

1. Gross motor coordination
   a. Can the child throw and catch a ball?
   b. Can he hop for a distance of ten feet on the right foot? On the left foot?
   c. Can he walk a tapeline heel to toe on the floor or ground?
   d. Can he walk straight backward for a distance of ten feet, looking straight ahead?
   e. Can he descend or ascend stairs with alternating feet in continuous steps?
   f. Is his walking gait regular, rigid, or uncoordinated?
2. Fine motor and eye-hand coordination
   a. Can the child color within lines?
   b. Can he cut on a line?

[1] Wretha Peterson, assistant supervisor, Montgomery County, Maryland, schools, cooperated in the preparation of this material.

3. Perceptual abilities
   a. Can the child do a two-piece puzzle?
   b. Can he sort 1-inch cube blocks according to color?
   c. Can he sort circles, squares, triangles, and diamonds?
   d. Can he reproduce tapped-out patterns, such as · · —,
      — — · ·, and — · · —?

Frequently there are gaps in gross motor development. If this is true, the teacher should provide a program to fill in the gaps. The following are appropriate activities to use. Have the child—

1. Jump on a bouncing board.
2. Balance on a 15-inch square balance board mounted on a 3-inch square block.
3. Walk a balance beam forward and backward, looking straight ahead.
4. Climb a ladder, and use the slide, jungle gym, and trampoline if available.
5. Identify body parts, e.g., respond to instructions to "touch your nose," "touch your eyes," "touch your ears," and so forth.
6. Imitate body movements, for example, place both hands on hips, extend arms forward at shoulder level, etc.
7. Step over objects.
8. Duck under objects.
9. Walk in spaces provided by laying a ladder on the ground.

Many of these children will be found to have deficits in finer muscle control, eye-hand cooordination, and/or perceptual abilities. The following activities will prove helpful for the above areas of development. Have the child—

1. Sort 1-inch cube blocks according to color. Sort paper squares, circles, or triangles according to color.
2. Reproduce a string of nursery beads. At first put on just a few beads, maybe only two or three. Give the child *only* the beads needed to reproduce the pattern given him. His *must*

look just like the pattern he is copying. Help him if necessary.

3. Use simple puzzles. The puzzle must always be finished before the child leaves it, with teacher's assistance if necessary.
4. Classify objects.
   a. Use toy objects for classification. Put all the people in one group and all the food in another group, etc. At first have only two classifications, using only about six objects each of which will fit into one of the classifications. More objects and classifications may be added as the child can handle them.
   b. Use picture cards for classification.
5. Sort cards with dots on them. Put all of the cards with one dot in one pile and all of the cards with two dots in another pile, etc. Follow same procedure as in 2.
6. Sort cards with different letters of the alphabet on them. Use same procedure as in 2.
7. Follow dotted lines to make pictures of geometric forms and objects, as:

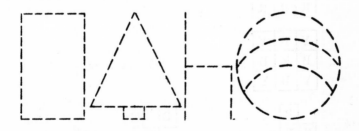

8. Sort forms—circles, squares, triangles—according to shape.
   a. Wooden forms, such as nursery beads, parquetry blocks, etc.
   b. Colored construction-paper forms.
      (*Note:* If this activity is difficult, all circles could be red, all squares blue, and all triangles yellow. Later the colors could be mixed, or all shapes one color, maybe black.)
9. Reproduce a simple block design, as:

R	R	R
Y	Y	Y
R	R	R

R = red   Y = yellow

a. Give the child the design made with 1-inch cube blocks and a tray with six red and three yellow 1-inch cube blocks. His design *must look just like the pattern.* Help if necessary, then give him an easier design next time.

b. Give the child a design made with 1-inch squares of colored paper. Provide a tray with the correct number of blocks of required colors.
(*Note:* Child may build on top of the teacher's pattern. Accept this, but encourage him then to build in the tray.)

c. Increase difficulty of designs as the child is able to do more difficult ones, such as:

R	R	R
R	B	R
R	R	R

R = red, B = blue

Y	B	Y
B	Y	B
Y	B	Y

Y = yellow

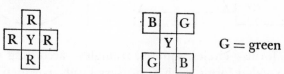

G = green

10. Use simple cutout stencils made of heavy cardboard. Later use the cutout portion to trace.
11. Use reading readiness workbooks, the page to be done being torn out each time. Frequently the page will need to be cut apart.

Sources of Materials

Following is a list of sources of materials useful in the activities just discussed:

From Beckley Cardy Company
      1900 North Narragansett Avenue
      Chicago 39, Illinois
      or
      Young Playways
      3404 Connecticut Avenue
      Washington, D.C.
      Colored 1-inch cube blocks for counting
      Parquetry blocks
      Large wooden beads of assorted shapes
      Sifo Puzzles
      Match-Me Reading Readiness Cards (Kenworthy)
      Kenworthy Perception Cards
      Kenworthy Little Cards (alphabet)
From Young Playways
      Primary Word Builders (boxes of letters)
      Primary Number Builders (boxes of numbers)
      Desk seat work charts
      One-inch Mosaic Color Cubes
      Go Fish (consonants)
      Go Fish (consonant blends)
      Dolch Picture Word Cards
      Match-Word Reading Game (Kenworthy)
      Phonics Bingo
      Dolch Vowel Rummy (Sets 1, 2, 3, and 4)
      Picture Word Builder (Milton Bradley)
      Number-Rite
      Colored Counting Sticks (assorted sizes)
      Consonant Lotto
      Vowel Lotto

From Houghton Mifflin Company
    2 Park Street
    Boston 7, Massachusetts
    Getting Ready (pages perforated for removal)
    Getting Ready Practice Book (pages perforated for removal)
    Learning Letter Sounds
    Tip; Tip and Mitten; and Big Show (three preprimers with one workbook and teaching manual)
    Jack and Janet (primer with workbook)
    Up and Away (first text with workbook)
    Come Along (second text with workbook)
    On We Go (consecutive second text with workbook)
From Phonovisual Products
    The Volta Bureau
    1537 35th Street, N.W.
    Washington, D.C.
    Phonovisual Manual
    Consonant Workbook
    Vowel Workbook
From McCormick Mathers Publishing Company
    1440 East English Street
    Wichita 1, Kansas
    Speed Boat; Jet Plane; and Jato Car (phonics books with teacher's guide)
From The Steck Company
    Steck Avenue and Grist Boulevard
    Austin, Texas
    Working with Numbers (Books 1, 2, and 3)
From J. L. Hammett Company
    2393 Vauxhall Road
    Union, New Jersey
    Say-it Addition Game
    Say-it Subtraction Game
    Say-it Multiplication Game

Say-it Division Game

No. 750 United States Map Puzzle Plaque

Washburne Individual Addition Cards

Washburne Individual Subtraction Cards

Washburne Individual Multiplication Cards

Washburne Individual Division Cards

From Whitman Publishing Company

    1220 Mound Avenue

    Racine, Wisconsin

    Fun with Birds (workbook available)

    Day by Day with Science (in Help Yourself Series; workbook available)

Guidelines for Teachers

The teacher should remember that along with careful structuring, the provision of opportunity for success is the foundation on which the school program is built. This is most important because these are children who up until this time have met with failure in many of their academic pursuits. If at any time the teacher gives a child work too difficult for him, the child should be helped to complete the work correctly. It is important that the work be completed even though the child needs a great deal of assistance.

The teacher should evaluate carefully every piece of work he gives the child so that discrepancies between the level of the child's performance and the expectations for performance can be minimized. Be available to give the child help if he really needs it. Each piece of work should be correctly completed before another is started. *Remember, earned success is vital to this program.*

As the child progresses on through the grades, use as many concrete materials as possible, being careful to choose materials, such as blocks and colored sticks for numbers, which do not carry strong emotional components. Tear out pages in workbooks as long as it is necessary. If given the whole book, the child may be tempted to do the whole book and go rushing on ahead, or become so upset at seeing so much work to be done that he will get frustrated and do nothing.

Some emotionally disturbed children respond well to the creative arts, both as recipients and as creators. Before they can write, they may express themselves with paints, chalk, clay modeling, etc., as well as by dictating stories, poems, and songs to the teacher. They may even compose melodies as well as the lyrics. The added ability to write down their stories, poems, and lyrics is quite rewarding to many emotionally disturbed children.

The children may grow in knowledge and composure by doing simple, well-directed experiments in science, such as watering one plant and giving one plant no water; or by doing a simple, well-directed project in social studies, such as one on the theme "How Thanksgiving Came About." This would probably include reading and reporting. The reporting might be written or oral, and/or might involve various forms of art work. Music would probably be included.

Gradually the child taking part in the program can be brought back to the academic work and experiences which are appropriate for his grade-achievement level. Once progress to this point becomes evident, the child needs to have little if any modifications in the curriculum or the instructional materials. After he is able to maintain earlier gains in the regularly used textbook and this is supported by comparable gains in social and emotional development, consideration may be given to trying him out for part of the day in a regular classroom. The pay-off is how well he can demonstrate the gains recognized in the special, more sheltered environment when he is brought back into a typical school setting.

SUMMARY

The organization of special classes for emotionally disturbed children requires the understanding, acceptance, and efforts of each person in the school system who will be in any way responsible for the program. Of particular importance is mutual agreement on the educational procedure by the administrative staff, the director of special education, psychologist, principal, and teachers of the school in which the class is located.

Care in consideration of the number of children in the classroom, in selection of the children, and in bringing the children into the class is also imperative to the smooth functioning of the class. Scheduling and programming of educational tasks require intensive preplanning. Exercising certain practical controls over the learning environment can greatly reduce unnecessary classroom conflicts and disorder.

6

PERSONNEL CONSIDERATIONS

The increased recognition of the problem of emotional disturbances in children and the discovery of effective educational techniques will undoubtedly provide momentum for special classes for years to come. If present indications are read correctly, the need for special classroom teachers of emotionally disturbed children will probably triple in the next five to ten years.

Since teacher-training sequences specifically designed for emotionally disturbed children are virtually nonexistent, much of the teacher education for these classes will have to be done through in-service and summer workshop programs. The selection of the teachers will probably be made from among those who are already having successful experiences as regular classroom teachers. In so far as present knowledge indicates, there is no reason to believe that the basic competences needed by teachers of special classes for the emotionally disturbed should be very different from those needed for general classroom teaching. However, teaching a special class of children with emotional disturbances ranging from moderate to severe degree does require an extra degree of perseverance as well as understanding beyond that provided in basic teacher training. In addition, there is some evidence which indicates that personal characteristics are an important factor in teacher selection. The major objective here is to provide basic considerations for the selection and training of teachers and ancillary personnel involved in the education of these children.

TEACHER SELECTION

Personality Factors

Making positive statements about factors of personality as they relate to successful teaching of emotionally disturbed children is a risky business. Conflicts exist in this area of thought—conflicts that are to some extent a result of philosophical differences concerning the approaches and methods to be used in teaching children with emotional problems. An approach which stresses a permissive or nondirective educational framework may stress certain personality characteristics among teachers, whereas a more structured setting may stress other traits. Personality criteria for the selection of teachers are today highly subjective. For that matter there is little if any experimental evidence relating a given set of personality traits in teachers to their effectiveness in teaching emotionally disturbed children; and if one thinks of personality as learned factors of behavioral responses, there is no reason to believe that the necessary traits for teaching cannot be learned from training in the majority of instances.

At the same time, there are certain definable traits that in the experiences of the authors have tentatively been shown to yield relatively good immediate results in special class teaching. These characteristics as they have been observed in teachers lose some meaning when put into words; yet the tentative observation to be made is that teachers of emotionally disturbed children should display the following basic traits in their teaching:

1. A calmness in the way they respond to and deal with the problems and conflicts of children

2. An unshakable stability in all phases of their relationships with children

3. An attitude of fairness and sincerity with children

4. A firm belief in the potential of all children

5. An unyielding firmness in holding limits once set and clearly defined

6. The ability to apply and direct teaching materials in an orderly manner

In addition to these specific traits, it is believed that teachers of these children should live a comparatively self-actualizing life, in Maslow's sense of the term, outside of teaching. That is to say, these teachers should hold a realistic view of themselves and their relationship to others and to their environment; they should be self-accepting and accepting of others; they should be spontaneous and creative in their activities and have a hearty and enthusiastic outlook upon living and working.

It is disconcerting to hear it said that teachers of exceptional children work so hard because they are completely devoted to these children. Teachers should live full and useful lives outside of their classrooms. For teachers to spend all of their waking hours preparing materials, scoring papers, planning lessons, or being concerned in other ways with teaching cannot, over the long haul, yield constructive returns for themselves or the children they teach. It is easy for teachers to become emotionally bound to these children and expect to be able to solve all of their problems for them. This kind of excessive altruism can lead to trouble for all concerned. Emotional responses to children in the classroom lead to conflicting and unstable treatment which can actually compound the problems. The teacher who becomes this involved with the child's progress cannot help but reflect deep concern and disappointment when the child falls back a little. The emotionally disturbed child depends upon a stable setting, with ample opportunity for him to make an evaluation of his progress. This is difficult to provide when the teacher is emotionally unstable.

Teacher Competences

Method of child study. Among the most important competences teachers of the emotionally disturbed need is the ability to understand and use scientific methods of child study. Prescott has offered educators a most systematically scientific and inclusive approach to studying children. A teacher with supervised experiences in using this method of child study along with the underlying philosophy put forth by Prescott can significantly increase his understanding of behavior and learning characteristics, as well as gain a better perspective on children's emotional and educational needs.

To teach all children, a knowledge of the physical, intellectual, emotional, and social factors and processes is essential. This is particularly true in the case of the emotionally disturbed child.

Physical factors. The teacher should be able to detect and understand some gross signs of irregular neurological development and organic brain involvement, if present. Through objective observation, teachers can become equipped to note and take into account growth rate and maturity level; and some defects of gross and fine eye-hand motor coordination and some abnormal features in physical health and appearance can be detected. The teacher will need help, however, in interpreting signs correctly and in gearing educational methods accordingly.

Intellectual factors. As much knowledge as can be gained of each child's intellectual functioning, both quantitative and qualitative, is needed. A certain sophistication about intelligence is extremely important. It is expected that teachers know enough not always to accept IQ scores at face value and know how to qualify scores for particular children. Evaluating intellectual ability through critical observation is often essential to designing the child's educational program; indeed, its value may rival the validity of objective tests.

Emotional factors. Teachers need to understand aspects of development that affect emotional adjustment and to seek understanding of the causes and remedies for problems related to development. They should be aware of the possible meanings associated with emotional outbursts and demands. An awareness of how the child views himself and those around him is equally important.

Social and cultural factors. Teachers should be able to understand the influence of a child's social and cultural environment upon his development. Continuous exploration of parent and peer relations is important; these relations should be well understood by the teacher.

Learning disorders. Learning disorders may accompany, cause, or exaggerate emotional conflicts. Teachers must be able to detect learning disabilities and have an understanding of the multiple causes of them. To be able to make a differential diagnosis of education and learning is no simple matter. Teachers should be familiar with techniques of discovering disorders in learning and behavior such as perceptual-motor incoordination, hyperkinesia, dissociation, and impulse disinhibition. In addition to recognizing these learning and behavior difficulties, teachers should be familiar with the modifications in the presentation of materials and subject matter which are indicated.

Methods of teaching. Emotionally disturbed children, whether in regular classes or special classes, require some special teaching techniques and an individualized curriculum. The teacher needs the ability to determine where the child can achieve success academically and develop a sequence of educational tasks based upon this information. This calls for a wide range of competences. The teacher should be able to interpret and synthesize psychological and physical data and keep anecdotal records. Diagnostic and remedial education skills are important for teachers of these children, including a thorough understanding of subject matter and order of presentation for grades 1 to 8.

Usually these children are placed in special classes which, of course, are ungraded. They are grouped according to academic achievement and social development. An understanding of social interests as well as chronological, emotional, and intellectual development thus is essential in maintaining appropriate groupings.

A wholesome amount of sensitivity on the part of the teacher to each child's frustrations in learning seems very important. Teachers will be continuously working toward increasing the ability of these children to cope with the irregularities and conflicts they encounter. This is done through careful planning and through recognizing where the child should be placed with respect to his adequacies in dealing with frustrating stimuli and his abilities to accomplish the educational requirements.

Parent conferencing. Working with parents is an essential part of a program for emotionally disturbed children; and certain aspects of the parent-teacher relationship can be carried over in the parents' child rearing practices. (See Appendix A.) Suggestions about assignments and suggestions that parents establish routine consequences for behavior infractions rather than harsh punitive measures and provide regularity in the daily routine are a few concrete aids teachers can offer parents. The rationale for these suggestions, however, must be well understood. It can sometimes be difficult to convince parents of the value of these techniques. Many times it is helpful to have follow-up interviews with parents in order to assess their regard for the suggestions that have been made in initial efforts to engage them in working cooperatively and broadly on the educational program.

Teachers need to have skills in counseling with parents to the extent that changes may be expected in the way parents handle their children. Also, it is necessary that teachers be completely objective with parents. The temptation to sugar-coat the problems their children may be having should be avoided. It is much kinder and more potentially constructive for teachers to be frank about a child's progress.

TRAINING AND PROFESSIONAL EXPERIENCES

Educational experiences. The specialized training program for teaching emotionally disturbed children should be presented on the graduate level. The undergraduate program should offer an elementary education major with at least one semester of full-time student teaching. It is highly recommended that a minor in human development and child study be required.

The following educational experiences, in addition to those provided for in the elementary education sequence, are considered essential for these teachers on the undergraduate level:

1. Observing and dealing firsthand with emotionally disturbed children; keeping anecdotal records of the children's behavior and the adult interactions with the children

2. Planning and developing teaching methods and curricula for emotionally disturbed children based upon child study data

3. Interpreting and synthesizing psychological, neurological, pediatric, and educational reports

4. Teaching in a special class for emotionally disturbed children under the supervision of a qualified teacher

A considerable amount of sophistication is needed with the observational technique. Much subtle but vital information can be gained through trained observations of a child's physical growth and development, through discerning characteristics of perception, conceptual thinking, learning, and fine and gross motor coordination, and through noting emotional characteristics and social adjustive techniques. Such a broad understanding, moreover, can be gained only through actual experiences with children in various settings. Individuals involved in teacher training have for some time recognized the need to provide more experiences with children for teacher trainees, but only a few colleges have taken concrete steps in this direction. A very good case could be built for replacing perhaps half of the formal course work with supervised actual teaching experience during the last two years of teacher preparation.

Professional experiences. A minimum of one year's experience in the regular elementary classroom is recommended for teachers of emotionally disturbed children. It is important to know how children without emotional disorder respond, solve problems, and relate to peers and adults. Moreover, experience with conducting organized, meaningful activities of an academic nature for the full day with a large group of children can be gained only in the classroom, and this experience is the educator's backbone: without it he is insufficient to his task. It would be ideal if beginning professional experience in the special class could be on an internship basis, for a minimum of one year, and could be under the supervision of a qualified teacher of emotionally disturbed children. The shortage of teachers in this specialty will, however, preclude such a program for some time. As the situation now stands, the best that can be hoped for is to have an in-service training program conducted by the supervisor of special education for the school, perhaps involving regular conferences with the school psychologist.

Conferencing with professional personnel. Teachers should have experience in conferences with other professional personnel including not only the psychologist but the physician, vocational counselor, school nurse, and speech therapist as well. This experience should include an opportunity to present educational reports on a child before a panel of these personnel. The reporting of objective observations on children under controlled circumstances offers information that is basic to many decisions regarding the educational progress of children. Experience in interpreting the reports of the other members of the professional team in conferences is also essential.

Teachers can make a vital contribution through their reporting of a child's behavior and educational progress because of the amount of intensive experiences they have with individual children over a long period of time. If the recording of the behavior is reasonably objective, such data may well be the bases for the evaluation and planning of the whole team.

OTHER SCHOOL PERSONNEL

In one way or another, all school personnel affect the success of any class, especially a special class which requires extra effort and understanding. This does not mean that specialized personnel are personally responsible for the success of a special class, but it does mean that their *integration* into the general effort can be effectively or poorly done. Since specialized personnel have unusual functions to perform and since their work is all geared to the welfare of the child at school, their services in the interest of a special class are manifold.

The services which highly trained personnel can perform include the following specialties:

Visiting teacher. The visiting teacher is primarily a mobile contact between the school and the home. Such a teacher is not an attendance officer, although attendance at school may be an issue that arises from time to time with a child; neither is a visiting teacher a social worker who visits the home. He or she has a far more integral task to perform. Learning to view the child as a product of the home which affects his adjustment and progress at school is the aim of the visiting teacher. A visiting teacher can be an extremely important contact between home and school, interpreting to the home the requirements of the school and interpreting to the school the strengths and weaknesses of the home.

In the interest of selecting children carefully for the special classes for the emotionally disturbed, it is important for the visiting teacher to visit the home, to assess the parents' co-operation potential, to explain the project in broad terms to the parents, and to act as an interpreter to the school of the parental potential. This is a far more important role in selecting candidates and activating classes for the emotionally disturbed than it is with special classes for the blind, the orthopedically handicapped, or the mentally retarded. In these groups and, indeed, in nearly all nonemotionally disturbed groups requiring special education, the manifest nature of the disability is so clear that little doubt exists that the children need special help and special facilities. With the emotionally disturbed child, on the other hand, attitudes are still rampant that all the child needs is "a good licking" or "to be sent away if he doesn't act right." Other extreme attitudes indicate an equally unrealistic position, e.g., that the emotionally disturbed child needs only more love.

It is important that the parents have some realization of the means and bounds of the special class. The visiting teacher can explain such limitations to the parents. Often, or at least on occasion, the special class may be an alternative to putting a severely disturbed child in a residential institution or foster home or to bringing about some other relatively drastic reshifting of the child's life. Special class placement and all that is involved should be *completely* understood by the visiting teacher.

The parent may want to ascertain the quality of the education in a special class, the child's chances to avoid stigma if he is put into a special class; is the child expected to make normal progress or is the special class simply a "custodial action meant to keep him out of other people's hair." (Also see Chapters 8 and 9 in this connection.) The visiting teacher may meet all kinds of unreasonable parental attitudes even when parents are trying to be helpful in constructive ways. The prejudices of the general public regarding emotional problems are still blatant, and school personnel face them no less often than the staffs of child guidance centers, adult mental hygiene clinics, and hospitals.

The visiting teacher can continue to be a go-between for parents and school, if need be, long after the special classes have been activated. Sometimes children have to be taken out of even the especially constructed atmosphere of the special class, as when, for example, a child has to be removed from the home owing to a breakup of the home or to other extenuating circumstances; in such a case the visiting teacher can interpret conditions to a court, to social agencies, or to parent surrogates.

One of the most rewarding duties of the visiting teacher is that of assisting the return of the child to his regular class. Here the visiting teacher can interpret the move and the family's readiness for it to the school; and the new teacher and new principal can be similarly apprised of the child's assets and limitations as he moves into his more normal school environment. Keeping track of the child who has made such a move and being ready as a "one-person task force" to aid in the solution of crises that may develop are other rewarding duties of the visiting teacher in this setting.

As a program of special classes for the emotionally disturbed gets under way and settles into a predictable role in the total school system, the visiting teacher can aid other staff members in ferreting out and evaluating children who may need to be referred to such classes. The visiting teacher can act as a first-line screening person to help teachers, principals, and others decide upon the propitiousness of referring a child to a special class.

Psychologist. Psychologists are also integral to a program of this type. The school may want to do a good deal of testing on the referrals to any special class. As long as some important criteria are followed (see Chapter 4) in selecting children for special classes, the psychologist will need to be consulted and probably some amount of first hand testing will be needed. Criteria relating to achievement, intelligence, and general symptom complex will need to be evaluated by the psychologist.

The psychologist may make a number of visits to the classroom of the to-be-referred child to observe his behavior and to talk with the principal and teacher about the child's general eligibility. At such a time, preliminary testing may be done, or previously existing tests may also have to be evaluated by the psychologist in the light of the demands for special class placement.

Two other very important functions may fall on the psychologist's shoulders in such a program. First, he may have over-all charge of the program. Because of his training in testing and research and his role as a psychotherapist or counselor, the psychologist's skills are made to order for such a program. He may find himself functioning in one or many or all of these capacities, depending upon the composition of the professional staff of a school system and upon the availability of various specialized personnel.

In the program reported upon in this book, the special education adviser (Dr. Haring) headed the project in an over-all administrative capacity and acted as an on-the-spot adviser to all school personnel, including the classroom teachers. The consulting psychologist (Dr. Phillips) helped design the study and acted as a visiting consultant to the classroom teachers and as the group leader in the parent discussion groups. In other settings these roles might be reversed or be found to overlap. It really matters little what the specific titles of the professionals are so long as their various roles relating to child, school, and home are well met.

In larger school systems it would probably be possible for the psychologists to design and oversee the entire study but employ personnel to carry out the specific roles mentioned above. The division lines will vary from one school system to another, but in all serious and respectable projects some regard will have to be had for research, for service requirements, for contacts with parents, and for the technicalities of selecting children and following through on the day-to-day amenities involved in carrying out the program.

Coordinator of special education. Usually such a program as discussed here cannot be initiated without the perseverance and over-all planning of a high administrative official in the school system. Yet most officials in traditional positions do not have the training or interest to initiate or follow through on the many details inherent in programs in special education. In one way or another, then, the coordinator of special education has to initiate and carry through such projects; schools without such coordinators are likely to suffer in the quality or quantity of special education studies, particularly in the area of service to emotionally disturbed children.

In training, the coordinator is an expert in education, more specifically in special education. As a specialist of this type, he may be best suited to an administrative or supervisory role; but many coordinators are intimately concerned with the educational problems of selected special groups such as the emotionally disturbed, and may take a very specific role in a program of this type.

The coordinator of special education may have a very high level administrative role to play in the whole school system, and usually carries on a variety of projects with classes for the brain-damaged, physically handicapped, mentally handicapped, etc. Thus his actual duties in such a project as here described will depend upon the interest in this area of work and the time available to supervise it.

Like the psychologist, the coordinator may act as a face-to-face advisor to the classroom teacher. He will also have to explain and interpret to principals and others the behavior of the children and how the program attempts to remedy educational ills. In addition, his role involves matters of budget, hiring personnel, and presenting programs to school superintendents or school boards in the hopes of interesting them and in obtaining money for projects. He may also (with the psychologist) devise and propose research projects for presentation to agencies which provide research grants.

Principal. As indicated previously (Chapter 5, page 86), the principal is an individual who can make or break a program of special classes for emotionally disturbed children. One reason this is true is that precedents do not exist for special classes in this area as they do for the mentally retarded and the physically handicapped. New pathways have to be sought, and this is sometimes a painstaking and perhaps temporarily unrewarding task. Money and services are not available for the emotionally disturbed child's education as they are for the mentally retarded or the physically handicapped. Unseen or nonobvious difficulties do not bring out the sympathies and supports that the more obvious handicaps do. Hence a principal who is willing to have special classes of this type in his or her school is usually a farseeing and realistic individual. Not many principals would have put up with the initial disorder and discouragement and seeming impasses that were encountered in the early days of the authors' project discussed in this book.

What can the principal do? He can support the project. He can act as a counselor to parents and teachers troubled with the problems presented by the youngsters. He can protect the integrity of the children in the special classes against the criticisms of those who decry such a program. And he can make available space, equipment, time, administrative effort, and other tangible and intangible services which will advance the successful operation of such classes.

Sometimes a strong and respected principal can appeal to the school administration to look in on, and see for themselves the usefulness of, special classes for emotionally disturbed children. A "before-and-after" view of the children can be presented by the principal, who might know the children over the years better than any teacher or school psychologist.

In a sense a principal's school is his castle, and within limits the castle can be used in support of projects in special education. The principal who is ready, willing, and able to take on such projects and to make them part of the educational program of the school can not only contribute well to the education of the children in question but can also make long-range contributions to education and to general knowledge of services of this type.

Teaching assistant. The teaching assistant, or assistant

teacher, who may also act as a substitute when the regular classroom teacher is away, has to know about, understand, and support the general purposes of the special class. As a helping hand he can aid or hinder the general progress of the classroom structure. An assistant who overindulges the children, who cannot say yes or no and mean it, who inadvertently opposes the general structure of the classroom can be a distinct liability. On the other hand, the assistant teacher who supports the general structure can act as a bulwark to the regular teacher in times of stress and strain. There were a number of instances where the assistant teacher, acting in a quiet but firm manner, kept the classroom discipline from getting out of hand, in the study principally referred to in this book.

The teaching assistant can often aid a child's solution of difficult problems where the child has to work alone or for long periods of time on something that is very requiring or tedious. The assistant can simply be present, be available, keep a watchful and stabilizing eye, and see that the child gets through to a successful solution of his task.

When he acts as a substitute for the regular teacher and the tasks of the whole class fall upon him, the assistant teacher can offer the same kind of continuity and stability that were present before the substitution. Therefore, whenever possible, it seems highly desirable that the assistant teacher be a continuous adjunct to the regular teacher. The regular teacher is bound to be absent upon occasion, and the special class program can be greatly injured by the insensitive and clumsy efforts of an outright substitute who knows or cares little about the purposes of the program. In just a few days time the hard-earned success of many weeks and months can be lost if the class is left to a poorly prepared teacher. On the other hand, the teaching assistant with a background of regular presence can often lessen or even preclude the disruption of class routine. For these reasons the assistant teacher needs to be included in the training of teachers for such special classes; a pinch hitter needs to know the rules of the games just as much as the regular team member.

School Physician. The school physician's role is, of course, to pass judgment on the physical well-being of the candidates for the special class. This role is usually less clear-cut in the case of emotionally disturbed children than it is with orthopedically handicapped, blind, or other demonstrably physically disabled or handicapped children. However, the physical well-being of emotionally disturbed children is of consequence to the school and to other children. Children who are known to have physical handicaps, whether subtle or obvious, may be included in classes for emotionally disturbed children, but in most instances their inclusion would be of doubtful value. The school physician can pass on the desirability of such inclusion and can help screen out the child who has a major disability of a physical nature and may have a secondary or associated emotional problem.

It is, of course, the school's business whether to mix emotional and physical handicaps. It is better, in the opinion of most special education experts, to have separate classes and to have still a third type of class for overlapping cases, e.g., cerebral palsy children who are emotionally disturbed and children with sight and hearing difficulties and emotional problems. The size of the school system and the extent of the special education program will, in most instances, determine whether overlapping classes are activated. In any decision along this line, the school physician's estimates are of considerable value.

The school physician can often aid the school in interpreting its program to professionals such as other physicians, nurses, and welfare workers. It is also of value for the school physician to realize and to state the realization to the public that emotionally disturbed children may present the personality and behavioral complaints they are known to have without there being any demonstrable physical basis. Sometimes superficial and almost quackish treatment is proposed for the emotionally disturbed child; in such cases the school physician can stand ready to assert that if there is a physical-health cause for emotional disturbance, it is probably not what the quacks may represent it to be.

It is sometimes easy for professional workers without medical training to overlook medical problems in the emotionally disturbed child. Problems with vision, hearing, skin disorders, and other relatively common complaints may be attributed in superficial thinking to "emotional factors." Sometimes the word "emotion" gets to be a very littered grab bag, and a wise school physician can help prevent this and aid in securing treatment for hearing, vision, and other problems which may be wholly independent of emotional disturbance.

Bus driver. In the study on which this book is based, a healthy respect was gained for the role of the bus driver. In many instances conferences and phone calls between school officials and the bus driver had to take place in order to bring matters of conduct on the school bus under control. Sometimes problems that were smoldering in the classroom broke out on the bus, probably because the amount of control necessary to handle the problem was absent. The bus driver's job is mainly that of driving the vehicle, not ministering to the fights and feelings of the children. However, sometimes the children's actions and emotions supervene and some constructive interfering is necessary.

In the study, the pattern was to have the bus driver report immediately to the parent if the child had been involved in any misconduct on the school bus. Since the bus which transported the special class children let them off near their homes, and was usually not full, some time was fortunately available for this service. Likewise, if a problem developed on the way to school, the bus driver reported it immediately to either the principal or the teacher. In this way problems did not accumulate, and they did not defy solution. Usually the youngsters in conflict were brought in to the teacher or the principal immediately upon arrival at school whether the problems had occurred on the way to school or the day before on the way home.

As would be expected, the bus drivers were urged and helped to deal firmly with the children in order to maintain continuity between the school and home programs. They were also taught to realize that more than the usual amount of problems might arise with this group, that they were to try to handle each problem immediately if possible, and that they should report each problem to the proper officials regardless of their own success in handling it. In this way very few problems arose that could not be dealt with in a short time. The bus driver became as integral to the program as anyone else. It was realized that, like other incidental personnel, the bus driver had to help in maintaining firmness and consistency in the school program, that the presence of a too yielding person in this job might do the program irreparable damage.

Helping teacher. By the term "helping teacher" reference is made to physical education, art, music, handicraft, and other teachers who come into a classroom at appointed times but who do not have any sustained responsibility for the children. An art teacher, for example, may cover several classes in a day, spending a half hour or an hour in each class, sometimes instructing teachers as well as students. The helping teachers in the program referred to here came into the classroom one or two times a week, usually in the afternoon, for a period of from twenty to forty-five minutes.

Since the regular classroom teachers were always present, except when the youngsters went out to play with the physical education instructor, there arose very few discipline problems. In addition, the recreational work, whether indoor or physical education, was usually viewed with great relish by the children. The recreational period was often held up as a kind of prize which the children could engage in provided the day's work was reasonably well accomplished. The fact that the recreational periods came in the afternoon allowed them to be a logical aftermath of the endeavor to meet the responsibility to get one's work done.

INTEGRATING SPECIALISTS' WORK

What does one do when he has all the observations of all the specialists? How are the findings integrated? How can meetings intended to gather and impart information relative to a given child be prevented from deteriorating into a vast hodgepodge? It has been necessary to be very mindful of this problem. There are too many instances in which all conceivable bits of information are gathered and no integration or workable plan emerges.

In selecting children for special classes, it is important to cover all aspects of the child's development and present status, at least in broad outline. It is important, as has been emphasized throughout this book, to know the child well, so that the specific tasks and behavioral limits that are established are as germane as possible. But while gathering of information is useful, the integration is still more important.

The first way to avoid confusion is to keep the criteria for special class inclusion clearly in mind; viz., matters pertaining to intelligence, age, achievement, and social and emotional condition should be kept explicit. If a child fits the criteria, well and good; if he does not, then a decision that is equally firm and reasonable can also be made. To proceed to make decisions without using explicit criteria is folly, and the staff that moves off in as many directions as it has members is bound to confuse the issues.

A second way to avoid confusion in the contributions of the various specialists is to hew closely to the achievement aims and behavioral limits set up for the special classes once the classes are started. If a child is not progressing well or if he seems not to fit in, the first questions asked should be about his actual day-to-day and hour-to-hour handling. Here the coordinator of special education or the psychologist can act as a moderator and chief decision maker. Decisions are, of course, subject to error, so they should always be subject to appropriate change when necessary. But some member of the special education staff ought to hold the final key to a decision. If his judgment is poor, this will be revealed; if it is good, encouraging evidence ought to appear.

Such a policy of data gathering and decision making may appear to some to be too arbitrary or too authoritarian. It is believed, however, that a closer look at the complexities will bring a different verdict. The psychologist or coordinator of special education is presumed to have the knowledge and experience necessary to integrate such a special class program for emotionally disturbed children just as the physician in a hospital setting coordinates and acts upon information obtained from various hospital laboratory tests, from the nurses' observations, and from direct contact with patients.

The usefulness of the various specialists cannot be denied. Their contributions to the pool of knowledge about a child are of inestimable importance. But the information will not come to one with the proper labels attached and will not integrate itself. Thus, if it is not properly and practically integrated into a forward-looking program, the information does not help the children in concrete and discernible ways.

SUMMARY

Special classes for the emotionally disturbed child cannot exist without proper selection and training of teacher personnel. While personality characteristics associated with effective teaching are not clearly understood, experience with special classes for the emotionally disturbed leads to an emphasis on the teacher being task-centered, and handling emotional upsets and underachievement in a matter-of-fact, unemotional "back-to-work" manner.

Teachers should have knowledge of the physical, intellectual, emotional, and achievement backgrounds of students; but the manner in which such knowledge is implemented and applied at the level of any child's daily work is very important. The daily educational experiences should be carefully planned; conferencing between the teacher and other professional personnel should be made possible, so that a constant corrective factor can be applied to the classroom situation.

Other school personnel—visiting teacher, school psychologist, coordinator of special education, helping teacher, teaching assistant, principal, school physician, and even the bus driver —are important both for their particular skills and for their ability to promote the various important aspects of the child's daily program at school.

The manner in which all these personnel are integrated is important. Conferencing must not be a conglomeration of ideas, facts, and fictions but must lead to an integrated, practical program geared to the child's daily classroom requirements. An over-all theory or set of guidelines becomes necessary for this coordination.

7

EDUCATIONAL METHODS AND
MATERIALS FOR SPECIAL CLASSES

During the early stages of the kind of educational program described in this book, almost complete control over the classroom environment is necessary. The structure that is an inherent part of this program for emotionally disturbed children must be established immediately and held to firmly. This requires certain modifications in the classroom and the number of children in the class. Related suggestions about helpful practices for the regular classroom teacher have been included in other chapters. The methods and materials referred to in this chapter have been found useful in making modifications for the special classroom.

THEORY

It may be helpful first to give the reader a view of the theoretical framework from which the teaching methods referred to in the following pages derive. To this end, the theory of personality and psychotherapy known as *interference theory* will be briefly explained. This theory has been adapted to classroom use, and forms the basis for the thinking in this book [28–40].

No one ordinarily wants to change or eliminate behavior that is basically healthy or that is individually and socially useful. One may want to improve upon it—but not eliminate it. On the other hand, undesirable (individually or socially injurious) behavior one does wish to eliminate, and many methods of therapy have been developed as means of altering or doing away with it. The method used here, interference theory, employs certain concepts and techniques which differ from those of Redl, Bettelheim, Pearson, and other writers discussed in this book. To make this difference clear in relation to the theory itself, only a short discussion is needed.

Two major techniques have been used to eliminate disordered behavior: *extinction* and *interference*. To extinguish (uncover, desensitize) disturbances, care should be taken not to reinforce that which is to be eliminated. Extinction had its first and perhaps simplest presentations in the original experiments of Pavlov. When the dog in Pavlov's studies had learned to pair the sound of a metronome or a bell with meat powder, the sound alone came to produce salivation (as a readiness for eating, originally associated in the hungry animal only with the meat powder). This familiar paradigm has come to be known as *conditioning,* a simple and direct form of learning. Extinction, a simple form of unlearning, was found to arise from not reinforcing the association. Thus, to extinguish the salivation to the sound of the metronome or bell in the Pavlovian study, the sound was continually presented without being paired with the meat powder. In time, the sound lost its conditioned value, and would no longer arouse salivation in the animal or would do so feebly.

In many forms of psychotherapy and other attempts to overcome pathological behavior, extinction (uncovering) has been the primary method used. In the unpunishing context of the therapist's office, the patient tells over and over again his ills and woes and comes to view them more neutrally. That is, he extinguishes his emotionally undesirable reactions to his former experiences. This form of therapy has served as a prototype of almost all psychotherapy developed since Freud. There are some, but very few, exceptions to this generalization.

Consider next interference as a method of doing away with unwanted behavior. Suppose someone knows the standard keyboard of a typewriter. Suppose further that he wants to learn a new and improved system of typing. How does he do it? Does he first extinguish the old standard keyboard system? Hardly. In fact, one could not think of a convenient or useful way to extinguish a complex skill like typing. Suppose, as further illustration, a person wished to learn a new way of speaking— perhaps a new language associated with a permanent move to a foreign country. How does a person in this situation overcome his penchant to use English, and how does he learn the new language? Does he extinguish the ability to speak and write the English language, assuming for the sake of argument that he never expects to use it again? Certainly not. He *interferes* with old habits and gradually builds new discrimination that forms new habits.

A similar interference-centered, relearning model would be followed in redoing or in relearning complex behavior as in learning to walk and speak differently as a part of training for acting, learning to solve problems through improved mechanical or mathematical methods, and so on. It could even be argued that extinction itself is a simple kind of interference that just inhibits the old response rather than builds up complex and compound discrimination of a previously unknown type.

The position taken here is that interference is a relatively simple, easily employed, economical, and easily tested method of changing behavior. But one has to be careful how the interference is carried on, and one has to take clear account of the total structure within which the interference is to take place, e.g., know the attitude structure and skill level of a child in reference to arithmetic in judging the best way to proceed to help him overcome faulty habits with, say, long division.

Thus, the theoretical structure in this book takes its cue from an interference standpoint. The methods proposed here, in their stress on limits and on appropriate task setting, stem from an application of the interference position. The reader will quickly recognize the general approach toward classroom behavioral and achievement problems as the over-all plan and discussions in this book unfold before him.

THE LEARNING ENVIRONMENT

Although numerous, the characteristics of emotionally disturbed children are familiar to most educators. The anxieties and tensions such children experience are manifested in many ways, but among the most commonly observed behavior symptoms are hyperactivity, aggressiveness, destructiveness, distractibility, inattentiveness, disinhibition, and withdrawal. Emotionally disturbed children rarely display one symptom; they are more apt to show a combination of the disturbed types of behavior mentioned above.

The first and most essential rehabilitative step to take for children who display these symptoms is to modify the educational environment to whatever extent is necessary to provide a suitable learning setting. How is this done?

Reduction of stimuli. Within the framework proposed in this volume, the most obvious way to reduce tensions in the beginning is to reduce, whenever possible, environmental conditions that may create tensions. It has been believed for some time that children who are distractible and inattentive respond to a marked reduction of stimuli in the learning environment. The less auditory and visual stimulation there is (and this includes the stimulation of social interactions), the less distracting the setting is for focusing attention on the material to be learned. And, of course, the more stimulating the material to be learned, the greater the possibility for holding attention.

In the beginning stages of teaching emotionally disturbed children, in so far as possible, one should remove from sight all that is not directly related to the particular material the children are expected to learn. The teacher should place before each child only that which he is to attend to; when he is finished, the materials should be taken up and supplanted with new materials. Distractions are to be minimized; a precedence and a predictable routine are to be established immediately.

Reduction of activity. Educators know children well enough to be aware of their active nature, particularly when the stimulation to activity is great. Most children enjoy activity. At the same time, most children can be expected to return to the classroom after recess and settle down quickly. Hyperactive, aggressive, emotionally disturbed children, on the other hand, cannot settle down as quickly. Therefore, when expectations call for concentration, one should not expect the emotionally disturbed child to settle down and concentrate without proper preparation. Eliminate unnecessary activity. All activity should be reduced in every way possible until it is obvious that the youngsters can cope with it. This includes eliminating the possibilities for leaving the seat and walking around the room. It requires regularly planned "seventh-inning stretches" but not vigorous activities during periods of academic learning. Highly stimulating physical activity during controlled study produces chaos and does not in any way contribute to the learning process.

Reduction of group participation. Aggressiveness and destructiveness are frequently sparked by group activities. It does not take much interaction for these children to create enough spark to start a fire. In the beginning of an educational program for emotionally disturbed children it becomes apparent that they are not ready to participate with each other in a group. Group participation is desirable, but only when the children can profit from it.

A specific emphasis on solution or resolution to a problem should always be held uppermost by the teacher. For the first few months, at least, all academic-learning activities should be planned and conducted individually. Gradually, small-group work may be attempted, but the teacher should be quick to recognize when a child is not yet ready to share his work.

The above suggestions for controlling the situational influences amount to reducing the learning environment to its most fundamental form, and the removal of all situational stimulation possible, except for the controlled stimulus of material to be learned, is important. In addition, having only one stimulus at a time allows the learner to avoid being confronted with too many choices or decisions which may act as distracters rather than promoters of learning.

TEACHING METHODS CONDUCIVE TO LEARNING

Basic Assumptions

To present specific methods of teaching prefaced with phrases like "should use" and "ought to" is a most dangerous thing for educators and psychologists to do. Everyone is aware of the dogmatic, lower-jaw-projected attitude this represents. Yet when one thinks of all the procedures and techniques teachers have to select from for use in a large variety of circumstances, how is it possible to list a half dozen or so which nearly always work? It would be unrealistic to suggest that any given set of anwers could be used under any circumstances, at any time, with any child. However, the assumptions on which the present volume is predicated must be listed and evaluated.

Only four basic assumptions are made here which must hold before the following material can have validity. These assumptions are:

1. That the teacher's essential motivation, beyond earning a living, is the utilization of the natural learning process of children to the fullest possible extent.

2. That the teacher believes that all children have potential for learning useful, constructive skills which can be utilized now and in the future for the benefit of themselves and society.

3. That the teacher employs, throughout his teaching ex-

periences, efficient and complete methods of child study. All information that can possibly be integrated will prove to be useful in gaining a thorough understanding of children, but it must be information that is properly and forcefully integrated.

4. That the teacher responds warmly, sensitively, and empathically but with firmness, fairness, and consistency to all of the children he teaches.

These assumptions are far from novel; they can be found in almost every manuscript on the education of children. Yet they are difficult to find embodied in specific teaching methods. They must be regarded as broad principles rather than specific guidelines. They have been interpreted by many educators and psychologists to give rise to a very permissive classroom environment, especially for emotionally disturbed children. Previous programs have emphasized adjusting the curriculum almost entirely to the child, or sugar-coating learning to fit the child's disturbed state. On the other hand, the point of view expressed here is that while modifications are always in order, there is a practical limit to the amount of modification of the curriculum that can be entertained. The value of endless modification of requirements is doubtful. Likewise, permission granted to a disturbed child to "act out" his anxieties and aggressive impulses can be detrimental. Neither the curriculum nor society can permit the endless and profitless acting out that much current theory states is desirable.

Specific guidelines are, therefore, called for. Having humane attitudes toward children and wanting to educate them and see them mature into responsible adults are useful motivations for teachers. But more specific aids to classroom teaching are needed.

Specific Guidelines

Some concrete and specific ways in which the above assumptions accumulate into specific classroom guidelines are the following:

Limited dilution. While some dilution of subject matter may be needed at the outset, there are specific limits to the desirability of this. Subject matter in more or less pure form has real value for helping children overcome their learning and behavior problems. The academic-tool subjects very importantly stimulate the child to come to terms with himself, to meet the normal demands of his educational environment, and to prepare for the future.

Concreteness. Material to be learned should be made as definite as possible—the more specific, the better. The value of a concrete assignment in arithmetic or reading lies in the fact that follow-through until completion is easier to accomplish here, for both student and teacher, than in a more abstract assignment.

Developmental stages. Once the child's developmental level is at least functionally determined, the reading and number skills and concepts can be given to the child in terms of this level. It is absolutely necessary that the child have reached a readiness for the material he is expected to learn and that the material be presented to him at his achievement level. The subject matter can then increase in difficulty by increments consistent with the child's forward progress.

Immediate scoring. Each task that is assigned should be scored upon completion whenever possible. This gives the child an on-the-spot picture of how he has done (immediate reinforcement) and an opportunity to see and correct his errors if he has made any.

Achievement. Steady forward progress is easily perceived by the child when concrete subject matter is used. A special effort should be made by the teacher to make sure the child knows where he was yesterday, where he is today, and where he can be tomorrow regarding his progress. To be able to see the gains he is making can be a most satisfying experience for him—so satisfying, in fact, that he may become intensely involved in the learning process. This is the manner in which motivation is promoted.

Means to an end. A casual inspection of the proposed curriculum for emotionally disturbed children might lead the reader to believe that it is similar to a traditional-subject-matter curriculum; and obviously the subject matter itself does remain essentially the same: it is not disguised or sugar-coated. If specific learning disabilities are observed these are of course treated. In the beginning the program is restricted, with little room for choice of activity. At this stage the emotionally disturbed child responds best to a structure that is defined, constant, and simple. The child must be able to solve simple conflicts before he can go on to the more complicated ones. If first things are not kept first, then poor achievement and loss of motivation follow.

It is important to be certain that the child can complete the assigned learning tasks. It is not helpful to make it easy for him. The child knows what he can do, and he wants to preserve and enhance his sense of achievement. In fact, it seems necessary to expect him to accomplish, so that he will think well and realistically of himself. Through experience grow confidence and realistic self-appraisals. Gradually the child becomes more involved and interested in his own achievements. He then requires less imposed structure because he can take over for himself; he gains more freedom to make choices. As this freedom of choice and the responsibility for choice increase, the child is on his way to being able to return to his regular classroom.

Teaching approach. The purpose of the program described here is to help the child gradually become more realistic about his behavior and more accepting of the demands of his environment. It is a matter of the child expanding the scope of his interaction with the requirements of his environment. As he begins to cope with his problems more adequately, the child gains confidence in himself.

The teacher's role in this readjustment process is a major one. The consistency of the teacher-child relationship is the function upon which to build. The teacher offers the much needed stabilizing influence by his consistent responses to the youngster. He corrects for the refractory errors the child makes by responding the same way each time the child's behavior or performance deviates from expectations. Through this constant reflective feedback the child can see concretely where correction is necessary. In short, the teacher is confirming desirable behavior and failing to confirm that which is not desirable.

Expectations. Tasks leading toward a carefully planned goal must be worked out for each child. The expected performance should be based upon a thorough knowledge and understanding of where the child is developmentally and how fast he can progress. The educational tasks that are assigned are an essential part of the program. They form the basis around which growth toward emotionally healthy performance can evolve.

The teacher should make sure that the child understands what is expected of him and that he lives up to expectations. At the start of each day the child can be given a list of the educational tasks he must accomplish. He can be given necessary instructions, told the location of materials, and requested to proceed with the assignment. Assignments must be broken up into a series of short tasks; as he finishes each task the child is to be instructed to have the teacher check his work and then go on to the next task.

Follow-through. In the beginning the child may show some resistance to the requests that are made of him to start working. This is to be expected, so the wise teacher should be prepared to cope with the problem. This program depends upon the child accepting the teacher's demands. If the teacher is aware of the child's ability to do the assigned task, his refusal can be viewed as another attempt to have his demands met and to reject the demands made upon him. The teacher has the choice of permitting the child not to do the assignment or insisting that he complete the assigned task. To yield to his demand is to unintentionally promote disorder. The child must come to grips with the responsibility of completing assignments. During the initial stages of the program the teacher must follow through with the child to make sure that he does the assignment exactly as he was asked and that a precedent for doing work is established.

Consequences, not punishment. If a child refuses to do the task assigned or refuses to accept the structure and limits set, punitive measures are generally not satisfactory. *Consequences* are a more constructive approach to motivating the child.

Specifically, consequences operate in several ways: having to redo poorly prepared work; not being permitted to move or to play and take part in other activities until the necessary obligations are met; letting a child lose his turn if he's not ready at the appointed time or if he forces himself forward; and having specific rules which operate with objectivity, finality, and clarity that apply to most or all conduct infractions by the child.

In using consequences, it is necessary to intersperse in the child's school day activities which he enjoys doing. Children usually enjoy recreation, art, and music activities. In addition, responsibilities assigned by the teacher, such as running errands and leading the other children to lunch, are useful anchorage points. Careful planning in imposing consequences can be quite effective. One can expect to be prepared to put into use some system of consequences because children who have been allowed to run away from tasks will not take hold without some struggle. No matter how much the material to be learned is sugar-coated or to what extent the approach is based upon the interest of the child, the fact still remains that there will come a time when the child will have to do tasks that are not pleasurable to him.

It is a mistake constantly to bend over backwards to make sure that the child will find academic learning fun. The hard work of learning can be established as being somewhat satisfying but usually not recreational. The most intense phase of this program is the initial stage of convincing the disturbed child that he must accept limits and demands imposed upon him and reducing the unreasonable demands he may make to keep from doing assigned work. The use of consequences will prove more effective and less apt to increase tension than the use of verbal threats and punishment.

Reduced verbalization. As a general rule teachers talk a great deal more than is necessary. Verbalizing is the most abstract method of getting across a point. Wherever possible *show* the child instead of telling him. Excessive talking on the part of the teacher often seems to condition children not to listen. Set the precedent of giving instructions once. Make sure the instructions are well organized, clear, and to the point. After the instructions have been given and understood, it is reasonable to expect the child to get the job done without having to repeat the instructions. When the child will not face up to his fair share of the responsibility, urging and coaxing *as influence techniques* are usually futile. A good rule to follow is to do at first what you would have to do later in order to get over to the child the consequences facing him. This attitude on the teacher's part saves a lot of time and avoids encouraging the child to play the game of testing the firmness of the educational requirements.

The motivation associated with a child's refusal to do tasks which are well within his abilities may stem from his feeling that he can win out over the teacher's request for him to work. This is the sort of matching strength which leads to a dead end. It should be discouraged immediately without argument. Give the child ample time to get started. If, after one reminder, he has not begun, impose appropriate consequences; and even though the consequences are imposed, make clear that the child is still expected to finish his assigned work. Do not assign new tasks or change the activity for the child until he has completed his preceding assignment. Going ahead depends upon the successful completion of prior assignments.

Response to misbehavior. Even though every effort has been made to control misbehavior by reducing group activity and increasing classroom structure, some misbehavior will occur occasionally during the initial phases of the program. At such times it may seem easier, as well as very tempting, to overlook behavior which you cannot accept. Unfortunately, results from educational experimentation where the child's inappropriate assertions have been confirmed are frightfully discouraging. Yielding to the disturbed child's demands as expressed in impulsive, hyperactive behavior results in a failure to come to grips with the important issues at hand.

It is not realistic to expect the child to become more tractable unless a well-structured pattern of behavior is expected from him. If the adult in charge, usually the teacher or the parents, nods approval to behavior that everyone knows cannot be appropriate, the child has no course but to continue to behave inappropriately when the impulse strikes him. Contrary to the assumption that children gain satisfaction from "acting out" impulsively, children become less satisfied and more impulsive when permissive, loosely structured conditions prevail. The child actually gains support from knowing exactly how he can behave.

As the child gains appreciation for his ability to respond with greater control and maturity, he gradually releases himself from the need to depend on imposed structure. From this point on he begins to provide his own controls. This maturing into self-control is, of course, a relative matter since, as adults, all of us could improve in this regard. One should not expect perfection from the youngsters, and care should be taken not to rush them too much. Expecting too much progress can threaten gains which the child has made.

Make-up work. It has been observed frequently that when children are absent from school owing to illness and other causes, they are not required to make up missed work. It is important that firm structure be maintained in this respect as well as in daily achievement and disciplinary issues. The child who returns from an absence should be required to make up his missed work as soon as posssible, allowing for gradual make-up if the child has been out of school for a protracted period.

If a child is not required to make up missed work, he tends to develop a careless attitude toward assignments in general.

This may promote the use of school absences to get out of difficult assignments. The development of close home-school contacts can, of course, sew up such gaps in the child's thinking and acting and preclude failure to finish normal assignments.

Returning to the regular classroom. The special class, as stated before, is considered only a temporary arrangement for emotionally disturbed children. The children in such a class will not, in most instances, require special class placement throughout their school experiences. Unless there are learning impairments other than emotional and behavioral adjustment problems, special classes of the nature described here will not be expected to be necessary for any one child for more than three to four years. The objective of this program is to return the child to appropriate intellectual and emotional functioning in the regular educational program as soon as it is legitimately possible. Placement back in the regular class should be considered the climax of all the work and planning that has preceded.

Return to regular class circumstances should begin gradually, and the elementary school in which the special class is located is the first and most logical place to start. The child can be placed back in the regular class for not more than an hour or two a day in the beginning. As he is brought into the routine of the regular classroom, his time there can be increased. The teacher should make the most out of the importance of this "new" classroom.

Except in rare instances, return to the regular class should not be attempted during the first year. However, if the plan outlined in this book is followed, two or three children in a class of eight or ten may have progressed well enough to return to regular classes during the first part of the second year; and another three or four children may be able to return to regular classes by the end of the second year. The two or three children remaining from the original class, if they are not progressing well, may signal the possible existence of learning disabilities in addition to emotional disturbance. If sufficient progress is being made in the special class, however, almost all of the children should be returned within a three-year period.

Selection of regular classroom. One way to help assure the success of the child's regular class experience is to pay particular attention to the selection of the teacher of the regular class in which the child is to be placed. This regular classroom teacher should have many of the same competences and characteristics of understanding as the special class teacher for the emotionally disturbed. Indeed, when establishing special classes for emotionally disturbed children, it is desirable to have several regular classroom teachers work occasionally with the special classroom teachers, so that many of the special class teachers' techniques can be employed with the child when he goes back into the normal classroom setting.

Follow-up. It is advisable to follow up the progress of these children for the remainder of their classroom experiences. There is no reason to expect difficulty, but it is interesting and informative to see how well a child copes with his adjustment problems throughout his total school experiences.

SUMMARY

The theory underlying the structured classroom environment was reviewed briefly. Older methods of treating emotional disturbance depend more upon what is known as *extinction.* Newer methods rely more on what is called *interference* in judicious ways with the pathological and immature processes characteristic of the emotionally disturbed child.

The newer method of relying on interference, then, presupposes certain changes in the classroom environment of the child, as well as changes in the teacher-student and the parent-child relationships. The learning environment of the classroom must include the following types of changes: reduction of stimuli, reduction of activity and of group participation so that new directions can be found in these respects, and initial concentration on individually conducted academic learning.

Much emphasis falls on the teacher and his method of teaching and handling the emotionally disturbed child. The teacher's basic assumptions must be recognized and clarified in terms of the over-all objectives of the special class. The teacher must carry out a number of constructive and articulate activities including the following: diluting the subject matter at first so that a successful start can be experienced by the child; concreteness in presentation; the use of stages of development of complexity of subject matter; the use of immediate scoring (reinforcement); steady and continuous recognition of achievement; clear expectations and follow-through in relation to the child's work; the use of consequences (not punishment); the reduction of verbal stimulation; firm attitudes toward missed and make-up work; continuous follow-through on broad requirements; and proper orientation toward the time when the child can return to regular classes.

8

HANDLING SPECIFIC
PROBLEM SITUATIONS

The classroom teacher of the emotionally disturbed is constantly bringing up questions about how to handle specific types of situations. It is reasonable and logical that the teacher would raise such questions since even the experienced teacher cannot be expected to cope with all conceivable problems, especially with emotionally disturbed children.

There are two general approaches useful to other educators in helping the teacher of special classes for the emotionally disturbed come to grips with typical problems.

First, ask the teacher how he or she handles the circumstance in question. The first and foremost question to be put to teachers (and parents: see the parent discussion protocols in Appendix A) when they have asked about handling specific problem situations is: "And what did you do?" or in other words "How did you handle it?" The reason for this is to encourage the teacher to give more thought and consideration to the assumptions he is working on, and also to give the special education consultant or school psychologist more information which can be used in helping the teacher.

When the teacher states what he did in a given problem

situation with a child, the first thing that comes to light is what did *not* work. When it is known what can be eliminated, or what probably does not work for that teacher with a given child in a given type of circumstance, one knows better how to proceed.

An example is the following conversation between a teacher and a consultant:

TEACHER: I can't seem to get Johnny to quit teasing others.

CONSULTANT: When does he do the teasing?

TEACHER: Usually he begins the day this way. Or he may do it when he's tired, or even when he's finished some work and feels he can let down for a time.

CONSULTANT: Usually when he's not well occupied, when he is idle?

TEACHER: Probably that's the main reason.

CONSULTANT: And what have you done to control this with Johnny?

TEACHER: Several things: scolding him, depriving him of his free play period, having him sit closer to my desk—oh, lots of things.

CONSULTANT: And how do they work?

TEACHER: Usually not too well, except for the moment. I turn my head or get busy with something, and away he goes, off to tease someone else.

CONSULTANT: You mean he actually leaves his seat, roams about, physically approaches others?

TEACHER: No, not necessarily, but he may do that, as at the end of a work period when he wants to have a seventh-inning stretch.

CONSULTANT: Controls have worked only momentarily?

TEACHER: Uh-huh.

CONSULTANT: Let's think a minute. Suppose you assumed at the start of the day that Johnny was going to get into this kind of trouble sooner or later.

TEACHER: Yes—

CONSULTANT: Suppose further that you said to him, "Johnny, I know you have a strong tendency to bother others when you are not busy. Today, I am going to keep you very busy; but when you are through with your work for the time being, I want you to rearrange the books on the bookshelf, put them in alphabetic order, and put the magazines in order according to their dates." That is, you give him something to turn to instead of idleness. You structure the situation further for him at a time when he's previously been prone to get into trouble.

TEACHER: You mean I'll have to keep after him all the time like that?

CONSULTANT: No, not all the time, but a good part of it for a day or two until you establish another pattern for him. When he knows for sure that you can and will keep him busy, he'll tend, in time, to develop his own motivation and direction after you've given him this kind of direction. If you feel he really does need a stretch, then by all means let him have it, in the form of an errand perhaps. But just don't leave him idle and completely open to his own poor judgment in this kind of situation.

A large number of similar situations come easily to mind. The child usually develops his own pattern of reacting to leisure time, perhaps by not wanting to do any work, by boasting about his successes, or by competitive and teasing exchanges with other children, and so on through a thousand and one daily episodes. The trick, if it can be called that, is first to know the child's tendencies and then to take action which challenges his assumptions; or to take action which allows him to develop a different perception of the situation. But in most instances, the teacher has to take the first, structuring steps.

The *second* general approach to helping the teacher is to notice and to point out to the teacher his own instances of successful handling of other problems and draw him out about his reasoning in these successful instances. Any given teacher will have a variety of successes and failures in coping with specific types of conduct or emotional problems in the classroom. A moment's reflection on the positive successes—how they were envisaged and how the teacher took decisive and constructive action—will aid in applying the same reasoning to other circumstances in which, as yet, the teacher has been successful. The following conversation between a mental health consultant and a classroom teacher of emotionally disturbed children will illustrate this point:

TEACHER: I've been able to work out a lot of problems with Bobby, but it is hard to know how to handle him when he gets his temper going.

CONSULTANT: Give me an example.

TEACHER: The other day, Bobby came into the classroom after an errand to the office for me. When he came back in, he found someone had "borrowed" his crayons and he jumped at Mike accusing him of taking the crayons. Mike came to his own support and told Bobby to "lay off" accusing him unless he was sure of his facts. This infuriated Bobby all the more since his first effort to pin the crime on someone had failed; he now had to look further for the culprit. Then he turned to Oscar, who sits behind Bobby, then to Gene, who sits behind Oscar, not really waiting to find out from either of them what their story was. He also did not call on me for help but tried to take the matter into his own hands. He was furious by this time, and I had to ask him to leave the room and stand in the hall until I could find his crayons and until he could calm down. He stormed out, slammed the door, and burst into tears.

CONSULTANT: And then what did you do?

TEACHER: I didn't to anything to Bobby. I just asked who had his crayons, and when I found them I asked Charles, the boy who had them and was about to give them to Bobby when Bobby stirred up so much fuss, to put them back on Bobby's desk.

CONSULTANT: Yes, and then what followed?

TEACHER: Well, by this time Bobby had calmed down and was asking to come back into the room. He was still out in the hall, you know.

CONSULTANT: Yes.

TEACHER: So I let Bobby come back into the room. When he entered, he saw his crayons back on his desk and asked who put them there. I nodded to Charles for him to answer Bobby, which Charles did. Then Bobby got mad at Charles and threatened to beat him up after school and made a lot of other threats as well.

CONSULTANT: How did you handle Bobby's continuing temper and accusations?

TEACHER: I guess I just didn't handle them; I felt it better to let Bobby calm down. I didn't say a word when Bobby got irate

at Charles, and neither did anyone else. Bobby then took his
seat and sat there silently except for gasping—you know how
a child will give short gasps after a hard crying spell?

CONSULTANT: Yes.

TEACHER: Well, he gradually settled down over the next ten to
fifteen minutes and slowly got back to work. But what bothers
me most is that this happens every few days—two or three times
a week on the average—and I don't seem able to control it.
The temper just has to spend itself like a hurricane without
my being able to use myself and the classroom setting to control
or modify it—with Bobby, that is.

CONSULTANT: So, all totaled up, Bobby evades your possible discipline and outmaneuvers you, so to speak.

TEACHER: Yes, but I would gladly do things differently if I knew
how.

CONSULTANT: I know you would, and I am not criticizing; I'm just
trying for the time being to understand what happens and
what you actually do. Let's set this aside a moment, and now
let me ask you how you handle other problems with Bobby.
Give me an example.

TEACHER: Well, he used to sass me a lot and talk back and throw
verbal threats at me. He hasn't done that for several weeks
now, so I guess we've largely overcome this problem.

CONSULTANT: How did you handle it when he sassed you?

TEACHER: I realized that he sassed when he had a subject he didn't
like, such as spelling, or when he had to get down to any work
he disliked. I told him at the beginning of each day how we
would proceed, that is, that we would spend the first half hour
on arithmetic, the second on reading, the third on spelling,
and so on. I gave him a chart of the day's work—his work,
that is—but it was, of course, similar to the routine of the
others in most respects. I told him that if he complained about
the spelling in the form of sassing or talking back to me, I
would take five minutes off his recess time for each sass. He
tried me out a few times and then began to control himself. I
could see, on a few occasions, that he was about to build up to
some verbal salvos to throw at me, but he caught himself, and
then, you know, he just buckled down so well it really surprised me. He has gotten to be a much better speller, and now

he keeps track of his spelling results and keeps a chart for himself.

CONSULTANT: So you really *do* have some good techniques for coping with Bobby's temper—and that's the real problem with the crayons too, you know—and all you have to do is think them out a little more clearly and extend them to other situations like the upset you just talked about.

TEACHER: I guess I felt he had been wronged by Charles, or someone, and I was rather sympathizing with him and his upset, and before I knew it, he was off.

CONSULTANT: Perhaps so. Anyhow, you gave him more emotional space than you intended for him to take. He felt you would not stop him, and at the same time there was no apparent answer to his lost crayons, so away he went with his emotional tornado, spewing destruction everywhere. He wanted someone to rectify his loss right away.

TEACHER: He was really demanding restitution, punishment, atonement, and everything else he could ask for, all in one bunch, wasn't he?

CONSULTANT: And he felt righteously indignant about what happened. The pitch here is not that Charles was right, but that Bobby's excesses neither correctly coped with Charles's infraction nor got back the crayons. The whole thing was a mess, and nobody was helped. I think, therefore, that what you can do hereafter, if you agree with me, is to try to see in advance these upsets building up. Assume that they *will* occur again and try to be generally prepared. Step right in if Bobby's lost something or felt some wrongdoing, and get him to tell you first what has happened before he begins his storming. Then, if you know what's wrong, you can quiet him and proceed to rectify the situation. If he, in his demanding, tries to take the law in his own hands, so to speak, you can first warn him, then isolate him, telling him that you will proceed with the matter *after* he calms down. This gives him the responsibility to *cooperate* instead of just fussing; it gives him an out, that is, a solution to the problem, but he has to cooperate and control himself first. When you get this point over to him, perhaps over a period of time, he can and will see that his own control is important in fair play to himself and in solving the problem he faces.

TEACHER: I see. I just didn't get to the heart of the issue. I was myself so overcome by Bobby's temper that I too lost sight of the real issue.

CONSULTANT: Exactly. Therefore, Bobby's demands and his explosiveness at the time, with you not being able to do any useful thing at the moment, until you sent him from the room, led him to take matters even more in his own hands. Then, after he came back in the room, he still showed his indignation at Charles and again picked up the matter, although he was pretty much exhausted by this time, too.

TEACHER (*laughing*): Yes, he was. He was exhausted the rest of the morning, too. One day after a big upset just before noon, he wore himself out so much that he went to sleep after lunch.

CONSULTANT: Somehow he has interpreted his temper as a necessary condition for getting problems solved—as he sees them. We can change this by recognizing a legitimate problem and helping him with it but also by not letting him damage himself and others as he selfishly and narrowly throws his weight around.

This teacher had really made a lot of good progress with Bobby, but she had simply failed to generalize her techniques to other situations with the youngster. She had in her armamentarium the correct solution but was not applying it appropriately. She had let Bobby's temper upset her and this handicapped her control in the classroom.

A problem situation in a classroom, or elsewhere, usually involves two or more people. It is important to know what a child does that starts off a problem; but of equal or greater importance is to know how the adult in charge handles the child, so as to appreciate what works and what does not work in controlling such circumstances. In a sense, what the adult does in response to the child's upset determines whether the child will change or not. In most cases the child will not change spontaneously, unless involved in only minor or passing episodes;

so it is up to the adult to structure, or restructure, the child's behavior and his social dynamics, in order to add a constructive, problem-solving element. In this same connection, a hypothesis as to why children persist in disturbed behavior is offered: the fact that the social situation does not permit or require doing the right thing at the right time. *Constructive intervention* can be expected to modify any problem, theoretically, by gradually bringing under control the relevant considerations. So far as present knowledge indicates, no child is so intractable that he cannot be helped, assuming the proper and relevant elements are brought in. This is equivalent to saying that one can solve a problem if he has the proper tools and applies them correctly.

OTHER PROBLEMS

How many different problems do children present at school? A careful delineation of all that have been recorded in the literature or in the minds of experienced teachers would fill a book larger than this one. There is, then, no purpose in trying to catalogue all possible problems and situations. But there is purpose in trying to break them down into convenient categories, so that the reader can knit problems and solutions together in an economical manner.

Aggressiveness vs. Withdrawal

Two commonly observed poles, two common but widely different response categories, are aggressiveness and withdrawal. The same child may use now one, now another. Or a child may react rather consistently with one of these polar responses. How is it possible to understand these reactions in a general way?

Aggressiveness usually consists in attempts to dominate others. Many adjectives and phrases are used to describe aggressiveness (not to be confused with normal aggressiveness or ascendance): bullying, threatening, dominating, teasing (in some instances), lording it over others, taking advantage of others who are younger or weaker, sassing, fighting back at disciplinary controls, sneaking or furtive noncompliance, going on a sit-down strike, passive noncooperation, and so on.

The overly aggressive child is saying, in effect: "You can't make me do that." Or "I'll do it *my* way and show you." Other equivalent states or attitudes may be involved, adding up to aggressiveness against an object or goal set by another.

How can these reactions on the child's part be coped with in constructive ways?

There are two general techniques useful in handling aggressiveness. First, the holding up of cherished goals, activities, etc., until the child has calmed himself or until he has performed the desired behavior. This is not bribing or cajolery. It is realistically saying: "You may have your deserts when you have performed adequately." Or "You may be 'paid,' or receive a reward, when you have properly completed your tasks." The reward is then held up until the child makes reasonable effort at compliance. For example, free play periods are held up until the child completes his assigned work.

In instances of holding up rewards, the adult is inherently in control. The adult does not have to give in to the child's demands; the work must be done. In discipline with the unruly child it is important for the adult to recognize this type of strategy and to be able to act accordingly. Once the child knows and appreciates the situation, the adult has but to await compliance. But the adult must search for and rely upon opportunities where he can maintain control. This strategy establishes a "beachhead" of control which can then allow progress toward better and more pervasive management of the child.

The first strategy gives rise to the second strategy: indirect control. The old saying "You can lead a horse to water, but you can't make him drink" applies very well to disciplinary measures. Determine what *can* and *cannot* be controlled; those things that cannot be controlled should be, for the moment, overlooked or dealt with indirectly. But what is meant by indirect control?

A child may play unfairly on the playground or elsewhere.

One may not want to intercede at such a time, or may feel that the child is so completely in control himself that it is unwise to try to intercede. In such cases, a mental note can be made and indirect control exercised through, say, not permitting participation in a forthcoming game, or in some other future event in which the child desires to participate.

A child may work his problems in arithmetic incorrectly just to get to the next activity. Instead of making him do his arithmetic right, or correcting each problem—he can stall you off this way and keep you "on the outside looking in"—just ignore his actions, but hold him to reasonable performance before he can be permitted to go on to his desired activity. "If you don't do it now, you have to do it later" can be the teacher's attitude. This shows the child that the adult will not battle with him on a "yes-you-will–no-I-won't" basis, but simply, indirectly take the attitude mentioned.

Another indirect method consists in a general plan of discipline designed to teach greater respect for requirements without challenging the child on his own terms. Keeping greater control over a child in the classroom or on the playground—keeping an eye on him—is preferable to figuratively letting him run away only to be hauled back again. If he is allowed to escape from the rules of the playground or the classroom, he is reinforcing his own unilateral actions; to preclude the opportunity, yet not to enter into a contest about whether he will or will not deviate from rules and requirements, is to save a lot of wear and tear on the teacher and to reduce difficulties in the relationship with the child.

Many times a child wants his teacher to contest him. If the adult is aware of this attitude and permits a contest only when he has actual or potential control over the child, the child will be brought under control sooner. He will not be as prone to challenge thereafter. In this way the teacher is not wasting energies by trying to make the child comply at every step but is indirectly controlling him through surveillance of the situation, so that he cannot "escape." In this manner, compliance will be faster than if the child is controlled only after the fact.

The withdrawn child may appear to present a different case. He is not aggressively maintaining his control, but he is covertly, or indirectly, maintaining control. The withdrawn child says, in effect: "Play it *my* way, or I don't participate." Or his behavior may mean: "I am uncertain of my performance, or success; therefore, I'd rather not participate at all if I cannot win, or be successful on my terms."

Here is an instance calling for indirect action. The withdrawn child should not be directly confronted with a kind of "shock treatment" based on threats, punishments, etc. Rather, he should be approached through the careful setting of *minute* limits and achievement goals. Often cajolery and even some tricking is to be legitimately employed if it can start a small amount of participation. However, the teacher should be careful not to set a procedure of cajolery or strong enticement because this tends to reinforce the child's covert terms: "I'll participate only if I can be *certain* of winning" or "You guarantee it for me, or I won't play."

Placing a very withdrawn child in a class of not too aggressive but somewhat ascendant children will tacitly set some precedent and will show him that participation can be fun. To solicit or cajole beyond the point of showing interest is not to be recommended except on a very tentative or limited basis.

Once the withdrawn child begins to participate and loosens up his demands on the teacher (or on others), the way is beginning to open for setting more definite structure or limits. But this must not be undertaken too readily. The assumption must be kept in mind by the teacher that the withdrawn child *does want to participate*. It is not a case of no motivation; rather it is a case of very unilateral or narrow motivational terms: guaranteed success. Related to this demand on the part of the withdrawn child is his actual experience of failure. However, he does not know how to let down his terms without losing face, and this is where the skill of the teacher comes into play. The teacher must be able to induce limited participation at first as if no contingencies or guarantees were implied. Just the fun of participating must be enough.

The person who has observed emotionally withdrawn children knows how tentative they can be, how they can participate in a seemingly open way one day, then rigidly withdraw the next. It is as if they remembered their old selves and their old ideas and resorted to them again. It is not unlike a person learning a new keyboard system on the typewriter after having become used to an old method, only to return to the old method when in doubt.

The skillful handling of the withdrawn child may take a lot of time. Sometimes a whole semester may go by before a withdrawn child begins to participate in any routine manner in the classroom. It is up to the teacher to keep a watchful and alert eye, to provide stimulation when the child is ready, and gradually to work toward the same kinds of specific limits set for less withdrawn children but to do so judiciously. The reason for setting limits in the usual fashion is to avoid keeping alive an artificial environment or relying too much on artificial motivation for the withdrawn child. One may alter the rules of the game slightly at first in order to get participation, just as one would modify the presentation of any new skill in order to acquaint the novice with his own potential and to give some success to him.

The very withdrawn child lacks confidence; he is insecure. But he is this way owing to his lack of participation; and, in turn, the lack of participation keeps him from learning new evaluations and developing skills. Once the teacher can bring about participation, some real progress can follow. Once the vicious circle is broken, new attitudes and skills can develop.

Boys vs. Girls

Contrasting boys and girls as to emotional problems is not of the same order as pointing to the behavioral poles of aggressiveness versus withdrawal, but to separate boys and girls in discussion of emotional problems of children is common nonetheless.

Behavior problems occur with boys three to five times as frequently as with girls. This may be true for a number of reasons: because limits are set more easily for girls; because our society expects and encourages aggressiveness in males, but sets less clear limits on propriety, and because in physiological and metabolic ways boys may be inherently more active.

A special class for emotionally disturbed children is likely to have many more boys than girls referred. But when girls are severely emotionally disturbed, their pattern is not likely to be less serious or less socially and educationally significant. They have to be treated in the same general manner as boys, and similar limits and requirements have to be set for them.

Girls are perhaps more likely than boys to be fastidious, to be demanding upon *themselves,* and to carry these traits to excess. They may clamor for approval, for notice, for rewards for their efforts, and be dismayed, withdrawn, or "hurt" when the expected approval is not forthcoming. Very seldom does one find aggressive girls—girls with aggressiveness comparable in intensity to that of the most "acting-out" boys.

In our society girls also tend to try harder to please. They tend to be socially and emotionally more mature than boys and to take on more mature responsibilities, such as doing their schoolwork acceptably and following rules and regulations; at adolescence they are less often found among offenders against the law than boys.

The type of girl most likely to be referred for special classes for emotionally disturbed children will be the very overprotected, "weak," immature, dependent youngster. Such a child may be withdrawn, relatively unable to carry on for herself, and, often, lazy about schoolwork and schoolroom responsibilities. Thus the task the teacher will face is that of blocking off small amounts of work that can be successfully completed, which in time can lead to larger and larger amounts of work done in qualitatively better ways. The building of initiative, self-confidence, and self-discipline all go hand in hand in educating such an immature and dependent child.

Some would urge that special classes should separate boys and girls, but there seems to be no inherently good reason for this theory. In the regular classroom in most schools boys and girls attend classes together. A special class, even if it contains only a very small proportion of girls, will still preserve some of the normality of the typical class by having girls included. This does not work any hardship on either boys or girls as far as is now known.

Older vs. Younger Children

Age per se seems to present no special or particular types of problems. The same general range of problems is encountered in the first grade as in the sixth or seventh grade. The differences are mainly differences of problem intensity; in addition, there is the perseverance and subtlety of the older child, who can find more ways of demanding by indirection. The general psychological position of the teacher would seem not to change except that she needs to be more alert, resourceful, and persevering in bringing the older child's problems under control.

Sometimes younger emotionally disturbed children are more respectful of teachers, school authorities, and of the consequences of not behaving. But these are more the characteristics one finds in younger children in general, not criteria by which the younger and older children can be separated in regard to matters of emotional maturity and adjustment.

Internal vs. External Controls

Some children are internally too controlled. That is, though they have strong feelings against someone or something, they keep them under so much control that it damages their general happiness and adjustment.

A youngster who is overcontrolled is more likely to be "nervous," to show habit-training problems expressed in going to the toilet too frequently, biting fingernails, displaying tics and other nervous habits or symptoms, sweating palms, lack of confidence in social situations, and so on. The overcontrol stems from an effort to do well and to present one's self favorably to others, as well as an apprehension that the intentions and efforts will not prove successful. Hence the concern of "How am I doing?" Overcontrolled children try too hard to please and keep themselves in an anxious state in order to please.

Unfortunately, many of these children go unobserved by their teachers. A disproportionately small number of them is likely to be found in a special class for the emotionally disturbed. It is not because they do not belong there but because they are usually so cooperative that they escape notice and their emotional problems remain unobserved or improperly evaluated.

By contrast, the child who lacks controls is so common and so easily observed in our society that to try to define him further is to elaborate upon the obvious. Suffice it to say that such children do need direct and specific controls and need to be taught self-control through outer, external controls first being established.

Children who are overly controlled may present a special problem. How are limits to be set for them? They already expect too much of themselves, do they not? They already try too hard to please and hence do not overstep the limits of propriety as do most other emotionally disturbed children.

Thus the problem of limits and controls with the overly controlled child is subtle, but its solution is nonetheless needed. The overly controlled child may often try hard only on some tasks or only when it pleases him. The control is finely and narrowly chosen; it is not generally versatile and resourceful.

Also the overly controlled youngster seems often to *demand* praise, to work only for praise, and to feel little satisfaction in the task well done. External rewards, seemingly for the sake of rewards, are held uppermost. Hence there is a rigidity in performance, a narrowness and a self-centeredness in putting one's self to tasks. Motivation is high, but it is often unrealistic and narrowly applied. If the motivation and efforts do not pay off, the child is crestfallen, severely defeated, rather than left with the feeling that the more realistic effort is required.

The teacher, then, will have to notice how such a child acts upon his motivation, how he evaluates his results, how stably he pursues his tasks in the face of defeat or failure, and how well he shifts with new evidence or new requirements. The teacher will need to prevent the child running away with the ball, or acting too unilaterally about his work. Setting realistic goals instead of fantastic ones, setting flexible goals instead of rigid ones, and setting goals in terms of the tasks rather than in terms of the ego demands of the child will be important. Having careless work done over may be required, even though this seems to be inconsistent with the overly conscientious attitude of the child. (Here again, the conscientiousness may be too narrowly applied, and may have strings attached.)

The overly controlled child may fool the unwary teacher. The good intentions may misdirect the teacher to paying attention only to avowed purposes rather than also to end products. The wise teacher will learn in time that the too conscientious person may, indeed, be very unsure of himself and very dependent upon approval. To improve this condition, more emphasis should be put on the task and on the rewards inherent in doing a job well.

Many other subdivisions of behavior could be pursued, and many polarities could be discussed: introverted versus extroverted children, submissive versus dominant children, rigid versus flexible children, and so on. But the value in discussing various polarities would be found, not in describing the contrasts, but in developing ways of meeting the traits and characteristics at a practical educational level in the daily work of the classroom. If the general types of approaches stressed in this chapter and throughout this book can be kept in mind, any special problems of a child or group of children will not preclude the skillful teacher from knowing how to set tasks and limits or from knowing how to firm up the social and educational structure of the classroom.

SUMMARY

This chapter gave a brief view of how the teacher can handle specific upsets in the classroom. Objectivity in handling the disturbed child is important. Commiseration, blaming, scolding, lecturing, and other ineffectual activities are to be avoided; in their place should exist a matter-of-fact, unemotional attitude. Teachers usually do a lot of constructive things without necessarily realizing it; their problems can often be solved by referring intelligently to their other more successful encounters with emotionally disturbed children. The consultant's role is to monitor these encounters and to help the teacher rise to his best in handling all types of classroom disturbances, of which there are typically many with the disturbed child.

Many types of classroom problems could have been listed. For sake of brevity and to convey a problem-solving attitude, only a few polar dimensions of classroom activity and related needs were listed: aggressiveness versus withdrawal; differences between boys and girls in emotional displays and demands; differences between older and younger children; and internal versus external controls.

Consonant with the general viewpoint held in this book, it was pointed out that the variables used to describe maladjusted behavior are less important than the means employed to constructively control and redirect the child.

9

WORKING WITH PARENTS

It is a trite but true statement that work done with parents can be extremely beneficial to a child's welfare. The concerns in this chapter are both to exhibit some examples of how the home and school can work better in the interests of the emotionally disturbed child's development and to help the school to cope better with his parents.

Often the parents of emotionally disturbed children are difficult for the school to work with. This may be true for a number of reasons. The parents want something done to help the child; the school wants something done too, but the two may not agree on methods and procedures. It is also common for parents to feel the school bears the main responsibility for the child's school disturbances, although these disturbances are closely related to the problems the child has at home. And the emotionally disturbed child may bring down on himself a lot of criticism, peer difficulties, and social problems that spring from his emotional problems—troubles that the school may have great difficulty in preventing. Parents may feel because of laxity or unfair treatment at school, the child has a harder time than he otherwise would have, and that this makes his adjustment and his education more pressing problems.

All of the above attitudes are at least partially representative of the positions of the parents and the school. The purpose in this discussion is not to take one side or argue one point or another. It is, rather, to specify what the school *can* do in the way of working directly with parents of emotionally disturbed children so that all will reap a profit. It is not assumed that the school can settle *all* the child's problems; it is simply asserted that in the context of the type of special class recommended, the school can further aid the child's growth and maturity by setting up a program of working with parents in the general manner recommended here.

Rather than separate the school and the home in arguing about who caused what in the child's behavior, let us pose an alternative set of questions: What can be done both in the home and at school that will help the emotionally disturbed child? How can these two vital resources be brought together in a constructive, consonant program? Such cooperation is an important objective to pursue.

Once the parents have agreed to the placement of a particular child in a special class, strong effort should be made by the school to keep the parents both *informed* and *involved*. This can best be done in two ways.

One way is by requesting that the parents attend periodic (perhaps monthly or semimonthly) meetings of an informal group discussion type, with the teacher and principal present. The meetings may be conducted by special education leaders, school psychologists, visiting teachers, or other school personnel who have the skill to do so.

The second way of bringing about parental involvement is by planning relatively frequent meetings between parents and the classroom teacher in two- or three-person conferences (which may be augmented to include the principal as well as the teacher). The reason for these conferences is to allow more time to deal with the specifics of the child's classroom academic work, to discuss and agree upon issues relating to homework, and to consider other items of a more personal nature, e.g., the child's language, his cleanliness, and so forth.

THE GROUP MEETING

What values exist in the parent group discussion meeting?

1. It lets the parents know that others have similar problems and allows a bond of interest and responsibility to grow between the parents, teacher, and child.

2. It allows the parents to know firsthand how behavioral and educational problems are handled in the classroom and provides a basis for *continuity* between home and school expectations and treatment of the child.

3. The group meeting allows the special education expert or psychologist the opportunity to select or work out better ways of coping with the child's problems with the help and understanding of both parent and teacher. This affords a kind of clinical approach to the child in a trouble-shooting manner that simultaneously reaches the ears of parents and teacher.

4. It allows the teacher and the principal a view of the parents in the group setting, which reveals the degree of interest, cooperation, and perseverance displayed by the parents. These evaluations of parental attitudes and degrees of cooperation can let the school authorities know more fully the size of their tasks with each child and the limitations under which they may have to work.

5. It affords the teacher considerable help in discussing each child's progress in a setting where all are presumably alert to the child's assets and limitations.

6. It affords the parents the same opportunity.

Should the group discussion meeting be a cathartic session? That is, should the group meeting be treated as a kind of individual therapy for the parents in the group setting? In each group the answer to this will depend upon the skill of the group leader and upon the composition of the group. If the group is very large—say, contains seven or eight parents or pairs of parents—not much time can be afforded each person. Time limits will preclude going into the personal lives of each individual parent or even each child. It is assumed, anyway, that the child's background is already well understood and that the classroom setting is itself a very therapeutic one. Also, if an opportunity is afforded parent and teacher to meet at times other than the group sessions, there is a chance then for the parent to go more into personal detail about the child. A further opportunity can be permitted the parents to talk alone with the group leader either before or after the group session or at some other convenient time.

A TYPICAL CONVERSATION WITH A PARENT

The structure of the group discussion meeting is such that a maximum amount of information and suggestion should get over to both parent and teacher in the time allotted; this limitation is helpful in promoting a concern for the child's immediate behavior problems at home or at school, as well as the child's day-to-day educational accomplishments. A brief excerpt from one of the recorded sessions that included parents, teachers, principal, special education personnel, and psychologist (group leader) will illustrate the point:

GROUP LEADER: Mrs. Y., suppose you tell us about your experiences with Carl in the last three to four weeks.

MRS. Y.: Well, Carl has been doing better in some ways and not as well in other ways. For example, he will get up and get dressed on time just about every day; but he has not wanted to come in after school, even after a play period of an hour or so, to get his homework done before dinner at six o'clock. I guess I keep after him and don't really get down to brass tacks as soon as I should.

GROUP LEADER: You mean you talk too much and don't take decisive action?

MRS. Y.: Yes, I guess that's the best way to put it.

GROUP LEADER: What do you actually do in trying to get Carl in after school at these times?

MRS. Y.: Well, I guess I am ashamed to say it, but I just call him and then wait awhile and call him again; and—well, this can go on several times, for maybe a half hour.

GROUP LEADER: He just thinks you don't mean business. There's no real difference between his coming in and his not coming in at these times, so why should he inconvenience himself if that is all the importance attached to your calls—at least he might seem to feel this way, don't you think?

MRS. Y.: Yes, I think you are exactly right. I just have to get him in by simply going right after him and not dillydally as I have. (*Pause.*) I see what you mean. You really have to make your word count for something if you want a child to respond.

GROUP LEADER: And it would be this way with almost anything, especially if Carl, or any other youngster, for that matter, didn't want to do what you requested. You've got to mean what you say and back up your words with action. You can see how a situation of this type might deteriorate your relationship with him if it continued or if it encompassed many other things.

MRS. Y.: Indeed I can! I've seen it happen with Carl before—that is, before these classes began—and I've seen it happen with my little girl who is only five. Boy, she can really throw the weight around when she wants to, she's got a temper like a witch. I don't want her to get to be as hard to control as Carl was last year in the third grade at A_____ School.

GROUP LEADER: Well, you can see our point here with the classes at school. We are not so much concerned with why a child acts in a given way—all children act in a way that makes them hard to control, or sulky, or whatever, to some degree—but with what you as a parent and the teacher can *do* to bring matters under control. The why of Bobby's behavior, even if we knew it, would only lead to the next question: what can we constructively do about it? In fact, that is the reason we have these special classes, and that is the reason why we meet with you parents. These are the two best ways we know to bring these "difficult" youngsters under control and give them some educational stimulation at the same time.

In this short passage the reader can observe that there is concern with handling the child's immediate behavior pattern that is creating a difficulty. The mother, Mrs. Y., was very quickly brought to see, at least for the time being in a general way, how she was failing to follow through on her controls with Carl. One could get bogged down in a long discourse about all the whys and wherefores of Carl's behavior, but this would not help. In an hour or so devoted to the problems of several parents and their children, the need is to come to grips in immediately useful ways. If daily contact is kept with the teacher by the special administrator and periodic psychological consultant contacts are kept with Mrs. Y. through these discussions, the values associated with this version of Carl's difficulty will be under constant test and revision. The daily life of the child at school and at home is a kind of proving ground of the adequacy in handling a child.

TROUBLE SHOOTING WITH THE TEACHER

Here is an excerpt from Carl's daily classroom activities. Compare the teacher's handling of him there. Note the advice the teacher receives from the group leader of the special education department.

TEACHER: Well, my worst problem this week has been Carl. He simply *won't* work. I have tried to handle him in a careful way, but he just defies and refuses to participate in learning.

GROUP LEADER: You mean he simply does no work at all at school?

TEACHER: Oh, no. I mean he does what he wants to do, then lies down on the job with the rest.

GROUP LEADER: For example.

TEACHER: Well, for example, he won't study his spelling. He likes arithmetic, and he does his daily work in that; then he just won't do the other things—reading, spelling, answering history or geography questions. He really could do it if he would.

GROUP LEADER: When does the arithmetic occur in the daily program?

TEACHER: First thing in the morning.

GROUP LEADER: So he gets his preferred work done, and as far as he is concerned, he's through for the day?

TEACHER: Exactly!

GROUP LEADER: What if you held off the arithmetic until he had done the other things, saving the arithmetic until last?

TEACHER: I could do that. I don't think it would help, though.

GROUP LEADER: Why not?

TEACHER: Well, I really don't know. I guess I have just figured he would be stubborn when he wanted to be, regardless of other things.

GROUP LEADER: And that may not be true, you know. You have let him call the shots, so to speak, by his saying what he would do and when. We have to put you back in control in this respect.

TEACHER: Well, I'm willing to try it; I'll try whatever you feel will work because he's certainly had me over a barrel lately. It has worsened the morale of the other kids, too. They see Carl not doing his spelling and reading, and they want to get out of something they prefer not to do. And it also worsens Carl's behavior; why, you know, he's been so stubborn on the playground that I've had to put him out of the baseball game every day this week. And at lunch he is so slow that I feel I almost have to feed him. Just lately he's gotten so ornery that I could just throw him out of class, if I dared to do so. (*Laughs.*)

GROUP LEADER: He's had you on the run in a lot of ways. He's gotten you off balance in one area—the arithmetic versus all the other schoolwork—and now he's extending his conquests to the whole school day. Pretty soon, he'll try to take over the whole class for you. (*Laughs.*)

TEACHER: Yes, I'll bet he would try it if he thought he could!

GROUP LEADER: Let's restructure and rearrange matters, then, so Carl isn't regulating too much. Let's put the must-do subjects first and tell him he's got to do those before he can go on to the arithmetic, or before he can go out for his recess period. A day or two of this will show him the reality of the situation.

TEACHER: O.K. We'll begin tomorrow morning with this, and I'll let you know in a couple of days how things progress.

This is an example of putting a child back into a routine that will be both educationally productive and emotionally and socially maturing, so that he does not try to have everything his own way in a destructive manner. But would not Carl in time come around by himself, spontaneously, the critical reader may ask. It is possible, to be sure. But it would be wasteful of everyone's time and energy to assume that a reliable, healthy, spontaneous correction would occur. It is better for the teacher to promote the occurrence of correction by adroitly and systematically planning the day in a manner that precludes Carl's unilateral actions. This can be done without open conflict with Carl, and it will aid the other children by showing them that the teacher is not to be overridden by any whimsey or impulse that one of them may hit upon.

The following conversation between the teacher and the group leader took place a few days later:

TEACHER: Well, I've got some good news to report today.

GROUP LEADER: What's that?

TEACHER: Carl is doing much better. At first he acted as if he were terribly hurt that I wouldn't let him do arithmetic the first thing in the morning. I simply told him he could do his arithmetic *after* he had done the other work, and that was really all I said. He tried a couple of times to put aside the geography and reading after he'd spent a little time on them, but I did not budge. He grumbled a little at his seat, looked up at the clock, and said, "I guess I'd better get this done before noon, so I can eat lunch with the others." Then he got down to work and surprised even himself with how much he could do. I didn't say a word to him about anything all morning, after the beginning discussion. Then, at noon, I told him I thought he had concentrated very well and I would look over his work and tell him later how well he had done. Then, about two o'clock, just a few minutes before the gym instructor came, I told him he had earned his baseball for today and that I hoped he would keep up the good work.

GROUP LEADER: Well, I guess you've learned as much from Carl as he's learned from you.

TEACHER (*laughing*): Yes, that's a good way to put it, and I think it is certainly true. I think, now that we have a better understanding, we can move on with better work and less nonsense from Carl.

If this situation with Carl had been allowed to worsen at school and at home—let us say owing to the parent and the teacher not having been ready or able to step in and structure matters—it might not have been long until Carl's behavior would have blossomed into a major conflict. This is how behavior problems are made; and it is the way they can get worse if not brought under constructive control.

There were no harshness, no unfairness, and no unhealthy attitudes or actions displayed by parent or teacher in these corrective episodes. Discipline in the harsh or unfair or authoritarian sense is entirely irrelevant, and it is precluded from the type of program instigated here. On the other hand, firmness, consistency, and fairness are promoted; but they are promoted in a manner that takes advantage of what the child is doing, of how he is evidently regarding the situation. Correction proceeds from an estimate of how the child is probably viewing his relationships and his obligations. Effort is made to move forward in a positive way.

These excerpts illustrate how, in a child's relationships with teacher and parent, the adult-child interactions can be made beneficial. This is what is really meant by placing a child in a *structured* situation. The child's individuality is preserved; indeed, it determines the *beginning* and the *end* points in estimating how to proceed with the child and in evaluating how successful the structuring attempts have been.

The child in this instance was taking advantage, one might say, of the looseness, the disorder, the lack of clarity in the relationships with mother and with teacher. When this looseness or disorder was viewed from the standpoint of how the child evaluated the situation, judging from his actions, then the adults concerned were placed in a position simultaneously to understand the child's actions and thought and to bring their own desires into focus. Instead of viewing the child as simply disturbed, stubborn, intractable, or "impossible," the adults took a view of the child which began with his perception of unsureness about what they desired and about what they could or would do.

Firming up the interaction dispenses with such looseness; it tells the adult and the child exactly what the child faces and allows the adult to know how to correct his version of what the circumstances require if the child's behavior or achievement is to be improved. In this way the child's own idiosyncrasies are viewed steadily and whole, but the adult, mature situation is also kept in mind as a good model to aim toward (knowing, of course, that it will not be completely attained). The adults in these instances move toward teaching the child to accept and act upon appropriate responsibilities.

Every interaction with parent and teacher, in the context of discussing the child's difficulties, is met in this manner. These general questions are asked: "Where is the structure loose?" "How does the child view the situation?" "Can we account for his behavior on the basis of knowledge of the structure and how he probably views it?" "Can we propose suitable intervention, in terms of fairness, firmness, and consistency that will correct the situation?"

A similar set of "prescriptions" can be communicated to parents. Since the school is running a program for emotionally disturbed children, the parental obligations can be clarified and extended by the school.

THE PARENTAL ROLE

What, then, are the parental responsibilities the school should keep in mind and try to communicate to the parents?

1. The parents should make a serious attempt to attend every group meeting. If both parents cannot attend, certainly one should. There will be instances where a child has only one parent and he or she cannot attend because of work, having to care for other children, etc.; but these are liabilities the school can know of and adjust to in advance.

2. The parents should try to understand the general purposes of the special classes and follow through on the school's suggestion on such matters as homework, handling behavioral upsets, handling problems of misconduct on the way to or from school (on foot or on a bus), and other specific matters which arise.

3. The parents should make the periodic conferences with the teacher consistent and integral features of their relationships with the school. Attending the group meetings is worthwhile and necessary, but the individual conferences are also important; one type of conference should not be regarded as taking the place of the other.

4. Parents should keep the school informed of any special plans involving the child, such as his having to go into a hospital for an operation, or any upsets that might arise in connection with the illness or death of a relative in the family, aged grandparents, for example.

5. The parents should not regard the special class as a permanent educational substitute for the child, but should hopefully view it as a temporary solution to a serious problem, with the intention to get the child back into his regular classroom as soon as it is feasible. There are, of course, instances where the special class arrangement may have to be a permanent one, but this is less likely to occur among a population of emotionally disturbed children than it is among the orthopedically handicapped, the retarded, or among those with sensory handicaps.

PARENT-TEACHER CONFERENCES

The recurrent parent-teacher conferences require further discussion. As has been stated, these conferences can be held as often as the school and the parent deem advisable. With normal children, they are typically held two or three times per year. Among the emotionally disturbed, it would seem that they need to be held more often, as often as once a month, at least at the start. The fact that individual parent-teacher conferences are supplemented by the group meetings may allow for less frequent conferences after the parent, teacher, and child are in fuller understanding of each other and after the objectives of the special class placement are well under way.

These parent-teacher conferences may include any items of mutual concern, and no limit as to topic should be placed on them in advance. They have typically concerned themselves with the following questions, among the emotionally disturbed:

1. Should my child have homework? If so, how much? How do I get him to do it? What if he fails to bring home the assigned work or fails to return it to school the next day?

2. What is the school's attitude toward misconduct on the bus or walking to and from school? Should our child report any complaints directly to the school, or should they be relayed through us?

3. Should we, as parents of youngsters who have trouble with each other, try to settle the problem or should we check first with the school?

4. Are grades to be given in special classes for emotionally disturbed? Will marking be on an individual-progress basis, or will students be compared with normals of the same age and grade placement?

5. Should a child be in psychotherapy with a psychologist or psychiatrist at the same time he attends these special classes?

6. How long will our child stay in the special class? How will we know when to change him? Will he go back to his regular school and class or to a different one? Will he lose a grade in such a transfer?

7. Will the change to a regular class, whenever it comes, be a detriment to a child's adjustment and school progress? Do the special classes make fewer demands and thus provide a "softer" program? Will any special class placement make readjustment to regular classes difficult?

8. Are children in special classes ridiculed as "dummies" or identified with other terms of opprobrium? If this is noticed, how can it be handled?

9. How long does a child have to stay in a special class? One or two years? Throughout the elementary grades? All through school?

10. Will attendance in special classes stay on a permanent school or other record and later, perhaps, injure chances for college, professional work, vocational placement?

While the answers to each of these questions cannot be given with complete certainty, the answers are generally that special class placement will probably have no adverse or permanent effect on a child. Rather, the opposite is anticipated and intended. A brief look at the likely answers to these questions will help, while we know full well that different schools will handle the problems differently.

1. Homework is not essential, but it is felt that it is advisable. It helps the child prepare for more demanding work, including homework, at the junior and senior high levels. It also aids the daily discipline of the child and helps him to follow through on his own to get work done. Failures to do assigned homework simply mean that adult firmness in viewing this item has to be made clear, that home-school relations have to be tightened up and assignments made to mean something.

2. Misconduct on the bus or on foot or bicycle on the way to and from school is bound to occur, and calls for appropriate actions. The details of giving proper attention to and handling problems on the bus, on the schoolground, etc., are similar to those outlined and discussed throughout this book.

3. It is better for parents to refer school problems to school officials. A school problem is any problem that occurs at school, on the way to and from school, on school trips, and at other school functions. Neighborhood problems, occurring after school hours, fall in a parental disciplinary pattern, of course, but for the sake of consistency and proper follow-through, the school is the best agency to handle problems like those mentioned. Often, also, the to-or-from-school problems have a way of breaking out at school, which allows the school to focus on the solutions.

4. Giving grades or not is a matter for school officials to determine. However, if standardized tests—intellectual, achievement, and emotional stability—are given, a set of national norms can be applied to the child's work and a general rating arrived at without too much local bias from the teacher or the school. Marking is probably best done on an individual basis, especially at the start of a child's tour in a special class; later, as the child gains educational momentum, resort to regular grading practices might be entertained without anticipated harm in most cases. In final analysis, matters ought to be settled on an individual basis.

5. The only reason to answer no to this question is that the special class for emotionally disturbed children, as herein described, is based on a highly structured classroom procedure. Most individual psychotherapy—but not all—is based on the theory of permissiveness, which is just the opposite of that stressed here. If one has a child in a special class and individual psychotherapy is also desired, a decision in the matter ought to be carefully considered. The parent has a right to put the child in any kind of program desired, but if a cooperative parent is informed fully of the purpose of the special class and if the class operates successfully, the need for individual treatment is largely precluded. Here, again, individual resolution of a problem of this type is strongly recommended.

6. The length of stay in a special class and the indications for change can usually be clearly worked out by an evaluation conference including parents and the following staff members: teacher, principal, school psychologist or special educational personnel. Several criteria might be studied. Has the child overcome most of his behavior problems and emotional upsets? Has the child progressed satisfactorily according to his ability level? Has the child developed satisfactory work habits, so that independent work and achievement are the rule rather than the exception? The extent to which these queries can be answered in the affirmative is probably the extent to which a positive decision to transfer the child to regular classes can be

reached. The transfer itself should not require a loss of a school grade. Whether the child, in the over-all process, has lost a grade, maintained his level, or even gained a grade will depend upon many other factors. The special class placement per se carries no particular implication in this regard.

7. If anything, the special class, as herein envisaged, requires relatively more from an emotionally disturbed child than would a regular class. But the tailoring to the individual child's needs and requirements is greater in the special class, and this fact has to be faced realistically so that the child is not prematurely returned to regular classes before he is able to bridge the gap.

8. There may be limited instances of ridicule directed at the child in a special class, but this is certainly a very uncommon event. In many observations of all kinds of special education classes, for children with physical handicaps as well as for children with unseen handicaps, derision by the so-called normal child has been very rare. When it does occur, it reflects a problem in attitude of the ridiculer, not a handicap or limitation of the special class.

9. Children will have to stay varying amounts of time in special classes, ranging from as short a time as a few months to several years. There is no reason, however, why a child typically would have to remain in a special class for more than a part of his elementary school period, unless he is gotten to very late or unless poor success is had with him in a special class. There is no reason now to anticipate that emotionally disturbed children would have to remain more than two or three years, on the average, in such classes. However, the individual factors associated with the child, his teacher, the manner in which the class is run, the availability of normal classes, and so forth must always be taken into consideration despite any generalization that may be uttered.

10. Again, the emphasis is on the approach to normality, the accent on the positive, healthy adjustment which the special classes for emotionally disturbed are bent on achieving. There

is, then, no reason inherent in the special class philosophy that leads to any later handicap in the child's vocational, scholastic, or professional life. Indeed, the entire movement of special education is to aid the child in reaching as full a degree of normality as his own limitations will permit. There is nothing second-rate about special class placement; hence no invidious comparisons can legitimately arise.

Generally speaking, the parent-teacher conferences will quickly get over the humps implied in these questions and get down to the daily work of helping Johnny and Susie overcome their emotional problems and gain in achievement, social maturity, and general mental health. The school is a social institution created by society to pass on the heritage of the past generations and to educate the child in matters of daily living. The advent of special classes in recent years serves as a broadening and strengthening of this service to society and its young. Today educators and parents are only beginning to realize that many possibilities for special education exist and that these will be encouragingly and challengingly put in effect as time goes by. The philosophy of special education is something the parent can be proud to have available for his or her child.

SUMMARY

Working with parents is a vital part of the structured classroom program. It is essential that parents at home maintain the same general conduct and achievement standards that the school maintains. Otherwise, the child is confused and further conflicted in his attempts to grow and mature. The structure must be as all-embracing as is practical and as is consonant with good judgment in controlling and redirecting behavior.

The values associated with group meetings are legion. They involve the parents in the process of maturing the child and display to the parents and the school their own assets and liabilities, as well as the probable growth potential of the child. Conversations with parents in the group meetings both illustrate and implement the methods of the structured classroom. Evident growth occurs in the parents through these conversations; their value is unparalleled in bringing about a constructive, forward-moving set of relationships with the child.

All is not well in the classroom just because a structured program is under way. Problems will arise, sometimes seemingly insurmountable ones. The teacher needs an "arsenal" of ideas and methods which he can gain from the mental health consultant through discussion and clarification of his interactions with children.

Parents raise doubts about special classes. Will they injure the child's educational or vocational future? Will he be labeled for having been in a special class? These and many other problems need to be covered with parents. The outcome of a properly implemented special program for an emotionally disturbed child is, in part, to minimize any future complications and to offset prejudices and misunderstandings.

10

GENERALIZING RESULTS
TO OTHER CASES

Questions may logically be raised as to the applicability of the methods prescribed here for more nearly normal children or for moderately disturbed children in regular classes. It is believed that the principles and procedures delineated for special classes for the emotionally disturbed will also apply to the psychologically more nearly normal children. The differences between the severely and less disturbed are matters of degree, it is hypothesized, not differences of kind or type. The severely disturbed child may, however, appear to be qualitatively different in his behavior. Experience with special classes and with classroom treatment of common disciplinary and achievement problems among more nearly normal children would lead to the belief that what applies to one group also applies to the other; but care must always be exercised in carrying out these applications and in considering as fully as possible the *individual differences* between children, regardless of a child's state of emotional health and possible diagnosis.

It is well known that diagnostic categories applied to behavior problems of children are unreliable. When the severely disturbed child is spoken of, the intention is not to refer to a precise category with clear-cut symptoms which anyone with professional training could recognize. The descriptions and categories in the behavioral and mental health fields are not clear-cut like the syndromes associated with common diseases or conditions like poliomyelitis, fractured bones, and appendicitis. In fact, most people question whether personality and emotional problems can be considered as disease groups at all. Therefore, in trying to apply the ideas in this book to the less severely disturbed child or to the normal child in the classroom with typical adjustment and achievement problems, the emphasis is put on describing *methods* of handling children, or on general approaches toward children, rather than on describing specific categories or types of behavior.

The application of the general ideas in this book to the more common adjustment problems in the classroom will be subdivided into topics having to do with everyday behavior. If the reader keeps this in mind and then thinks of how the generalizations and related statements might be tailored to the *individual child* he deals with, the results can be surprisingly germane. The teacher is urged to think first in terms of the generalization and then to apply it to given children under specific sets of circumstances.

GENERAL THEORY, OR GENERAL ATTITUDES TOWARD CHILDREN

Look forward to the child's development; think of what can be done with present behavior to alter it in the future, rather than be concerned about why and how the behavior developed.

The child does not belong to us as individual parents or teachers, although we may have him as our charge for a limited time; the child belongs to the world. Although rigid compliance is not sought, the child does need to learn enough compliance to get along and to use strength gained from compliance to bring about wholesome changes in himself and others.

Our actions as teachers and parents should have some long-term bearing on the child's development, at least by implication; for adulthood is not only the longest but also the most important period of life.

Remember that discipline, or structure, is not a negative condition—not merely a matter of restraint. Proper self-discipline promotes achievement, and achievement develops self-discipline.

Good discipline avoids resort to fear. One's actions should not be grounded on inspiring fear but on a realistic and understandable recognition of the child's gains and losses which are germane to his values and to his level of comprehension.

Schooling is integral to life. It is not merely preparation for life; it is a small piece of life itself. Everything that one does counts for something in his nervous structure and in his habit system. Therefore, the daily tasks of schoolwork and their level of success or failure are being "written into" the behavioral system and nervous structure of the child; they are rapidly becoming part of his life, not simply preparation for later living. Thus a person learns what he lives and continues to live what he has learned.

Avoid leaving too many decisions up to the child that have to do with his daily routine. Some teachers follow the dictum "If you learn, fine; if you do not learn, that is up to you." This attitude of purporting to leave a mature choice up to the immature student without teaching him the consequences of his action in more concrete terms is unrealistic; it is bound to cause the student trouble and to adversely affect society in many ways.

Many children have to be settled down emotionally and socially before they can be expected to engage in positive educational effort. In lieu of working, they misbehave; but as misbehavior is brought under control, opportunity for work and achievement is increased.

The first duty of the teacher is to know what he wants or expects from the child. The second duty is to recognize and utilize means for attaining these expectations. And the third duty is to go about correcting the child's malfunctioning in behavior and achievement in constructive and problem-solving ways. Don't belittle, don't complain, have the work done over until it is acceptably done.

One child gave his teacher a great compliment without realizing it: "She makes me *know* my history as well as read it."

Are parents typically too strict? Is this really the most common parent-child problem? Does it account for much poor achievement and misbehavior? This is doubtful. The opposite is more likely to be typical, viz., that parents are not firm and consistent enough. Consistent firmness and clarity of expectations preclude the need for excessive harshness. The answer to those problems which are due to excessive parental strictness is to smooth out disciplinary demands, not to take away the disciplinary control.

Although teachers have good intentions, they sometimes fail to teach the child the differences between right and wrong, correct and incorrect. There is too great reliance on words and too little effort to put forth concrete examples, to follow through, and to set consequences. A negative approach emphasizes failure rather than success and thus heightens a child's apprehensions and discouragements.

There is no strength in acquiescence. The child can learn neither the skills he needs nor good feelings about himself if he is allowed to get by with poor or minimal effort.

A good day's work is something of which to be proud. An attitude of simple nonchalance and matter-of-factness toward an irritating or demanding child is often a good remedy, especially if carried on within a generally firm attitude and conduct structure in the classroom.

Threats should always be used sparingly, but when used, should be threats that can be backed up with actual deeds that stay close to the infraction and serve as a corrective influence on the child.

Teach the child to get his work done before play time. Failure to do this sets poor precedents for work; this is a common error made by teachers and parents alike.

Remember at all times when dealing with most types of disciplinary problems: don't just talk—act! But let your actions be guided by an analysis of what is required for corrective influence on the child, not by spur-of-the-moment decisions.

In remembering to act, remember also to do first what you might later have to do, before you are driven to it because of delay or indecision.

Pace yourself carefully from the start with children. Know your requirements and let the students know these requirements in concrete, measured terms.

Avoid giving unlimited or unspecified times for completing work. Keep assignments clearly stated in terms of time, place, and other relevant conditions.

Never regard the child's behavior or attitude as a fixed quantity, unaffected by the attitudes of the teacher, the school, or the parent.

Absorbing failure constructively is a difficult matter. Try to put the child back on his own when he has failed; avoid letting him place his failure on you or on something outside his control. Center attention on what he did and did not do relative to the task; take his attention off his failure per se and put it on the improvement of his performance. This will be more useful than any amount of words or censorship anyone can use.

SPECIFIC CORRECTIVE PROCEDURES

There are a number of ways in which the teacher can cope intelligently and constructively with day-to-day problems. The following comments about these procedures supplement earlier comments in this volume.

Stop a bad habit or practice with the current or most recent episode, not with the next possible instance.

Recalcitrant children, especially at the elementary school level, can be handled constructively by sending them home to work for the remainder of a school day. With approval from school personnel and from parents, it can aid a child in several ways: first, by depriving him of his audience; secondly, by setting him down to his incompleted tasks in an uninterrupted way; and thirdly, by letting him know that the consequences of his action are in your hands, not in his hands.

In correcting inadequate or incomplete work, set your goals first on the completion of the original assignment. Do not double the assignment or add to it, as a punishment, before the child has completed the original task.

Failing a child for the whole school year is not usually a good disciplinary technique. It is better to proceed with daily corrective measures rather than to put all failure and correction into one general evaluation at the end of the year.

Task requirements are preferable to time requirements. Time can be wasted; amount and quality of work can be better controlled.

It might be desirable if every school had a "concentration room" —not the office, not the library, where distracting stimuli entertain the child, but a place of isolation where the child can be observed, be kept at work, and be challenged to put forth consistent effort and to complete work away from the distractions inherent in the social structure of the average classroom.

Do not "save up" the mistakes a child tends to accumulate; get corrective action right away. If the child is prone to make certain types of errors or to commit given conduct infractions, do not wait for the periodic six- or nine-week reports to obtain corrective action.

In case of chronic and recurrent disciplinary problems, think over what you might do; learn to anticipate that the child will continue to force you to action. Do not assume the child will not repeat his action; until or unless you intervene in a constructive way, be prepared for his recurrent behavior.

In order not to be at cross purposes with ourselves as educators and with the child's growth, we should decide what role we expect discipline to play in the classroom. Is it to be primarily a warning to others? Something punitive? An act of expiation? Several or all of these? Perhaps discipline should always produce a corrective influence, by and through the leveling of consequences which spell out the differences between the choices the child has open to himself. If discipline is properly regulated to fit the child's comprehension, its constructive use can be more likely.

If there is one single most important error we commit as teachers and parents, it is that of talking too much to children. We "yak, yak, and yak some more," as one child put it. Another child, who wore a hearing aid, promptly turned down the aid when he felt he was being bombarded with endless words of admonition. The more one talks, the less effective he is as a teacher or guide; too much talk may actually teach the child *not* to listen rather than teach him to attend and to act.

Set the behavioral limits and educational requirements early in the school year. Do not wait to set rules of procedure after infractions have accumulated. Greater respect will accrue you when as a teacher you begin with firmness and with clear purpose.

Children may vigorously protest assuming responsibilities. Later, when they learn to accept responsibilities, they enjoy meeting them. One can show the child by firmness and by confidence in him that he can and will perform responsibly. Children have to learn through example and firsthand experience that the sky will not fall on them if they do not always succeed and that reasonable effort can usually be followed by at least moderate success.

Remember not to threaten and then give in to the child. Think before answering no or yes, and be prepared to follow through on the answer. Words must always be capable of being supported by appropriate action.

Have the child make up as soon as possible the work he has missed, whether the missed work has been due to illness or other causes. Once a task is set, the responsibility to complete it should not be relaxed. If it is clearly evident that a task was wrongly set, then correction of the task should be made, but not without a substitute or alternate task.

When setting goals for and with students, be careful not to set them too far in advance; provide subgoals or short-term goals to aid interim progress.

What of the child who does alternately poorly and acceptably on the same general task at different times? Vacillation or oscillation may be due to lack of skill or to lack of application, or to both. As new skills become fixed, variability in performance tends to decrease; this should be an index of progress, and a clue to reasons for lack of progress with most skills.

Whenever persistent inferiority feelings are found, look for or suspect a too high aspiration level. Try to detect possibly high and even grandiose aspirations, and help the child to cut them back to reasonable levels; but at the same time help the child to actually beef up his concrete efforts and actual level of achievement.

Always try to operate on the principle "Do as I do." To keep proper expectations clear to the child, avoid the old error of "Don't do as I do, but do as I say."

As the coach or physical education teacher does, "bench" the child who fails to cooperate with group rules and efforts. Apply this technique to classroom and social activities as well as to playground and athletics.

Avoid letting the child throw in the sponge when the going gets tough for him. Do not assume that he cannot do what is required of him but that he simply prefers not to do it.

Hold him to his commitments, in games and in schoolwork, so that he learns to overcome hardships.

Avoid punishing the whole group in order to get at an offender. Punishing the group shows the teacher up badly, tells the students the teacher is stymied and outmaneuvered, and creates a loss of respect for the adult role. It is better to drop the issue at the time and wait for a later, well-discerned opportunity to find an offender and deal directly with him.

Exert great care in trying to handle circumstantial evidence of stealing and lying. Do not blame or follow a "third-degree" procedure when uncertain. Avoid trying to get a child to confess by grilling him. If no facts are available, let the matter drop temporarily and await further opportunities. If good circumstantial evidence is available, proceed from there to a correction of the matter, but keep attention on the facts and on the correction, not on a confession or moral victory.

When a child's stealing or destructive behavior has been clearly ascertained, have the child retrace his steps, make restitution. Do not harass the child with admonitions, advice, threats, shaming comments.

Breaking rules often leads the child to more and more guilt and weaker self-control; a destructive, vicious circle is thus created. Respect for the rules has to be taught, and firmness has to be followed in keeping the rules.

Overcoming emotional problems of children is often not a matter of rolling away a stone in their way—removing a block, so to speak—but is rather a matter of building up better *choices* as to the roads the child will follow, the small but important turns and decisions he makes daily.

Feelings and emotions loom less large when the individual has problem-solving skills available to meet life's contingencies. Negative emotions often are aroused when effective problem solving is poor or nonexistent.

The back-talking, "sniping," impudent youngster is best handled by not responding to him in terms of the face value of his remarks. He wants to distract and turn attention away from the requirement; if he can deflect the adult through sniping, he defeats the adult and at the same time perfects his own maladjustment.

LOVE AND RESPECT

What are the basic considerations for a child's relationship to the teacher and to formal classroom requirements? Since so much is said today about love and its effect on the child's welfare and since so little is said about respect, some dovetailing of these important conditions is called for.

Loving and being loved are certainly important in parent-child relations. But are they the answer to all problems? Do children misbehave because they are not loved? Sometimes both child and parent misuse love by using it for license. If love cannot lead to disciplined respect, it is too empty to be called love.

Respect may be more important than love. No one is going to love everybody, but a child can be taught to respect everyone, their rights, their differences. It is doubtful if sincere and mature love can exist without respect; love must be built upon fair and reliable relationships which, in turn, permit the greater fondness and affection to develop.

Love for a child should promote a firm, fair, and realistic discipline. Love and discipline are not opposites.

Firmness, fairness, and consistency in setting requirements for children, in the classroom as well as at home, make harshness and severity of discipline unnecessary; firmness is not to be confused with severity.

Perhaps too much emphasis is placed on having the child love his teacher and his schoolwork. Perhaps adults try too hard to appeal to the child, to sell him on his work. If he fails to respond, this is interpreted as an emotional problem, as indicating he is not sufficiently loved, does not feel secure. Is it not putting the cart before the horse to emphasize so strongly that the child love his work and his teacher? It would be more realistic to acquaint him first with his tasks, help him to successful achievement, then let his liking or not liking the various subjects be left up to him.

If we are truthful with ourselves, we will admit that it is difficult to love a child who is constantly a troublemaker. However, we can respect the child's individuality and attempt to use proper skills as teachers and adults to bring this individuality into productive fruition, rather than allow the child to show it destructively and worsen his social and emotional condition.

Be careful not to let the child's show of affection distract from the business of teaching him. Some children, in carrying on patterns of affection learned at home, tend to see affection as a way of getting out of responsibilities. In the well-known way in which mothering turns into "smothering," affection may be turned into "deflection," that is, used to circumvent mature responsibilities by the immature use of affection.

A complaining child may not be an unloved child. He may simply be trying to get others to shoulder his responsibilities.

PARENTS AND CHILDREN

The following comments are general guides to thinking about parent-child relationships as they affect the child's school behavior and achievement. They supplement comments in Chapter 9 and in the protocols dealing with parent group meetings in Appendix A.

Much of the friction between home and school stems from parents and teachers failing to understand and appreciate the role of the other. Parents are often on guard about the attitudes of teachers toward children; and teachers often blame parents too severely for common human shortcomings. From the standpoint of parents, teachers often describe a child's

problems without being able to come up with positive recommendations. This state of affairs ends in frustration for the
parents, who want to help the child but find no clear or open
paths.

From the standpoint of the teacher, parents frequently lack
interest in the child's schoolwork and behavior. Teachers
may try to get parents constructively involved in the child's
welfare but feel that the parents rebuff the school, saying
that the problems belong to the school, not to the parents.

Sometimes teachers dismiss a child's behavior as being "just
like his parents'," meaning to say that nothing can be done
about the situation. While children are certainly similar to
their parents in attitudes and actions, this does not preclude
constructive work on adverse attitudes the child may show at
school.

There is probably not enough constant feedback between school
and home to allow parents to know how a child is progressing, especially in the case of conduct and achievement problems. For children needing close supervision, the six- or nine-
week periodic reports are probably too infrequent to allow
for the firm requirements and follow-through necessary to
correct deviate behavior or poor work.

The teacher ought to know what kinds of help the parent offers
a child. It is one thing for parents to see that the child does
his homework and quite a different thing to do it for him or
unduly aid him. Parental supervision is not a bad thing, but
it should be put to the proper use; the teacher can often
specify to the parent what is and is not acceptable help.

Children often bring home very garbled versions of what a
teacher has said in class. In order to avoid complicated com-
munication problems, the teacher is safest who does not
comment on the child's dress, home background, or other
personal areas of the child's life.

Deciding when a child is honestly bored with schoolwork is not
easy. Many parents feel a child is bored owing to a lack of
challenge when in reality the child is simply not occupied in

doing the work he should do; he lacks skills and study habits rather than stimulation.

Should a child be given credit for work done at home instead of at school? Perhaps as a start toward developing better work habits or as a way of setting certain requirements, but not as a general recourse or dodge in which the child is allowed to set his own conditions of work and achievement.

Task requirements are generally preferable to time requirements. Time can be wasted, but the amount of work done can be controlled and the child can be kept to a task, or to a given portion of it, until acceptable work is done.

Watch out for a kind of "amazed ignorance" on the child's part. This is a common technique used when a child wants to get out of a responsibility. He may naïvely or experimentally take the position "I did my work but it didn't come out right." Or "I did the right thing, and I don't know what happened." Some guarded reality on the teacher's part will allow her to assess the genuineness of the child's remarks.

The child who is always complaining may be trying, in part, to get someone to do his work for him or release him from his responsibility. Hear his complaints, acknowledge to him that you know how he feels, but still hold him to his requirements.

Motivating the lazy child is not a matter of finding a particular cue to his attitude. It is more a matter of demonstrating to him that his bread is buttered on the side of activity and effort.

Observe carefully the child who makes a great start, with fanfare and pronouncements of good intentions, then finishes poorly or not at all. Help him cut down on his exorbitant expectations at first, so that his commitment is not so large; and then help him beef up his actual effort and performance at realistic levels.

Most mechanical aids to learning—visual aids, learning machines, reading improvement machines—are useful because they not only present material systematically but also set up disciplined and programmed ways of progressing toward the learning goals. The good teacher proceeds in a similar manner.

Common ways to improve the value of examinations are well known. But some uncommon ways need attention, too: give examinations often; give back results from the exams as soon as possible; require correction of faulty work; state clearly what exams are worth in arriving at a total grade; let students know the basis for grading, whether on a "curve" or absolute-score basis.

Boredom with classroom routine and lack of challenge may precipitate temper outbursts with some children. Try within limits to vary the pace; introduce explicit alternations in routine, so that the child is not put to the breaking point. Such alternations may be usefully planned to alleviate unnecessary tensions among a variety of handicapped learners.

Some children are, so to speak, good at rubbing out the lines that others draw but poor at drawing and following their own. In such cases, begin by not allowing the child to erase your lines and limits; as he respects and follows normal limits first set by others, he will begin to make and follow his own.

While teachers do not want to be such sticklers for rules that they take all the fun out of life, they do have to be aware of the implications both of easily broken rules and of rules so hard to follow that they cannot be kept. Both extremes misinform the student of the importance of rules.

Fear of schoolwork is not so common as strong reluctance to do the work because of a set standard of rigid performance. A rigid standard may arise from a perfectionistic expectation or from an unwillingness to make an effort without guaranteed success.

Watch for after-vacation and after-illness letdowns in the child's schoolwork. Old problems of lack of concentration, misbehavior, and other distractions may come back to haunt the child who has had a layoff from studying for a few days.

SUMMARY

Generalizing to other cases—less disturbed children or the common variety of classroom problems—is not without its value. The program for the severely disturbed child ought to have implications for all other children, exceptional and otherwise. If a program has to change drastically with each category of maladjusted behavior, then it is inefficient and ineffectual.

Children do not come to us in clearly defined types. Rather than make recommendations on the basis of type or category, we should put emphasis on the individual differences in the children and on how to cope with specific problem situations. These problem situations have given dimensions; to work with these dimensions is the important task.

In this chapter, the general theory was briefly reviewed and the discussion was extended to the less disturbed groups of children. Aspects of a generally applicable structured program were considered. These include specific corrective procedures, the roles of love and respect, and general guides to clear thinking about parents and their children vis-à-vis the school.

APPENDIX A.
PROTOCOLS FROM PARENT GROUP
MEETINGS

INTRODUCTION TO PARENT GROUP MEETINGS

The publication of the protocols of the parent group meetings serves several purposes. The first and foremost is to show the reader how the group discussions were conducted. This illustrates how the child's actual behavior was coped with in theory in the discussions and how the theory led to classroom practices and to recommendations to parents.

The second reason for introducing the protocols is to show the reader how continuity between home and school handling of the child was developed and maintained. As a result of the effort illustrated by the protocols, parent, child, teacher (and other school officials) were more or less successfully bound together in working consistently toward commonly shared goals.

Thirdly, it is hoped that the discussions will give the reader the impression that no matter how disturbed the child or discouraged the parents, there are constructive measures which can and should be taken. It takes no reading between the lines to note that this program passed through some critical stages, especially when the misbehavior of various children seemed to get out of hand and when parental cooperation and forbearance were in jeopardy. A constructive effort was made at all times to try to bring order into the disordered lives of the children and their parents. Effort was made to infuse the parents with a constructive and realistically optimistic notion of what they could do to parallel the school's efforts.

A fourth reason for the inclusion of the protocols is to convey a total sense of how treatment of the child's educational *and* emotional ills can be simultaneously worked on in economical and salutary ways. It would have been an easy thing to dismiss or exclude most if not all of these youngsters from the public school, to have said they were too disturbed to be dealt with in a public school setting. It would have been easy to have taken no educational responsibility for them, saying that the emotional factors had to be cleared up first. Obviously such a rigid position was not taken; results seem to indicate that the choice was not only a theoretically wise one but also one of immense practical importance to school systems, to classroom teachers, and to all parents of emotionally disturbed children.

The meetings were held on an average of once a month the first year and on alternate months during the second year. The recorded discussions took from fifty to sixty minutes. In this period each child whose parent was present (or whose parents were both present) got from five to ten minutes discussion focus. This may seem like a very small amount, and it is. But with the aid of the firmness and the structure in the classroom setting, even this brief parental discussion time proved useful. More time might have been desirable, but taking a backward view over the years which this study covers (it began three years ago at the time of this writing), it is evident that a satisfactory equilibrium between time allotted to parental discussion meetings and other factors was reached. In addition to the discussion meetings, the parents had access to the teacher for conferences or phone conversations.

In a few instances it was necessary for the authors to have some extra time with the teachers after the evening parent discussion meeting, in order to clear up up some problems in handling children, which were raised in the group discussion.

Usually, however, matters of great or persistent importance to the teachers were adequately covered in the frequent meetings between them and the authors.

Except for the first parent group discussion meeting, the teachers and the principal of the school attended each meeting. This helped give the parents concrete support for what they felt the problems to be; and it helped to show the parents that the school personnel were capable of handling the difficulties the children posed. Nothing was said about the children in private that would not have been said openly in the parent group meetings. It is likely that the parents felt this sincerity; it may have helped them to be more cooperative and enduring in the pinches.

Any of the details concerning the parent group meetings— the size of the group, the frequency and length of meetings— might well have been handled differently. Other schools with other classes with different compositions might handle the same general problems differently. No intention exists to stand on the actual minutiae of the operation, except as they illustrate as a whole the general importance attached to setting up and maintaining structure in the classroom (and conveying related attitudes and techniques to the parents). Thus, there is no intention to foster orthodoxy by this report. Indeed, it is preferable that the interested reader take from the methods and procedures presented here those that seem to fit other specific situations and requirements. Some programs for the education of the emotionally disturbed child do not include any parent participation. It is felt that the parent group meetings of this study, while they may not have been essential, were nonetheless important, and that such meetings, considered generally, would seem to accelerate a child's growth because of the added significance the home plays in the child's life. However, if the methods used here were to be employed in an orphanage, or in a boarding school without any parental participation, it would be expected that the classroom practices would remain essentially as reported here. The absence of parental cooperation would possibly restrict progress but would not stifle it.

FIRST PARENT GROUP MEETING, FIRST YEAR

DR. H.: Let me start off with a very brief introduction. Our common problem here is to help children with learning disabilities. What we are going to do in these sessions is not group therapy. What we will do is give you ideas and examples of the kinds of situations which we believe these youngsters respond best to, in terms of both classroom practices and your child rearing practices at home. We have in common, then, a concern with these basically average or intellectually normal children who have displayed learning disabilities of various types. All of these children—as each of you knows well in his own case—all of these children have had classroom difficulties, both educational and in conduct. But there isn't a youngster in this group who cannot achieve satisfactorily if we find the appropriate learning-teaching situation. We are convinced of this. If we can define and develop the specialized kinds of situations necessary for each child—and we believe we can, with your help—this will lead to gradually more successful school performance and better conduct on the part of each child. Of course, different children will respond differently—some relatively fast, some more slowly. But all can profit to a much greater extent than they have before. But this is not a promise; it is a goal toward which we feel we can work, and we want your help and confidence. Dr. Phillips, here, is to act as a consultant in this program. He and I will work with you parents here at the meetings, and we will work very closely with the classroom teachers day by day and week by week. We are all fortunate in being able to muster an interest in this program, free of additional cost to you. We know you will sustain interest and let us help you, as we think we can help you, in the matter of improving the psychological and educational positions of these children. Dr. Phillips will take over now.

DR. P.: Thank you, Dr. Haring. What I think we might do is to start off now by simply going around the table and letting each one of you, in a few minutes, describe the main difficulties which you feel you have with your child. We will discuss each one's comments a little bit, then move on to the next. You can take about five or six minutes each. Even though each of you needs more time, you will gradually get the idea of what we are trying to do and how we go about it, and how it fits your child and your situation. As Dr. Haring has already said, we want to contribute to overcoming the learning difficulties these children show. The reason we have asked you to come is that we want to help you handle the children the way we are trying to handle them at school. We want to develop *continuity* between the home and the school. We want you to know what we do, and how, and why, so that you understand and can cooperate more fully with us. If you do not like what we are doing or if you disagree with any particular methods, we want you to feel free to openly challenge us. We want to know when our suggestions work satisfactorily and when they do not. We should all be frank with each other. (*Pause.*) Now we can start over here with you first, Mrs. D.

Mrs. D.: Well, he won't come home after school, among other things. He wouldn't come in for dinner.

Dr. P.: You mean after school, or in the late afternoon? And what do you do?

Mrs. D.: I have tried everything.

Dr. P.: Exactly what did you try?

Mrs. D.: I would not let him watch TV for a week. I just took away things one at a time.

Dr. P.: You tried a little bit of everything, and nothing worked very well?

Mrs. D.: Nothing worked, but he was always very sorry and promised he wouldn't do it the next time.

Dr. P.: Would he promise you that he wouldn't do it again?

Mrs. D.: Yes, he did. But then his friends would come to the house, and he would go to their house.

Dr. P.: Was he angry with you when you punished him for not coming home on time?

Mrs. D.: No, he understood.

Dr. P.: But still it didn't actually change him?

Mrs. D.: No.

Dr. P.: Are there any other things which you feel—besides this not coming home after school—have been a source of difficulty?

MRS. D.: Well, he seems to forget when I talk to him. When I ask him to clean his room, come home on time, or if I ask him to do something, he would forget about it. I don't know if he is just not interested. When he was younger, he used to help me.

DR. P.: How old is he now?

MRS. D.: He is eight.

DR. P.: But he has been rather absent-minded about it, you might say. You don't think he was doing it out of any maliciousness?

MRS. D.: No, I don't think he was doing it on purpose.

DR. P.: Have you noticed in the last couple of weeks if he is still doing this, or has been coming home more regularly?

MRS. D.: Well, the school bus brings him home.

DR. P.: That is one way of doing it. What about after that, when he goes out to play again?

MRS. D.: He goes out and plays around the court, and if I call him he comes home.

DR. P.: So he is more amenable to your discipline?

MRS. D.: Yes, and he tells more about his school activities and what he has been doing during the day.

DR. P.: Now let us suppose, for your sake and the sake of the rest of us here, that the newness of this situation at school will soon wear off and he will start ambling down the road again in a few days. What do you think you might do if he starts being tardy about coming home?

MRS. D.: I don't know yet.

DR. P.: Let us think about it a minute. You say you have tried a lot of things before and none of them worked very well. Do you think you could find some one thing which means a great deal to him and then rather hold on to that—watching TV or a weekend movie or allowance or something?

MRS. D.: Well, he gets an allowance; if he is good, he gets one. His grandmother made him a wonderful proposition; if he would come home from school, behave himself, and clean up his room, she would give him a dollar a week. That went on for three weeks.

DR. P.: Is that in force now?

MRS. D.: No.

DR. P.: That doesn't explain his better behavior?

Mrs. D.: No, she just dropped it because I insisted on it. Because I don't want him to do anything for money.

Dr. P.: That's better. I am glad to see that because it is better to say, "When you have done something, there are certain rewards that are natural," than pay the child.

Mrs. D.: I don't want to feel that if he does something for me, he is supposed to get paid for it.

Dr. P.: What does he like to do best of all in his free time? What is his chief interest?

Mrs. D.: Right now he is very much interested in model airplanes and clay models.

Dr. P.: Does he buy them every so often?

Mrs. D.: No. I buy one for him every three or four weeks.

Dr. P.: You might use this as an incentive. You might say, "As long as you continue to come home every afternoon after school then possibly you can get a new airplane once in a while." But if he doesn't stick with this, then the airplane would have to be postponed for another week or two.

Mrs. D.: That wouldn't bother him.

Dr. P.: That wouldn't bother him any? What kind of thing is he interested enough in that if you took it away it would bother him?

Mrs. D.: Nothing that I can think of—nothing, really. But he has been coming home after school, and if he is out playing with someone I go out looking for him.

Dr. P.: Well, we have to move on; but think about this some more, so that the next time we meet, you can tell us about how things have been going and also whether you have thought of any consequences that might befall him if he doesn't do what he is supposed to. You see what I am saying. If you don't pay your electric light bill, they turn off your light. They don't send you a reward for paying it, but there are consequences if you don't pay it. This is the way life operates. We want to invoke these kinds of limits for the child; but we want them to be natural, and we want them to involve something the child is interested in.

Shall we move on? Mrs. A., you are next.

Mrs. A.: Well, I don't know just where to start. I used to have the same problem. Although lately, there are a lot of children right in the block that he can play with. But the main thing is, I am always so afraid he is going to hurt somebody.

DR. P.: You mean he is too rough?

MRS. A.: Oh, he is just as strong as an ox. I always have fear that every time he goes out of the house, I wonder who he is going to hurt this time.

DR. P.: What do you do if he does hurt somebody?

MRS. A.: I've talked and talked and talked. I don't know what else to do.

DR. P.: Did you have any consequences that befell him if he didn't do what he was supposed to do? You see, talk is cheap.

MRS. A.: Yes, I know.

DR. P.: The child does not respect it unless there are events that back it up; then the words mean something. If you don't have that, it just won't make much difference to some of them. What has he done in the past two or three weeks that has caused you some concern?

MRS. A.: I don't know. I do find that he has been better since he has come in this school, really. I noticed a big difference.

DR. P.: How have you noticed the difference?

MRS. A.: Well, oh, I don't know, the children seem to be playing in our yard all the time now. And before, they used to shun him. And tonight, I know there must have been fifteen running around the house. Cowboys and Indians.

DR. P.: And he didn't get into trouble with any of them?

MRS. A.: No. He did all right this evening. He seems to have spells, though, where he'd get along fine for three or four weeks and then he'd just go off.

DR. P.: Would you keep track—and all the rest of you, too—of things that happen in these intervening periods between our meetings, so that you can bring them up and have them sort of jell in your thinking, so we can be more efficient in discussing them. Think about these things. Tonight we are just breaking the ground, but later we can get more specific.

MRS. A.: We have so many problems, we went to the guidance clinic every week for fourteen weeks, and one person would tell you one thing and another would tell you something else. I am just as confused as he is.

DR. P.: Is it hard for you to put your foot down and try to stop him when he does something you feel is wrong—I mean really forcefully, clearly, let him know what you think and where you stand? Instead of saying, "Cecil, don't do that, Cecil, don't do that."

MR. A.: It doesn't seem to make too much difference to him. We can switch him.

MRS. A.: That doesn't do any good at all.

MR. A.: Well, within the last two or three years—well, I don't think I've switched him for about a couple of years. Then the other night we wanted to watch TV, and a certain program. He wanted to watch something else. I told him no. He made quite a fuss, so I took my belt to him. Tonight and the rest of that night he seemed pretty good. He even came and asked me first if this program would be all right.

DR. P.: Do you wait too long before you do something like that? Do you give him warning after warning before you finally take your belt off and crack him with it?

MR. A.: Well, like I said, it's been a couple of years since I've laid it on to him, but it didn't seem to do any good.

MRS. A.: But we were advised not to do this, that it wouldn't do any good. I don't know; I have tried everything.

DR. P.: Does taking privileges away from him help any?

MRS. A.: Well, like his coming in for dinner. I'd call and call and call him. Maybe an hour later he'd come in, and he'd be starving to death.

DR. P.: Then what would happen?

MRS. A.: I wouldn't warm his dinner. He'd eat it like it was because I don't believe in taking his dinner away from him.

DR. P.: Why not?

MRS. A. I just don't.

DR. P.: Well, he's got you coming and going, no matter what. He sure gets to you.

MRS. A.: We have an arrangement now. I call him one time; if he isn't within hearing distance, then that night he gets no dessert. He doesn't eat his dessert with his dinner; he eats it maybe two or three hours later when he's watching television.

DR. P.: Is this helping now, cutting out dessert?

MRS. A.: It seems to be. Well, last night I called him once, and he was down in the next block. He didn't hear me—I knew he wouldn't hear me—but I did my duty and he didn't get any dessert.

DR. P.: Personally, I would extend that to the dinner, but you don't have to do it if you don't want to.

MRS. A.: Well, I disapprove of putting him to bed with no dinner.

DR. P.: All right, think about it some more. But the point we want to make clear is that whatever you do should make a difference in his behavior. If you do it, you want to do it for that reason. If you don't do it, you want it to be for an equally good reason. But if he comes in late and still gets his dinner, chances are it won't make much difference. So do some thinking about that. Missing a meal isn't too bad. Most physicians say that if you miss one once in a while, it is good for you. Shall we move on? Mrs. K.?

MRS. K.: Well, most of our trouble with our youngster has been in school. He started out in California in September of 1954, and he was in that school until Thanksgiving, and I talked to the teacher. She called me to school twice. So when we came back here, I warned the teacher that if there was any trouble, to let me know immediately. And for that year and all of the next year, Larry was a good boy.

DR. P.: Where was he last year?

MRS. K.: He was at N———— last year. Last year was really the beginning of the trouble. He has been behind ever since we brought him from California. He came back here behind in the first grade after his two months out there. But last year, I don't—I couldn't tell you how many times the teacher called me to tell me that Larry would wad up his papers and throw them away, get mad at himself, throw things, and that he was disturbing the other children. We would punish him at first, but it didn't do any good. We finally decided that the teacher's personality and his just clashed. So I talked to the principal and he had his teacher changed, but it didn't take place until just a month before school was out.

DR. P.: So you didn't have a chance to tell if the change helped?

MRS. K.: But in that month the teacher had no complaints at all about his behavior; it was all right.

DR. P.: How is he starting off this fall?

MRS. K.: Well, now he has still a different teacher this fall in

N_____, and he was just changed a couple of weeks ago. He was performing in the same manner. If he couldn't work to suit himself, he would roll his papers up and throw them away and get mad at himself, break his pencil and then throw it, and have a temper display.

D<small>R</small>. P.: Does he do this at home? While he is working on things?

M<small>RS</small>. K.: Well, he doesn't throw things much. He gets mad at himself because things won't go into place just to suit him.

D<small>R</small>. P.: What do you do when he does that?

M<small>RS</small>. K.: I scold him mostly, but that doesn't do any good.

M<small>R</small>. K.: We usually take away what he's playing with.

D<small>R</small>. P.: Why do you do that? I'm not criticizing; I'm just asking. Do you want to stop his noise?

M<small>R</small>. K.: No, not necessarily. We want to teach him to control his temper. I mean we know that before he becomes an adult, if he is going to be a successful adult, he has to learn to control that temper.

D<small>R</small>. P.: What do you think would happen if you had him do over whatever it was that disturbed him at the time.

M<small>RS</small>. K.: We have done that with work. He did some work at home not very long ago. And the first paper he turned in, there was an erasure in every single word on the page, and he wrote a whole paragraph. So we made him do it again, and he got through it with only a couple of errors. It was very neat and well done.

D<small>R</small>. P.: Well, now, let's think about that for a minute. If you hadn't had him do it over again, the first thing he wouldn't have learned would have been that he could do it, and do it more satisfactorily. And that is what we want him to learn and gain the confidence for. The second thing he wouldn't have learned would have been a reasonable attitude toward the requirement, because if we had left things at the point where his temper dismissed these activities, then he would have finished with a bad taste in his mouth. This is not unlike training situations in the Air Force, where people are learning to fly. If the pilots go up and have some bad experience, they send them right back up again so as to erase, so to speak, the unpleasant experience and the fear and also to teach the pilot, in this case, that he can master these particular situations.

So you might think of doing that in trying to keep your own concern down. Don't get upset when he gets mad, but put him back to the task, and let him know that you feel confidence in him and that you know he can do it, and by golly, you are going to see that he does it. And if he has to copy that paper over five times, he's going to copy it over five times or till he gets it. You won't have to do that very many times. Do you see what I mean?

MRS. K.: Well, there are other things that we—little things around the house—that I can't think of right now.

MR. K.: I think one of the big troubles with Larry was that he had a teacher at N_____, called Miss R., who was an elderly teacher. She rattled him so much. She was one of those teachers who would holler and scream at the child. She rattled him so much he just didn't want to do anything when she was around.

DR. P.: He didn't want to cooperate?

MR. K.: He didn't want to cooperate, and the minute she'd scream at him he'd just stop completely what he was doing and freeze up. I asked him several times, "Why don't you just go to Miss R. and tell her that when she hollers at you that she just makes you freeze up?" He said, "I have, but then she screams at me for coming up to her."

MRS. K.: Well, she had us believing that Larry was just about the worst thing that could happen to anyone, and I know the child is not really that bad.

DR. P.: She was discouraged with him?

MRS. K.: Very much so, and Larry drifted backward. Miss C. tutored him the year before in reading and writing in the summertime with the thought that he could catch up last year, but she wasn't with him last year. He got along beautifully with her. And then he got this other teacher, and instead of going forward like she expected him to do, he drifted backward and ended up worse off at the end of the term than he was at the beginning.

DR. P.: We realize that unfortunate situations like you mention will sometimes develop. Please don't hold back mentioning adverse learning situations affecting the child. We are not here to criticize anybody, but we are here to speak the truth as we see it, in order to be of help to the children. So speak your mind and we'll try to sort out what is useful and what is meaningful. (Stated as a help to the parent—Mrs. K.—who was receiving some side line comments and criticisms to restrain herself as she was speaking the above recorded paragraph.)

MRS. K.: We considered taking some things away from him. The things he dearly loves most are cub scouts and sports. And at the time we were having so much trouble he was on the cub scout team, and we thought of taking that away; and then we thought perhaps that would be doing more harm than good.

DR. P.: When I speak of taking things away, I don't mean taking away a whole activity like scouting, but tomorrow's show or this afternoon's play period.

MRS. K.: Well, I did take away his ball glove about three weeks ago.

DR. P.: Yes, you can do that. You can put a bicycle or ball gloves in hock until something is finished, and then they come out again.

MR. K.: He has the toughest pair of hands in the neighborhood now from playing ball without gloves.

DR. P.: All right, let us move on. Mrs. E.?

MRS. E.: Frank has been very happy down here. He likes the situation; he'll come home and tell me he's won a race or something like that which he has never been able to do along with the other children. His coordination has always been very poor. But I think one of our biggest problems is, has been with —I guess you'd call it defiance. He'll wait until he gets us out with a group of people and then show off. He thinks we can't do anything about it.

DR. P.: That is why he picks that time.

MRS. E.: Yes, I think he knows full well that we can't do anything about it. Then also, if we have a rule about something—we have two other children—and we tell them that none of them can do something, he would look at us and keep his eye right on us and go right ahead and do it, with a look that practically says, "Well, what are you going to do about it?"

DR. P.: Well, what do you do about it?

MRS. E.: We take away his television, which seems to work very well.

DR. P.: Do you do anything at the time?

MRS. E.: Yes, we send him to his room usually. Something right away. Or send him in the house if they all happen to be playing outside. But it's strange the way he takes to discipline; he likes to be disciplined. If we tell him, for instance, he is going to miss five minutes of a program for a whole week, rather than miss it all in one day he'll go out in the kitchen and watch the clock himself and five minutes after the hour he'll go back in. But of course that doesn't always do any good, as far as changing the situation. Of course, we think he is slowly getting better in all this.

DR. P.: What is the most difficult thing to change, this business of putting you on the spot when you are in company?

MRS. E.: Yes. Then he gets very excited when he gets with other children or when other people come in. Goodness knows, there are always people at our house. It's nothing for us to have ten or twelve people in for the weekend. So we've had enough. It is not that he isn't used to people.

DR. P.: He is used to getting excited! Do you ever isolate him at those times?

MRS. E.: Yes. We take him completely away from the other children and put him in his room. And if he finds that he can't get by with it, that we can do something about it, he gets along fine. He'll come out and behave himself. But he has to know that he has to.

DR. P.: That's right. You have to put your foot down and be definitive. And if not, he thinks you are talking monkey business.

MRS. E.: And he'll look at you while he's doing something he shouldn't.

DR. P.: Right. There isn't a child in the world who wouldn't do this, providing the situation is stacked this way as he sees it.

MRS. S.: May I ask a question along that same line?

DR. P.: Yes, certainly.

MRS. S.: When I was out in the store not very long ago, I told my youngster if he didn't quit doing certain things like handling the merchandise, I would give him a spanking when I got home. He didn't stop, so I did give him a spanking when I got home. Should I have taken him to the lounge or someplace and given it to him then, or was I right in waiting?

Dr. P.: I'd say the sooner the better.

Mrs. S.: You mean, if there is someplace you can do it, do it.

Dr. P.: Right. Or another thing you can do a lot of times, depending on your shopping conveniences, is put him back in the car and make him wait there. Of course, that is a variable that won't be the same for all children, but it is something you can keep in mind. But I think, in your situation, you might be more definitive earlier. When people come in and he starts getting wound up and gets higher and higher, like the stock market, he is going to crash eventually. Anticipate him, and save all the wear and tear.

Mr. E.: We have found, in former experiences, if we nip it in the bud we have pretty well solved our problems. We've learned that over a period of years.

Dr. P.: Keep that in mind, and watch for these kinds of situations. Keep track of them in your own thinking, and try to line them up on the positive and negative side, and bring that information back with you.

Mrs. E.: I have noticed that he is much improved in the past months that he has been coming down here and we have much fewer situations like this.

Dr. P.: But when you do have them, they're difficult to handle at that time; so watch for them, and see what you can do.

Mr. E.: There is one thing I would like to mention along this same problem. When he is looking forward to something—for example, he has a playmate at school; they are great buddies. One day last week, he got home and went out to meet his friend. He found out his friend was going to someone else's house, and he came back to the house brokenhearted. I was home and tried to explain the situation to him. Finally I convinced him to go out and play with his bicycle, and after about ten minutes he was over it. But every time something interferes with something he should have, he gets terribly upset for a period of time. It lasts for about five or ten minutes, and then he is over it. Here is another example following the same pattern. He wants a hamburger and bun every night at dinnertime. Every night he wants to know if we are going to have hamburgers. He won't accept the fact that we can't have hamburgers every night; he still comes in and fusses. But we tell him that's the way it is going to be.

DR. P.: That's right. If you show him the firmness of your decision and that he has to make a choice, this puts the burden back on him instead of continuing his fussing at you and trying to get you to change the menu or pull his chestnuts out of the fire in some way.

MRS. E.: There is one other thing too. He doesn't get along too well with his playmates. I think part of that stems from the fact that he can't keep up with them physically. And when he can't, he gets antagonistic toward them, and then he says they don't like him. We have tried to tell him that if he wants other people to be friends with him, he has to be friends with them and play with them and not against them.

DR. P.: Well, in a lot of these instances which you bring up here there are not specific answers in the sense of skills or tricks or something; but as he is put back on his own more and matures more, then he will feel more whole in his own right, and he'll take his role with the other kids more adequately. This is just a kind of general maturing thing. Let's put that in the back of our minds and make some observations on it.

Let's move along. Mrs. H., let's go on with you since you are next in line.

MRS. H.: I think one of our big problems is to get Ira to get dressed in the morning and make his bed. He gets up and sits at his desk and draws or plays. He has been under a threat that everything is going to be taken out of the room. He got his final notice today. We'll see what happens if he pulls the same trick tomorrow morning. We will carry out our threat. He is generally a happy child. He goes very cheerfully to get the bus every morning and comes home equally happy in the afternoon.

DR. P.: May I ask what you have been doing about the morning dressing and getting the bed made?

MRS. H.: We just made a rule. He must get up, get dressed, make his bed, and have his breakfast; and then if there is any time left over, he can do what he pleases until bus time. But this is something that has happened only in the past two or three weeks. For a while he did get up and get dressed without much dillydallying.

DR. P.: Do you spend much time talking about it to him?

MRS. H.: Well, we tell him that is what he has to do.

DR. P.: Well, what if he doesn't get dressed? What do you do?

MRS. H.: But he does.

DR. P.: Well, how has he? Has he done it because you have stayed with him?

MRS. H.: No, I don't stay with him.

DR. P.: Oh, he's just slow about it.

MRS. H.: Yes, he is slow. Oh, no, I've never stayed with him!

DR. P.: So what he really does is put in his spare time early instead of having it after breakfast.

MRS. H.: That's right. But I insist he should put it in later because I don't want to spend my time cheering him on through breakfast so he can get the bus.

DR. P.: That is what I mean; you're in there pushing.

MRS. H.: No, only through his breakfast; by that time he is dressed.

DR. P.: What if he missed breakfast?

MRS. H.: Well, then he goes to school hungry. He certainly wouldn't stay home; I can tell you that.

DR. P.: You mean he would want to go to school?

MRS. H.: Oh, yes, I think he would.

DR. P.: You see, this is an ultimate anchorage point you have.

MRS. H.: I am sure that it isn't that he doesn't want to go to school. I think it is because he gets preoccupied with his sister.

DR. P.: I think you are probably right. What I was suggesting is to be careful how you put the pressure on him to move along. Keep in mind that actually he is rather robbing Peter to pay Paul all the time here. And you can put down the ultimate anchorage here, by saying that if he is not down to breakfast by such and such a time, he misses it, and if he keeps pushing things back, he'll miss the bus, and he'll have to stay home. Now you may not want to do that, and I am not saying that you should do it, but keep it in mind because you may have to. And it isn't a bad thing. You see, this would teach him to order these events prior to breakfast.

MR. H.: I think the only thing we might add to this is the tremendous improvement since he has been here. He is much more interested in reading now; and yesterday when I was helping my older son with his algebra, he took a paper and proceeded to put down what looked like equations, and I discovered he was putting down $10 + 20 + 80 - 15$ and had gotten the right answer, surprisingly enough. So there is much more interest on his part, and I think he really wants to learn for the first time in his life.

DR. P.: Let's go on with Mrs. V.

MRS. V.: Well, we have a lot of similar problems. We have the defiance. He has started to want to learn, and this keeps him happy in the school situation. His home situation is still not desirable; he feels so rejected. He says no one likes him and no one wants to play with him.

DR. P.: You mean in the neighborhood, with other children?

MRS. V.: Yes, he doesn't bother to go out and find out if they want to play with him. We have a terrible time to get him to go outdoors.

DR. P.: What do you say when he says the other kids don't like him?

MRS. V.: I tell him there must be a reason—that people have to be liked in this world and that you have to meet people halfway and do your part.

DR. P.: What does he say?

MRS. V.: He says, "Well, they're mean to me, and I wasn't mean to them." And I say, "You are, lots of times, because I've been around when you have been, and you can't act that way and expect people to like you. They won't."

DR. P.: Does this talking to him do any good?

MRS. V.: Well, sometimes.

DR. P.: Does it get him outside then?

MRS. V.: No. It doesn't budge him unless you do the arranging for him. You have to plan a program for him. If you do the calling of the parents and arrange for him to be with other children, then he will go.

DR. P.: You are his social secretary.

MRS. V.: That's right. I am his social secretary and carry out every plan. I find it is simpler to just take him somewhere. I took him to the zoo last week. I can't plan a social program every day, but I do try.

DR. P.: What do you think about not answering him when he complains about the other kids not liking him, and also not planning these things for him? I don't mean you shouldn't take him anywhere, but don't make a lot of plans.

MRS. V.: Well, he'd watch television all the time. And I think he watches entirely too much television now.

DR. P.: How are you going to break this impasse if you are going to keep on letting him lean on you?

MRS. V.: That is what I would like to know. I'd like to know what you'd suggest.

DR. P.: Well, I would suggest that you turn the television off and keep it off. Can you do that?

MRS. V.: I suppose I could have someone show me how to take out the tubes.

DR. P.: All right, take it apart. A lot of people do that. Take out a tube and then leave him on his own. Don't say, "Why don't you do this? You should do that. I'll take you here or there." Don't do that; put him on his own. He's like somebody who won't get into the swim; he won't know what he *can* do well. You mean well, and what you are doing is ordinarily satisfactory, but in his state of affairs he has got to learn to lift his own weight. You can't do it all the time. Does that make sense to you?

MRS. V.: Yes, except I feel sorry for him because he is rejected.

DR. P.: Well, I don't think he is *that* rejected, and I do not think that feeling sorry for him is either appropriate or valid. You see, it is not appropriate in the sense that it does not help him, and it is not valid because he is not really being mistreated. This is his version of it. And the reason he has this version is that he doesn't make sufficient effort himself.

MRS. V.: It is the same way with adults. He feels that they reject him too. Sometimes it amazes me. He feels Mrs. N. loves him dearly, but he doesn't feel everyone likes him.

DR. P.: He can get over this, not by you or me trying to talk him out of it, but by strengthening his confidence in himself through experiences and activities. You know there is an insurance company that puts out an ad saying, "With experience comes confidence." That is exactly true with a child or an adult. He has to have the kinds of experiences that will allow him to develop the confidence that he needs. And he cannot have them as long as he is watching television or depending on you or someone else to pull his social chestnuts out of the fire. So try your hardest. It may be difficult for you, and it may not work too well at first, but try as hard as you can the next few weeks.

MRS. V.: Well, should I suggest that he call someone?

DR. P.: I wouldn't even do that. Because the more you suggest, the more you take any kind of lead, the more he is going to look to you.

MR. V.: I think that sums it up pretty well. His attitude has seemed to improve since he has come to this school. We do have these intermittent periods of defiance and disobedience.

DR. P.: What do you do when he is that way? When he kicks up the dust.

MRS. V.: Not much of anything. That's been the trouble I think. I've been the one that carries the stick.

MR. V.: I'd say we do various things, probably not consistent. That may be one of the difficulties. Sometimes we try to reason with him, and other times we just put down a firm line. I think the firm line is better. I think part of the explanation of being lenient with him and attempting this reasoning, pleading process stems from a more or less subconscious sympathy or pity on our part for the fact that he doesn't seem to have the friendly associations which are normal among children.

DR. P.: You are making allowances all the time.

MR. V.: Yes.

DR. P.: And he can sense this, and so he pushes another inch, another foot. And all the time he is doing that, he is neglecting developing himself in this other direction.

MR. V.: That sounds reasonable.

MRS. V.: We have been working in the wrong direction.

DR. P.: That's right, Mrs. V. Think these things over; look them over in his behavior and in your relationships. By next time come back fighting with us.

Now then, Mrs. C?

MRS. C.: I have a feeling that my boy is older than the children who have been discussed here tonight.

DR. P.: How old is he?

MRS. C.: He is ten, will be eleven in November. He doesn't seem to have quite the same type of problems. You can't put a label on him that says "naughty." He never seems to do those things I would term as bad. I feel that perhaps his two greatest problems would be social and maturity, and maybe failure to complete a job. I don't know just how much progress he has made in school. I don't feel I have learned enough from him, and he hasn't been in school here very long yet. He doesn't seem to come home and discuss school very much, like some of the others have said. When I question him, he says, "Well, Mother, the teacher tells me I am making rapid advancement, but that is all she tells me. She doesn't tell me what kind of grades I am making." But I had the constant complaint last year that he never completed a job, and I had a feeling that he needed much more discipline than he was getting and that perhaps he forgot himself a lot. And that he was left to his own initiative altogether and the job was never completed. He does a lot of that at home also.

DR. P.: Give me an example of something recent at home that you've wanted him to do that he hasn't finished. Like mowing the yard, putting away his toys.

MRS. C.: I am afraid I don't ask him to do too many things.

DR. P.: Does he have any daily responsibilities at home?

MRS. C.: Yes, he has a newspaper route, and he takes care of that. That is almost all he takes care of. He is supposed to take care of his clothes. He still isn't very good at combing his hair, and I think if someone doesn't remind him to comb his hair in the morning, he'd get on the bus without having it combed. His sister once reminded him about it. I think he does depend on her to a certain extent. She is a few years older.

DR. P.: Does he depend on her too much?

MRS. C.: Perhaps he does. As much as he can get by with.

DR. P.: What do you do when he doesn't finish a task?

MRS. C.: Right now I come home so late he's been home quite a while before I get in, and I find that he has taken care of his newspaper route but he doesn't have his room in very good order.

DR. P.: What do you do then?

MRS. C.: I have discussed a period of self-improvement with him recently. I tell him that I think all people should have one period during the day when they should try to improve themselves. My daughter is taking typing at home; she's in junior high school now. She is doing very nicely. And he is supposed to be learning to play the clarinet. I think he goes in and gives it about two-and-a-half toots and that is the end of it.

DR. P.: You are working and come about five?

MRS. C.: Yes, I am working, and it is about five thirty when I get home. When I get home, of course, we rush in for dinner, and I have really very little time to actually get in behind him to supervise him.

DR. P.: How about in the morning? Does he make his bed? Clean up his room?

MRS. C.: Yes, he did until his daddy started to stay home. Now I think his daddy helps him and does some of that with him. I leave the house without checking to see if he does those things. His daddy has been home for about four or five weeks.

DR. P.: Can you check and see that he does these things each morning?

MRS. C.: Sometimes he puts his things away and sometimes he doesn't.

DR. P.: I know that children do this. We've gotten plenty of evidence here tonight. But I am suggesting that we tighten the screws a little bit, so that he begins to take more responsibility. Then when he takes more responsibility, he'll feel better. When he feels better, he takes more responsibility. He holds his head up and sticks his chest out—not literally, but this kind of thing. I think you described him very well; it is just a kind of general state of immaturity. It is nothing very specific, just a kind of general sagging. I think if you can put him on some daily chore which you can really check on and then really follow through on the consequences—loss of privileges or something like that—then he may straighten up a little bit; and I'd like to see you give it a whirl and see what you think about it. Do you understand what I mean?

MRS. C.: Yes, I do. But I think most of his problems are more in school than at home.

DR. P.: Well, you may be right. But I think we might strike a balance here between home and school.

MRS. C.: I don't know how much better he is doing now; for example, Miss M. stays behind him and sees that he does the job. But last year in school the teacher didn't have the time to stay behind him. She would simply hand out an assignment, and left the child to do the job, and it was never done. I am just wondering now—perhaps he will do very nicely this year because she is with him and she does things to create interest. He told me last night he completed his work very nicely. I wonder—when she turns him loose, say next year, for example, when he goes back into junior high school—if he will go ahead and do his work on his own, or whether he will wait for someone to push him into the job.

DR. P.: That is a very good question. I am glad you brought it up. We want to make this distinction. We want to distinguish between standing there all the time pushing a child and putting an *indirect* kind of pressure on him, if you want to call it that, through the consequences, through loss of something that is important to him. The telephone company doesn't call you about every week and say you owe so much on your telephone bill; if you don't pay it after a certain period of time, they turn off the service. Now that is comparable to what we want to do with the child. We want to treat him realistically, just as life will treat him when he gets outside, gets older. We want to put the consequences before him in a way that causes him to recognize them, so he will say, "I want to do this because it is to my interest to do it," rather than for someone to say, "Johnny, do this, do that," every five minutes. There have to be pressures because we all have pressures. If we didn't have pressures on us, I am sure we would be just as flabby as jellyfish. But there are various kinds of pressures, and we want the pressures to come back into the child and make him feel more as if he is taking the responsibility. You may have to build a lot of fires under him to do that. But that is what we want in this program. We don't want to say immediately that these children can go back to their normal classes. We don't think it will take long if we all do the right kinds of things. They may sag a little bit, yes, because being in a class of ten or fewer children, no matter what kinds of children you have, is different from being in a class of thirty-five or forty. There is bound to be some difference. We want to minimize it by teaching these children self-control and initiative. You may want to try some of these suggestions and let us know next time how they worked out.

MRS. C.: We also seem to have trouble in money problems. He never seems to be able to take care of a nickel. When he gets an allowance, it is gone immediately. My little daughter is just the opposite. She hangs on to her money; and she is going to be sure, if she spends a dime, she is going to get ten cents' worth of something. While he throws it around and has a tendency to lose it or something. Now that he has the paper route, I think maybe it is helping him a little bit. The other day he came in and said, "Mother, with this paper route I am beginning to learn how hard it is to make a little money."

DR. P.: That is exactly what I mean, you see. The route is putting pressure on him because he has to deliver the paper, collect from the people, and pay the route man for the papers he bought; and if the people don't pay him, he is left standing in the ditch. He has to fork out. What a wonderful learning experience that is. I think paper routes are tremendous. Wish all children could have paper routes.

MRS. C.: He also learned that he must have a method of doing things. He has been collecting for two months now. The first time he went around, he was so anxious to get his hands on the money that he didn't wait for me to come home, even though I had told him to wait and let me show him how to go about making the collection. He went out and he collected a few—didn't keep a record, didn't know just where he went, where he had gone. But then I showed him a little method to have his receipts all made out before he got ready to go, keeping his book in order so he would know who has paid him, and so on. When he came back he said, "Thank you, Mother, for your suggestions."

DR. P.: Well, that is a very good working model to go by. You have some very good instances of how to work this.

We'll move on. Mrs. DeF., would you like to take the last five minutes?

MRS. DEF.: Well, the big problem with my youngster is that I can't depend on him. I'd ask him on the phone from the office if he changed into his dungarees, and he'd say yes. Then when I get home I find that he hasn't done it. I say, "I thought you said you changed your clothes." He claims he didn't say that. He always denies everything.

DR. P.: What do you do when you come and find that he hasn't changed his clothes?

MRS. DEF.: Well, he always expects to have his Pepsi-Cola or something like that. If I try to talk to him about it, he always denies it. Another thing, he likes to take money. I've told him that the next time I would really punish him.

DR. P.: You mean from your purse, dresser, or something?

MRS. DEF.: That is right. He gets his allowance. He gets a dollar and fifty cents every Thursday. He denies that he does those things.

DR. P.: What does he do with all that money?

MRS. DEF.: That is what I would like to know. I didn't know he had been taking any.

DR. P.: No, I mean with the dollar and fifty cents allowance.

MRS. DEF.: Well, he just spends it foolishly.

DR. P.: Does he save any of it?

MRS. DEF.: No.

DR. P.: It might be that he is used to this money—easy come, easy go. And whether it is a legitimate dollar or an extra seventy-five cents, it still is all in the same category. He doesn't have enough respect for it.

MRS. DEF.: I have tried taking it away from him, but it doesn't bother him.

DR. P.: How is he in minding you in little things? In morning routines, etc.?

MRS. DEF.: In the morning he doesn't want to get dressed, he doesn't want to eat his breakfast.

DR. P.: And you can't let him lag and then let him suffer the consequences like missing the bus or school; you have to go off to work. Would you keep track of these things and bring them in with you in a summarized fashion? We'll get to you earlier next time and discuss them a little bit more.

SECOND MEETING, FIRST YEAR

DR. P.: Shall we start with you, Mrs. E.? Tell us what has been happening these past two weeks.

MRS. E.: Well, I think these are the best two weeks of Frank's life. He is no longer defiant when I ask him to do something; he doesn't try to see how much he can get by with. He is even eating different kinds of food. And too, he is much more reasonable. For instance, if we tell him he can't do something and we explain why, he accepts it so much better. And he doesn't get upset. We have tried to figure out why, and we have three reasons that we think this change might be attributable to. One, we think he is better-adjusted at school. We think this has definitely something to do with it. Second reason is, last week—first of all, two weeks ago—he asked that his bedtime be set back to seven thirty instead of eight. We almost fainted, as you can imagine. But then he decided he made a mistake; he would like to stay up and see "Zorro" on Thursday. Well, we said, "You do what we tell you, and we'll let you stay up." Well, he worked all week to stay up and see "Zorro." That seemed to be an incentive for him to behave himself. And then, his cousin told him that he could have his outgrown bike. Last weekend we went up to my home, and he got it. He is just in his element with that bike. He rides it before breakfast; and when I tell him to come in to breakfast, he says O.K., puts the bike away, and comes in. Now we feel that these past two weeks we have had no problems.

DR. P.: So he has done a lot of things in an improved way. He is accepting discipline, following through on his normal requirements, and his general level of activity and general attitude have improved.

MRS. E.: However, he told me this evening that maybe I wouldn't get a very good report from his school. So maybe if he is good at home, he can't be at school.

DR. P.: No, I think he is coming along pretty well, from what we have observed. His teacher isn't here right now, but maybe you can talk to her later if you want to.

MRS. E.: I would like to.

DR. P.: Do you see any particular application of the things we talked about, or does it seem to you to have just happened?

MRS. E.: Well, I think it just happened, but the three reasons I mentioned are the things we feel are the reasons for it. We were watching for something, an outburst of some kind or other. But he seems able to control himself better.

DR. P.: Do you think you have done anything any differently?

MRS. E.: Well, I don't think so; it is possible. I have been more relaxed with him. I think sometimes when you are, he reacts better. He seems to get along with other children better. I really believe that with the bike he feels more like one of them. The children he plays with are bigger, and they can do things he has not been able to do. But I think he feels that when he gets out with his bike, he can keep up with them. He doesn't ride as well as they do, but at least he's out there with them.

DR. P.: Well, that sounds very good. But keep your eyes and ears open for more opportunities to help him with his self control. Don't let down too soon in your vigilance. Mrs. A., shall we go on to you?

MRS. A.: Well, I really don't know what to say. We haven't noticed any particular difference one way or the other.

DR. P.: Have you had any special trouble with Cecil at home these past two weeks?

MRS. A.: No.

DR. P.: He hasn't been acting up any more than he had been?

MRS. A.: No.

DR. P.: What particular thing has he had the most difficulty with these two weeks, regardless of whether it represents any change or not?

MRS. A.: Well, one thing, he'll fight with his sister over the television. Even if there is nothing he wants to watch, he won't let her have the program to look at, and every night it is a fight.

Dr. P.: How old is she?

Mrs. A.: Fourteen. You'd think she would know better than to bother fighting with him, but she does. I have sent him to his room without letting him watch television, and the next night it is the same thing.

Dr. P.: Well, why don't you keep sending him to his room at this time or else divide the privilege of watching the television. Let one see it one night and the other the next night.

Mrs. A.: You see, she has so much homework she really doesn't have too much time to watch it. Once a week she'll want to watch one show, and then that is when he'll want to watch something.

Dr. P.: The rest of the time Cecil has it?

Mrs. A.: He and his father.

Dr. P.: Well, why don't you reserve this time for her? And this can preclude a lot of his tendency to create difficulty with others. Actually, he is a very good kid, but what he wants to do is—he comes up to a certain situation and wants to see how much he can overcome the other person, as he does here at school. The thing to do is let him know where he stands on this and regulate it a little bit. And let her have one or two nights to watch television, and see that he doesn't bother her. Can you actually step right in and not let him bother her? Send him to his room, or find something else to do. Do you think, if you did, that it would cut down on the ruckus?

Mrs. A.: Well, it probably would. I don't know if he'd try all the time, but it seems it happens every time she wants to watch something. There might not be anything on that she would want to see, but he won't let her even look at the program.

Dr. P.: He acts as though he owns it.

Mrs. A.: Yes.

Dr. P.: And this is what we don't want to foster. We don't want to keep this going. What other situations similar to this have occurred?

Mrs. A.: Well, I can't think of any other arguments like that.

Dr. P.: What about his own routine life—getting up, going to bed, coming in for meals, and so on?

Mrs. A.: He is doing real well. He gives me no trouble coming to dinner or taking his bath or putting his clothes away. He does it, he knows he has to do it.

DR. P.: Is this an improvement?

MRS. A.: Yes, it is.

DR. P.: So actually where he is on his own, there is some betterment; but where he has a chance to do battle with someone else over a privilege, as access to the television, that's where he strong-arms his way in.

MRS. A.: That's right.

DR. P.: All right, do you think you can try these next three weeks, before we meet the next time, to regulate him out of this situation? When your daughter is going to watch television, tell him in advance that on Thursday night, or whenever it is, he is not to bother her. He is to do his homework or read a book or something else. Can you tackle that?

MRS. A.: I'll try.

DR. P.: Let us go to Mrs. F. next.

MRS. F.: Well, I still feel I am most interested in seeing Fred make advancement in subject material and social activities. I feel he is making that advancement in subject material, as much as I could expect him to make. He still has a long way to go, and will for a long time to come. I had a talk with Miss M. a couple of times, and I do feel his muscles are underdeveloped and so on. He is very weak in penmanship; he is strong in reading. I am interested in seeing him come up to par, and I am beginning to believe he will do so by the end of the year, and I am hoping that he will. As far as social adjustment is concerned, I have very little opportunity to observe in the way that I think I should; that is, in playing with other children, getting along with other children, he is a poor sport. It is very hard for him to lose a game, and so on. And due to the fact that he is out on a paper route after school, and I get home very late from work, I get much less chance to observe that than I did have before school opened. He does have little problems that crop up now and then, like other children. For example, he wore a pair of pants to school this morning that he ironed himself, because he purposely forgot to change his clothes after school. He is expected to wear those clothes two days to school. He is supposed to change into the ones he wore the day before to deliver the newspaper so his fresh clothes will not be covered with newsprint. But I expect those little problems to come up.

Dr. P.: Did he get himself into a ditch or something and have to iron his own trousers this morning?

Mrs. F.: No, he is supposed to change his clothes each day when he comes home from school. Just like the other children, he will not do these things unless he is forced to do them. But when he failed to change his clothes two days in a row and had to have fresh clothes this morning, well then, last night before he went to bed he had to iron the pants he wore to school this morning.

Dr. P.: I see. But you're more interested right now in his academic progress. Do you think he is getting his feet on the ground in this respect? Do you think we are beginning to get someplace?

Mrs. F.: I think he needs a lot of work at home, which I am not giving him. At least I could help him a lot more, especially in writing.

Dr. P.: How much time could you spend with him on writing?

Mrs. F.: I spend very little, some days none at all.

Dr. P.: Could you get some regular time to do this?

Mrs. F.: It is very hard for one to do that when you work from seven in the morning until six at night and come home in time to cook dinner, and so on; and then it is almost time to see that they get to bed.

Dr. P.: How about on weekends? Could you do any then? Would that crowd you too much?

Mrs. F.: Well, I am not crowding myself. I could put forth a little more effort.

Dr. P.: Would you be willing to give that a try for the next three weeks and see what you get from it and tell us your observations and tell us how he responds, and so on?

Mrs. F.: I think I should do it. I certainly will try.

Dr. P.: Do you have anything else you want to comment on?

Mrs. F.: I don't think so.

Dr. P.: All right. We'll go on to Mr. and Mrs. K.

Mr. K.: I used to leave in the morning before Larry got up; but I understand that was the big problem, getting him up and getting him to eat his breakfast. Why don't I let my wife take it from here?

Mrs. K.: Larry was outside playing football about a week ago, and had fallen down and gotten his coat muddy. I didn't say too much to him, but his father did. I just kind of let it pass. But later on in the evening he came and apologized to me. That's encouragement. But tonight, I got home from work and got all kinds of bad reports about him. Their grandfather is there with them; he's home all day. This afternoon when Larry came home from school, the bus driver came to the door and said that Larry had been misbehaving on the bus—running around, opening the windows.

Dr. P.: Coming home from school or going?

Mrs. K.: Coming home from school.

Dr. P.: Was it just today?

Mrs. K.: Just today; that is the first bad report I've had since he has been over here. I asked Larry how he is getting along in school, and he says it's fine. He told me the other night that he had finished one book and was going to start another. And the other day a neighbor came to the house and said the children were throwing rocks. Well, I've forbidden my boys, both of them, to throw rocks. And Larry swore he had not been throwing rocks, that it was the other boys. However, he was with them, and I told him that when he is with a group of children who are misbehaving, if he stays with them, he will be blamed the same as they are. I whipped him for not coming home rather than staying around with the boys. However, that passed; he told me he did not throw any rocks. But now tonight, this trouble in the bus. The driver came to the door and told my father.

Dr. P.: What did you do about it?

Mrs. K.: Well, I decided that whipping him didn't make too much of an impression, so I took him in our room where he has no toys or anything at all, sat him in a chair in the corner, and told him to stay there until dinnertime.

Dr. P.: For how long?

Mrs. K.: It must have been forty-five minutes, I'd say.

Dr. P.: Then how was he at dinner?

Mrs. K.: Fine, but he doesn't take direction from his grandfather too well. His grandfather is an old man; he is seventy-five years old. He is stern with the kids sometimes, and he doesn't show any affection towards them, and they don't take direction from him very well.

Dr. P.: And also it would be easier for a child to get around an old person like that.

Mrs. K.: Well, he did spank them this afternoon. Larry talked back to him. Dad told Larry to put some toys away, and Larry got mad and started yelling; so Dad ended up spanking him, which he seldom does.

Dr. P.: What is the worst thing that could happen to Larry in the way of loss of privileges or opportunities?

Mrs. K.: Well, I told him I'd take football away from him today.

Dr. P.: For how long?

Mrs. K.: Well, I didn't tell him for how long; I told him not to touch the football until I said he could.

Mr. K.: His grandfather is hard of hearing; although he has a hearing aid, he has it turned down. And Larry has had a cold, and he's deaf as a post. And brother, when they get together, you have to go into the other room; they just holler at each other at the top of their voices.

Mrs. K.: I have an appointment with the doctor to see about Larry's ears. It seems when he gets a cold he is very deaf.

Dr. P.: Will he be out tomorrow?

Mrs. K.: No, my appointment is for three.

Dr. P.: Anything else that has happened?

Mrs. K.: That is about all, except that in the morning he is slow; he always has been slow. Yesterday and today he had to run for the bus.

Dr. P.: What if he missed it?

Mrs. K.: Well, I'd either take him or he'd have to stay home.

Dr. P.: But if he stayed home, he wouldn't be under your supervision, and it might lead to other problems. So it is better for him to get the bus.

Mrs. K.: Well, he has no objection to getting the bus.

Dr. P.: Is he doing more things for himself? Instead of you pitching in and aiding him, supporting him?

Mrs. K.: Since we were here two weeks ago, he has been making his own bed; yesterday he didn't get it made because he was too late, but this morning I made him do it.

DR. P.: Well, except for these two episodes, they have been two fairly smooth weeks. Do you feel you are getting your foot down about these things that have troubled you?

MRS. K.: Well, tonight I was very discouraged because I just didn't know what to do.

DR. P.: I think you did all right.

MRS. K.: I don't know exactly where to go. I have found that spanking him, for the moment, is impressive, but it doesn't last. And if I take television away, which I have done in the past, he'll voluntarily go in the bedroom, so that is not too impressive. But he does like football, and he wants a new bicycle for Christmas, or a football uniform.

DR. P.: You just might mention to him that if there are more episodes like this, it will postpone the realization of these things. And I think that is much more effective, if there is something he really wants, than to spank him. (*Pause.*) Well, it sounds like we are making some progress there. I would not be upset about these occasional backslidings because we are going to have them.

Mrs. D., you are next.

MRS. D.: My report is way down this time.

DR. P.: Well, he has been sick a lot.

MRS. D.: Well, one day I kept him home because he ran away. He turned the alarm clock off so I wouldn't get up, and then he left at two, and we didn't get home until nine thirty that night.

DR. P.: Where did he go?

MRS. D.: We don't know. We searched the neighborhood for hours. He has been going into Fairlington and also into Shirlington to the animal shelter with the other boys. I kept him home as punishment the next day, and the next day he had a cold. It had been very cold and rainy that night.

DR. P.: He was at school two days and missed three.

MRS. D.: Yes.

DR. P.: And this week, so far he hasn't been in.

MRS. D.: No. Thursday he was outside in his tennis shoes and just a thin shirt and caught cold.

DR. P.: So he has only been in school three days out of ten. That alone would disrupt his equilibrium.

MRS. D.: But two weeks before that, he doesn't come for dinner; he doesn't clean up his room. He is just away; I don't know where he is.

DR. P.: It is hard for you to keep track of him. Do you work during the day?

MRS. D.: No. I am home when he goes to school and when he comes home.

DR. P.: Does he have to report home before he goes out?

MRS. D.: He always comes home.

DR. P.: And then he takes off?

MRS. D.: Then he goes out till dinnertime, but he hasn't had dinner at home for two weeks.

DR. P.: Instead of coming for dinnertime, he just stays out.

MRS. D.: He doesn't come home until eight or eight thirty.

DR. P.: How about not letting him go off after school?

MRS. D.: Well, he has been sick. Sunday I had the doctor for him. Monday I went to the laundry room, and when I came back he was gone—cold, fever, and all. And today it was the same thing again. It was about two o'clock, and I looked for about and hour and couldn't find him.

DR. P.: What do you do when he comes home on these occasions?

MRS. D.: I spanked him with a belt. Before, we used to talk to him, but nothing helps. I don't know what to do with him. If I punish him by making him stay in the house, I have to watch him constantly. If I don't give him any dinner when he comes home late, that doesn't bother him either.

DR. P.: Was he doing this two weeks ago, before he got sick, or is he doing this because he wants to get out?

MRS. D.: He was doing this before he got sick. He's been staying out late, and we don't know where he goes or what he does.

DR. P.: He doesn't inform you at all about where he goes?

MRS. D.: Well, he tells us things, but they are not true.

DR. P.: Is he presumably in some boy's house?

MRS. D.: No, because most of his friends—I talked to their mothers, and told them not to let Evan in their homes after dark, to send him home at dinnertime, which they do; but he doesn't come home.

DR. P.: You don't think there is anything you can do at the time he comes home from school to watch him more closely, keep him from getting started on these trips?

MRS. D.: Well, I have; I have kept him in the house, but he is very emotional and he cries very easily.

DR. P.: Well, let him cry. It is better to have him crying, protesting that way, than running off.

MRS. D.: The first time he goes outside again, he'll be running off. He has been doing that since he was four years old.

DR. P.: My point is that if you can start controlling him after school, gradually increasing control—you can't do it all at once, that is impossible—but if you can, gradually try increasing control. Let him cry; let him be uncomfortable. He is merely protesting; don't feel sorry for him at this time. Don't give him any rope.

MRS. D.: I don't feel sorry for him at all. He has got me to such a point that I'm—I feel like just keeping him home tied to a chair or something. It is very uncomfortable around the other children, too. Last week we spent four hours looking for him in the rain. That is when he became ill. I left him at the neighbor's one day after school. She couldn't control him; he went away from her house. I just don't know what to do.

DR. P.: It certainly isn't an easy situation to cope with. But see what you can do about supervising him a little more closely when he first comes home from school. Just expect him to try to get out. Anticipate that he is going to try to get away, and gradually increase your supervision over him. It won't be easy to do, and it may not be successful, but there is no easy way, no magic wand you can wave to get him to stay home and mind. Unfortunately, when he's gone, he makes it a long time.

MRS. D.: He's gone sometimes from one until nine P.M.

DR. P.: Have the police ever picked him up and brought him home?

MRS. D.: Yes, in Washington about three years ago. He went away and stayed all day, and I got so worried. He was so young, and something might have happened to him. That is when I called the police.

DR. P.: This was when?

MRS. D.: About 1954.

DR. P.: Three years ago, and he has been doing this more or less
since then. Well, it certainly is a difficult situation; we couldn't
avoid recognizing that. Is there anyone else—friends, relatives,
or neighbors—who can supervise him better than you in the
afternoon?

MRS. D.: No. The neighbors are all busy, and I don't have any
relatives here.

DR. P.: Do you think there is anything you can do together? For
example, develop some activity together that would fill his
time in the afternoon?

MRS. D.: Well, he likes artcraft—plastic models, key chains, and
different things like that. But he only plays with them for a
few minutes at a time. Nothing he has can keep him at home.

DR. P.: And you haven't been able to find out what he does and
where he goes? Nobody has reported that they have seen him
any particular place?

MRS. D.: I spoke to one of the boys' mothers. He goes to the shelter;
it is far from home.

DR. P.: Have you talked to the people at the shelter? Do you
think it would help if you talked to them, described him, and
asked them to direct him homeward if he should come in?

MRS. D.: I can try.

DR. P.: You see, they could be cooperating instead of aiding and
abetting him in this expedition. Well, let's see what we can
do on two things: supervising him in some activity, and then
checking on any source of information as to where he may go
and seeing if you can obtain their help.
Mr. or Mrs. V.?

MR. V.: Well, I think we have experienced some letdown in our
boy somewhat in the last two weeks. The period just prior to
that he seemed to be getting along quite well, taking an
interest in school work and being a little more relaxed and
better-behaved at home. But in the past two weeks we have seen
more defiance. Well, he has been doing little things which
were characteristic of him earlier. Now just today we were
looking at him, and it appeared that he did not have on an
undershirt. We inquired as to whether he had gone to school
without one. Well, he had. And things like throwing things
under the bed and that sort of performance, you know.

MRS. V.: He seems to have reverted horribly in the past two weeks, and I am terribly discouraged with the situation. When we first brought him here, he was responding beautifully. He seemed like a changed child, and I was so delighted that they had sent him here. And now I am anything but delighted. I am just horrified with the situation because I think the boy is behaving worse.

DR. P.: How do you account for this? What do you think?

MR. V.: I don't think we really know. Now he has come home in the past two weeks with stories of commotions and fighting at school, involving especially Stanley and Cecil, and I sort of get the impression that they are sort of cross-fertilizing each other, these boys. Of course he doesn't mention his part in this, but I am sure he has a part in it. Now just tonight he went through quite a period of defiance. And we are trying to get him to sit quietly and read with his mother, and he kept protesting about this book which he had gotten from the library, which was a sixth-grade book, and he didn't read it. Well, we explained very patiently that we would tell him the words and it would be quite an interesting story. Well, he behaved so badly that his mother finally spanked him for his defiance and refusal to listen to reason.

MRS. V.: I really spanked him.

MR. V.: Now just about the time we began to get this quieted down and settled down for some more reading, there was a phone call, and Stanley answered the phone and said, "Thank you, goodbye," and hung up. And very shortly thereafter the phone rang again, and I picked up the receiver this time, and it was Mary, the bus driver. She reported that she had been very much disappointed in Stanley's behavior the last few days, that they had been close pals and he was somewhat a favorite of hers. He always sat near her up front, but he and some of the other boys had gotten to running up and down the aisle and leading the other children, and this had made her quite nervous and fearful that someone might get hurt. Today she got out of the bus to look under the hood. While she was peering under the hood, Stanley and some of the other boys walked around the bus and kept her out there for a while. Then she mentioned that on the way home he pulled the emergency handle in the bus. Well, I sat Stanley down and hammered him real hard; I don't mean I thrashed him, but I lectured him on the consequences of this kind of behavior and how and why he should do better, and reported what the bus driver had said. I thought her comments were very sensible and constructive. He quieted down after this discipline and read very nicely for about a half hour.

MRS. V.: Well, Stanley isn't completely selfish, I am happy to report. I had just about given up hope these past couple of weeks. I have a fast-beating heart, and after whipping him I could hardly catch my breath, and he was very alarmed because he thought I was going to be ill. And he said, "Oh, Mother, what have I done to you?" And I said, "Well, I am not sure. Sit down and we'll read." So he sat down, and he was very nice because he had thought he had harmed me, which I am pleased to note. But I am frankly very much discouraged these past few weeks; and if it continues, I can't see how we can continue to keep him here. I just really don't. Because he certainly is not showing improvement; he is showing deterioration.

DR. P.: I understand how you feel, and I know what you mean. These things just do occur, and we are doing our best to cope with them. However, the fact that we did get improvement just prior to these two weeks I think is encouraging, and I think we can get back to it again.

MRS. V.: Well, Dr. Phillips, yes. I would be glad to agree with you, except I can't spare—I can't sacrifice Stanley because others have to be rehabilitated. I can't sacrifice him completely, and if he continues to show reverting to the former behavior instead of the progress he had shown, then I can't see that it is going to help him in any way.

DR. P.: Well, we don't think he will continue to revert.

MRS. V.: Well, I hope you are right. But I am very discouraged; we both are.

MR. V.: It was quite disheartening. I went away on a little trip and I was really discouraged when I came home.

MRS. V.: And all the little things! Not one but several of the things he hadn't done for maybe a year or two—all these nasty things are cropping up. And if he is going to be exposed to children who behave in this manner, I don't see how we can continue.

MR. V.: Of course, as Dr. Phillips says, there may be a quick turning.

DR. P.: Well, he is probably better off where he is, even though I sympathize with your concern and agree with what you have observed. But still he is better off where he is than he would be in any other class.

MRS. V.: I don't know about that. We took him to a private physician, and the physician is very much opposed to this sort of school for Stanley. Stanley needs to have a good example set for him, not bad ones. And he responds to either sort of behavior. If he has a bad example, he is going to act that way, regardless of how much the teacher loves him and tries to work with him. She is going to be pretty helpless in the situation when she is faced with such things.

DR. P.: I agree with you. I think you are right. We are trying to set a good example for him, though. It isn't that we are not trying, not doing anything. We are just having some trouble. We are ready to admit it, face it, and do the best we can.

MRS. V.: You see, our doctor didn't want him in this sort of thing in the first place. He was very much opposed to it. We had been told by Arlington schools to take him to a reputable man, and we did that. We followed their advice, and then we didn't follow our doctor's advice. It has been most disheartening to me because I didn't realize it was going to be this sort of setup. And I might as well just put my cards on the table.

DR. P.: Well, I am glad you do. We want to know exactly how you feel. As I said last time, we are going to have discouraging and difficult periods to go through. This may be an opportunity for growth; it doesn't have to be just discouraging. I am not gainsaying a thing you said. I agree with you, and you have just reasons for concern; but we still have our sleeves rolled up, and are going to keep working.

MRS. V.: If his condition doesn't improve shortly, we are going to have to make other arrangements because I think—well, my physical health won't permit it, and I simply cannot cope with it.

DR. P.: Well, let's do the best we can. But we want you to feel free to let us know if it isn't improving or is getting worse or if it is improving. All right, shall we go on to Mrs. H.?

MRS. H.: Well, I am afraid the bus driver must have had a tough day today.

DR. P.: I am sure she had.

MRS. H.: Just for curiosity, did she report back to you?

DR. P.: She didn't report to me personally; she reported to the school people.

MRS. H.: Well, I just wondered. About two I heard a couple of toots of the bus, and I went out to see what was going on. She was having a pretty tough time.

DR. P.: It was one of those free-for-alls, and unfortunately, today it was too free and too all-inclusive.

MRS. H.: Well, I know. It was just one of those days. I may also fill you in on something. This morning the bus broke down at the top of our street.

DR. P.: Yes we know.

MRS. H.: But apparently she got out to check the water, and I guess that is how she got locked out.

MR. V.: That is the same incident I told you about. She said she didn't wish to complain to the school people, so she was calling the parents. Her attitude was very good.

MRS. H.: I thought she deserved a gold medal. I also was kind of flabbergasted and didn't know exactly what to do with Ira. But I had quite a talk with him. I told him that rather than joining in the fun, he might have helped Mary, and I didn't think what he had done was very nice. I told him if we heard any more complaints—we have a long-handled brush at our house that has a wonderful effect. However, I don't use it until I have warned him first. So he has been threatened, and if I get any more complaints, I'm afraid I will have to use it.

DR. P.: How about other than today, these last two weeks?

MRS. H.: This last week, he had the flu and was quite sick. He was awfully good at home. I have no complaints there. He now gets dressed in the morning and eats his breakfast, which he had not done for a while. But he is fine now. I have no complaints there.

Dr. P.: You haven't had much "breaking out," then, or unruly behavior?

Mrs. H.: No. He has not been bad at home.

Dr. P.: Do you feel you have been handling him any better, in discerning things about him?

Mrs. H.: I think now I can pretty well tell whether he has had a good day or not. Today he wasn't very happy when he got home. I think he is pulling his own, and I am not unhappy about it. Can you think of anything?

Mr. H.: Well, this has been a difficult two-week period because he has been home most of the time and hasn't been under any influence.

Mrs. H.: Well, I'll tell you he did act up Sunday. But I think he was just plain bored. He'd been home a solid week, and this has happened many times before; it is not unusual. All the other children do the same thing. I mean all of ours. After they have been sick, when they start feeling better, they start acting up.

Dr. P.: Sure. That's one way you know they are better.

Mrs. H.: Of course, I was very happy when he went back to school on Monday.

Dr. P.: Would you say that the last two weeks, although they have been somewhat atypical, he has been better than the previous two or four weeks?

Mrs. H.: Well, he doesn't dawdle as much in the morning. I take my husband to work early, and when I come back he's dressed and ready for breakfast. This is a relief.

Dr. P.: He does this on his own, while you are out?

Mrs. H.: Yes.

Dr. P.: How about minding you and meeting critical situations?

Mrs. H.: I think it is fifty-fifty.

Dr. P.: Where can we stand some improvement on that? Is there anything you are not sure about, not doing as well as you might, that we'd need to talk about?

Mr. H.: Well, I have been thinking the same thing that Mrs. V. mentioned. I think that Ira is just as impressionistic as most other boys his age. His sister usually sets him off—his sister is six—and the next thing we know, we have two bad children instead of one. The story I have gotten, at least my interpretation of the incident in the bus, I would say was just a case of one kid doing what other kids were doing. I disagree on one thing. I think it is very difficult for one kid or any part of the group to say to the other children, "I'm not going to stay with you; I am going to help the bus driver." They just don't do it. You don't know if you are punishing him for anything or whether he was just an innocent bystander.

MRS. H.: There was one incident today when his lunch box went into play in the bus. So I decided, rather than have anybody injured, I would give him a paper bag hereafter.

MR. H.: His lunch box hit the driver. He said it was on his side and one of the boys took it and threw it. The driver turned around, and of course it was his lunch box, so he got bawled out for it. But he says he didn't throw the lunch box.

DR. P.: Yes, that is one of the difficulties in these free-for-alls, as we all recognize. You cannot tell where the blame belongs or if there is any blame. It is like a mob reaction, you see. You cannot pin it down.

MRS. H.: Well, I think the driver had a very bad day today.

DR. P.: She sure did.

MRS. H.: I think it started off with the bus breaking down and ran right through. I was very unhappy at the time, but I think I am seeing it a little better now than I did before.

DR. P.: Well, we are going to have bad days from time to time. I am just trying to be realistic, and we just have to swim through this. And of course, we are going to try to get them to be less frequent and less intense and have a quicker recovery.

MR. H.: I think his interest is decreasing. At one point he wanted to read stories to me, and he wanted to hear stories in the evening. Now when I ask him if he would like a story or see something on television, he'd prefer watching television. He doesn't seem to have as much interest in school as he did before. There seems to be deterioration there.

DR. P.: How about this last week? Did it pick up any after his illness?

MR. H.: He's only been back Tuesday and Wednesday.

DR. P.: All right, keep your eye peeled for those kinds of things and tell us about them the next time we meet.

We have a few minutes left; does anyone want to add something? Anyone have any second thoughts he wants to bring out?

MRS. V.: I have lots of them, but I don't think they are dependable.

MR. H.: I have one thing that might be of interest to the others. About a week or so ago, the phone rang and a voice said, "Is this Mr. or Mrs. H.?" I said, "This is Mr. H." The voice said, "This is Stanley V. I was wondering whether Ira was going to school on Monday." I said, "Well, he's sick and I am not quite sure if he will be going or not." He said, "I am calling because the bus driver wanted to know." I said, "Well, we have her telephone number, and we'll call her if he isn't going." He said, "She and I are very good pals, and I told her I would check and find out." I said, "Well, thank you very much. Let me have your telephone number, and I will get in touch with you." It was a very, very glib conversation, and very gentlemanly. I was very impressed.

DR. P.: It just shows you how much he is capable of, and we don't want to let a few bad days destroy our goal here. I think we can be realistic and optimistic at the same time.

MRS. V.: How long do you think the probationary period should be, doctor? How long do you think we should allow?

DR. P.: Things to simmer down?

MRS. V.: Yes.

DR. P.: I would be the wisest man in the world if I could answer that for you. But I would like to see us be very flexible and liberal through the first semester anyway.

MRS. V.: If I can stand it.

DR. P.: Well, what can you do? We are all in this together. We are all working at it, and we have just got to stand it.

DR. H.: You mean his behavior in the past weeks has been the worst it ever has?

MRS. V.: Well, just as bad. It has reverted until I was so beside myself—he had been so much better.

DR. H.: Then you don't think you have lost anything, in terms of what you had the last two or three years?

MRS. V.: Well, I would say this. After taking him to Dr. M. and after having gone through the summer with him, and then after Mrs. O. had him for the first two weeks of school, I'd say we have lost ground considerably.

DR. H.: Then it would seem he is about where he was last spring. This changing behavior did not happen just last summer; the events of the summer did not change Stanley's behavior permanently.

MRS. V.: Oh, no, Dr. H., I didn't mean to imply that Stanley had become a little angel. But I say the improvement was considerable.

DR. H.: But it was noticeable. I know exactly how you feel, how upset you become, because I know how tremendous an anxiety it is to live with an unreasonable situation. This is exactly what we are trying to correct. We will have some pitfalls, some backslides, and so forth. But what we are doing here is exactly working in the same direction you are, whereas in another classroom situation they are not working in the same direction. At least we can say that your goals and our goals are the same. I can say definitely too, that the behavior of Stanley is fairly representative of what we are working with here. We are all in about the same situation.

SEVENTH MEETING, FIRST YEAR

DR. P.: Mrs. A., since your name is first here, do you want to tell us about the last month?

MRS. A.: Well, he seems to be getting along better with the other children and he is playing with them more in the evening, but the last few weeks he started some sort of whining. He goes into a cry that really isn't a cry. I don't know what all that is about.

MRS. W. (teacher): He has been doing that at school, too.

DR. P.: What is he fussing and whining about?

MRS. A.: Everything and anything he can't have his way about or he can't have right then, he goes into this little act.

MRS. W.: I seem to find that it is a little more sincere than that. At least I think it is. For example, if he misbehaves and I tell him he will have to go to the office, he will cry; and they just don't strike me as being crocodile tears.

MRS. A.: Well, he does this about little things at home.

MRS. W.: Oh, I see. Maybe he thinks he is getting away with this at school simply by being apologetic about it and it is working.

Maybe he is transferring this to the home. Do you think that is possible?

DR. P.: Could be.

MRS. W.: I want to make this point. It isn't his tears that have moved me, but it has been his apology. From what I can gather from his past history at school, at times before when he was disobedient he didn't seem to feel very sorry for it. I assumed that now there was a sign of progress.

MRS. A.: He is always sorry, but he has never shed a tear. He goes through the act, but there are no tears at home.

DR. P.: What do you think he is trying to get at these times with his whining in the afternoon, just some sympathy?

MRS. A.: I don't know; if it is, he hasn't gotten it. I don't know what's happened.

DR. P.: Well, you know kids will try things. They'll have little runs on certain kinds of behavior. A child will wake up in the night for a few nights or stutter for a month or so. They'll pick up all kinds of slightly devious behavior; and if you are not too alarmed about it and treat things fairly sensibly, just as you would in the case of a physical ailment of some sort, this will correct itself in a short period of time. So I would think your advantage lay in treating this rather casually, maybe asking him what he is whining about but not expecting to give in and not talking him out of it. Treat it as matter-of-factly as you can.

MRS. A.: But he has played with the other children, and he has been helping these two little girls out on the paper route. Yesterday he came home and said they are selling magazines now, so I don't know just what is going on.

DR. P.: He is taking more of a role with the other kids, isn't he?

MRS. A.: Yes. In fact, several days there the children came and knocked on the door and wanted to know if he could play. The first day he didn't say anything; but the second day he said, "You know it makes my heart feel so good when somebody knocks on the door and wants me to play." He does appreciate it when somebody will play with him.

MRS. W.: He is playing much better with the other children at school too. They have been out as a group in the playground.

The first week it worked beautifully; there were no problems at all. This last week there was a problem, but I don't believe Cecil instigated it. He is doing much better in the classroom too.

MR. X.: I don't mean for this to be a testimonial for Cecil, but last week when I came down in the morning he was coming to school, and he stopped his bicycle to let two girls cross in front of him. That didn't seem like the behavior of Cecil consistent with his past behavior.

MRS. A.: His sister went to camp last weekend, and she wanted to borrow his scout knife. Well, he told her he didn't know where it was, and he went on and on. Well, he came home from school Friday before she did, and he comes out with his hand behind him and slipped something into the bedroll. He said, "I bet Nancy thought I wouldn't give her that knife, but I fooled her." He had been thinking about it, whether he should give it to her. He acted as though he didn't know where it was, but the first thing he did when he came in the door was to get the knife. Well, that's progress, I think.

DR. P.: That's fine; just keep up the good work, Mrs. S.

MRS. S.: How long does it take Alvin to do any work at school?

DR. P.: What are you thinking of specifically?

MRS. S.: If he is reading or doing his work and he doesn't know a word, if I make the mistake and tell him the word, then he acts like he doesn't know every other word he should know.

DR. P.: Passing the buck?

MRS. S.: Yes. So then, well, I learned that finally. Now I make him sound out every word until he gets it. For example, I have been trying to see how far he'll go. He was sounding out "man." Well, I knew as well as he did that he knew it. I have heard him read it over a million times. But he said he didn't know it. So I said, "Sound it out until you get it." So he kept sounding it out, over and over again. "Do you know it yet?" He'd say, "No, but I am trying." He did that for an hour and a half. I timed him to see how long he would do it. And every once in a while I'd ask him, "Do you know it yet, Alvin?" And he was saying "em-ah-en." I told him to put it all together and say the word. He kept repeating it over and over, and I said, "Alvin, you're not hearing yourself very well. Say it a little bit louder." Dinnertime came, and I asked, "Alvin, do you know what it is yet?" So I had him say it a couple more times, but he still didn't know it.

DR. P.: He was holding out on you?

MRS. S.: What do you do with him? He took that for an hour and a half. The only way I got him to tell me, it was dinnertime and he came flying in, and I said, "Where are you going, boy?" He said, "I want to wash my hands." I said, "Oh, no. Do you know that word yet?" He said, "No." I said, "If you are real hungry, you'll tell we what the word is; and if you are not so hungry, then I think it will take you a little longer to find out what it is." He went in there and turned right around and said, "I think I know what it is, Momma." I said, "You do? What is it?" He said, "Is it 'man'?" What do you do?

DR. P.: You see, when the die is really cast, he comes across with it. From what you said a while ago, you have just realized that he was doing it.

MRS. S.: Well, that was these past two weeks. First few weeks he was doing homework, he was still doing homework at six o'clock in the evening, and he started at five after two. That's how long it was taking him. Now I have it down to about five o'clock.

DR. P.: But don't you see? If you put him to the task, you have got to keep him there; and if he is being slow out of lack of skill, this will gradually improve; and if he is being slow because he wants to get out of it, he is learning that you are not going to let him out of it.

MRS. S.: Well, there is another way, too. He hates to go outside, absolutely hates it. That is the worst punishment you can give him. And I have been thinking that maybe he is doing this because he knows if he takes long enough to do his homework, it is too late to go outside.

DR. P.: All right, good observation. He is trying to put the pressure on you or maneuver the circumstances some way for support for what he is doing, and you have to realize this and beat him to it.

MRS. S.: How do I do that?

DR. P.: Well, what does he want to do besides stay in?

MRS. S.: Absolutely nothing.

DR. P.: How about sending him outside then and saying he can come back in when he is ready to buckle down and get the work done? And that you will give him a certain amount of time, and if he doesn't get it done he goes back out again?

MRS. S.: Those are the days that everything seems to be fine and dandy outside, and he is very willing to stay out there rather than come in and do his homework.

DR. P.: Then you may have to get something that is more consistent or stronger than staying outside. You've got to find your anchorage point, a stronger one.

MRS. S.: There isn't any. He doesn't have any.

DR. P.: I think there is. I think what you are saying is that you have changed your pace to some extent and he is not used to it yet. He is still testing you to see if you really mean it, if you are going to be consistent. You may have to stay with this for several weeks or a couple of months for him to realize that you really are going to stick with what you say. This is a very characteristic thing. Then he will make the adjustment and go on.

MRS. S.: Well, the only thing—I don't know, it was just like today. I said to him, "Well, Alvin, I'll have to go to the meeting tonight to see how you are doing in school." I didn't say anymore. When he came home from school, I said, "O.K., let's get the homework done." And he just went to it. We did more work today in an hour than we've done in a month.

DR. P.: Are you serious when you give him these requirements, or do you have a twinkle in your eye and your tongue in your cheek?

MRS. S.: No. He knows that when he comes home from school, he starts on his homework. And if he is doing homework until bedtime, he stays right there with his book until that homework is done. He could stay there until midnight; it doesn't bother him.

DR. P.: It may bother him more than you think. He is doing this partly to put you off. Don't let this get him out of the task. Well, let's see how he is doing about a month from now.

MRS. S.: But make him stay right there until he does it?

DR. P.: Once you set the requirement, you hold him to it.

O.K., let's move on. Mrs. K.?

MRS. K.: Well, as far as school goes, I think Larry is getting along fine in his work. But we did have rather a sad experience a couple of weekends ago. Larry had been playing with a neighbor boy—let's see, it was Saturday. She called me up that evening—they are Catholic, and she was preparing the youngster, who is seven, for confession the next day—and it came out that he and Larry had been to the drugstore and had taken some kind of guns out of the drugstore. So I confronted Larry with it, and he finally admitted that he had taken them. He had left them outside; they had broken them. The next morning his dad took him up to the drugstore and made him pay for them and admit what he had done and return the merchandise back to the druggist. I hope that will be our last experience along that line. As far as I know, nothing like that has ever happened before. I never heard of it. But he is not allowed to go to the drugstore any more without an adult or his older brother.

DR. P.: Well, you handled it quite well. You made him retrace his steps. This is much more constructive—helping a child correct something like this—than it is merely to badger him and lecture him.

MRS. K.: We didn't spank him; we talked to him. I was much more calm about it than my husband. But Larry is inclined to fib a little to me now and then; and at this point, since he had admitted it, I wasn't going to spank him and make him afraid to tell the truth to me next time. I figured that making him retrace his steps and pay for it with his own money would be enough punishment. He was sent to bed that evening, and he cried for a long time.

DR. P.: How has he been otherwise?

MRS. K.: Otherwise, he has been fine.

DR. P.: O.K., Mr. E.?

MR. E.: Well, Frank is O.K. at home. The only thing he does do, and he has done it perhaps less, recently, but he still does it— his crocodile tears and whining when things don't go his way. I have a feeling that by now he should know he isn't going to get by with it. Tonight—we usually eat about six thirty— he wanted to see a six o'clock TV program, but we were ready to eat. But since he normally sees it, I said, "All right, if you'd rather see that and eat your dinner cold, you may do it." At six thirty I called him. "If you are going to eat, you'll have to eat now." I hear him stomping around down in the basement, turning off the TV, stomping up the stairs. I told him either stop that or go to his room. He came in the kitchen, and by that time he was mad, so I changed the subject. But he does that fairly often. I don't know if that is a sign of his immaturity or—I feel that by now he should know he doesn't get by with it.

DR. P.: Well, he may just try it because it is the first thing that occurs to him. And when he finds that it doesn't get him anywhere, he apparently drops it. But I think it is more significant that he doesn't keep it up, that you handle it well, and that he just briefly tests you. That is more constructive and more significant than the fact that it occurs. I wouldn't worry about it occurring as long as you feel you can handle it. It will gradually drop out.

MR. E.: One thing I would like to ask, how does he get along with the other children in school?

MRS. W.: All right. The trouble I have with him is at lunch. He likes to play too much, so I have to send him back to the room sometimes when he finishes his lunch.

DR. P.: A lot of this is ordinary child's horseplay. It's not anything to worry about. It is just something to keep in tow and not let get out of ordinary limits. The sheer occurrence of these things we have to regard as normal and healthy and not particularly alarming unless they get way out of hand, which they are not doing now.

Mrs. M., you are new. Do you have some idea of what we are doing here? Would you like to tell us about your child?

MRS. M.: I am very well pleased with Nathan's behavior since he has been coming down here. He has improved at home. He is the one who gets after me. I come home from work; we eat supper, do the dishes, then I sit down with him. He can look at TV, do anything he wants to do until about six thirty or six forty-five. Then he gets me aside. I try to get him to get me aside. If I think he is not too anxious, I tell him I'm too busy, but he says he can't wait. "You know I have to go to bed at nine. I have to get my reading done. I have to do my paper."

DR. P.: In other words he has taken this responsibility?

Mrs. M.: Yes, that is exactly what I want him to do. This is his project; I can't live his life for him. I can't do his learning for him; I can't do his memorizing for him. When he grows up his boss can't do it; nobody else can do it. He's got to learn that. He used to tell me he couldn't see why people wanted to go to college because it was hard enough to get one diploma. What in the world did they want with two?

Dr. P.: How was he before? Can you contrast this sort of circumstance with a few months ago?

Mrs. M.: He was not interested in words; he wasn't interested in school. He'd get sick; if anything unpleasant happened at school he would vomit, he'd get so nervous and upset. He's vomited so violently I would have to take him to the doctor. But he seems to be adjusted here much better.

Dr. P.: How do you feel he is coming along in his schoolwork? In terms of achievement.

Mrs. M.: He seems to be able to read. He gets an interest in books— *A Tale of Two Cities, Ivanhoe.* He struggles through them himself. He likes that.

Dr. P.: He takes a lot more initiative; and he has only been here about six weeks?

Mrs. W.: Does he ever complain at home about feeling nervous?

Mrs. M.: Sometimes. Has he been nervous this week or today?

Mrs. W.: No, not this week. But a couple of weeks back he appeared to be quite ill at ease, and he wasn't able to concentrate; and he would say to me, while I was working with him, "Oh, I feel so nervous."

Mrs. M.: I explained to you before, I go to work about seven, and Grandma gets him off to school. And if she gets up on the wrong side of the bed, God help him! I think that many times she sends the children off in a state of nervousness. Like Monday night, before I got home. When he got home from school after playing outside, he came in all upset about something the kids had done because it hurts and he got upset. And right away he gets dizzy and falls on the floor; but I know that is purely emotional, psychosomatic. And his big brother gets all shook up and picked the kid up and takes him upstairs and puts him to bed. He's mad at Grandma, too. So

Grandma is on the defensive, and I not only have Nathan to handle, but I have Grandma to handle too. And I try to keep peace in the family back and forth all the time. But I certainly don't approve of that; that is no way to handle a child.

DR. P.: This may be the reason he comes to school nervous?

MRS. M.: Yes, nervous and upset. But he is very fond of his grandmother, and that is where the confusion sets in.

DR. P.: Can you do anything about this, talking with her?

MRS. M.: I have tried for years. But she is older than I am, and I am reminded of how old I am and that she is still my mother and I can't talk back to her.

DR. P.: You are in kind of a bad spot there.

MRS. M.: It has only been in the last few months that I have stood on my own two feet. I say it is too bad what you think, but my kids come first before any relatives, I don't care how close they are.

DR. P.: It might help a little.

MRS. M.: I don't know if it helps Nathan, but it sure helps me.

DR. P.: It helps you, and it helps Nathan too. (*Speaking to the teacher.*) You might keep that in mind, Mrs. W. When he comes in visibly upset, you might try to elicit some comment from him; if he is free to talk about whatever has upset him, the talking to you might dissipate some of the tension.

MRS. M.: He seems to like his brother more than he used to. He used to say, "I hate Keith." I have been after him for this ever since last summer. I used to say to him, "Don't say you hate him. Don't you like him?" He'd say, "No."

DR. P.: All right, we'll see how things are the next time. Mrs. H.?

MRS. H.: Well, we haven't had a behavior problem, but Miss M. has been putting us through some afternoons with the arithmetic. But it has been a little better since we have gotten down to two pages a day; four pages was more than he could handle.

MISS M. (teacher): Well, you see what happened, he had two pages to do one night, and he didn't take his book home. So the next day when he came in, I told him that since he didn't take his book home, he'd have to do three pages tonight as punishment. So when he came, he hadn't finished it. I said he'd have four more to do tonight.[1]

MRS. H.: You see, he goes to bed at eight. He is really very tired. He starts working in the afternoon. Actually, maybe only two days out of the month I won't be home when he comes in from school. He will sneak out then and play. I don't blame him; I would do the same. But on other days, I make him go up and do his work. He gets baffled by the problems he has to read. I don't really think he understands them. As a matter of fact, I have to read them two or three times to get them through my head.

MISS M.: Some of the problems are difficult; and I have told him, if there are some he can't get, just to leave them until the next day when I can help him with them.

MRS. H.: What I finally did, I read a couple of them to him. I tried to show him what he was supposed to do and to make him do the next problem.

MISS M.: But I am so pleased with this book, because it is different and he gets to read something more advanced while doing arithmetic, too.

MRS. H.: I have noticed that he can read practically any word. I noticed one day he was reading out of a book he had at home; and I realized—and I think he realized—that he could read everything in the book. He just had to sit down and figure it out syllable by syllable. So when he was ill, I tried to give him a pep talk, tried to build up his confidence. I think he realized that he could read better.

DR. P.: This way he is learning that he can do these things, even though there may be technical problems.

MRS. H.: It is simply a matter of getting it through his head that he can do it. I think before, we all agreed, he got defeated before he started. But I think he is beginning to have a little confidence that he can do it.

---

[1] The teacher's position was actually modified here. She might have kept adding on page after page, day by day, eventually having to admit defeat. It was suggested that, instead of letting herself in for this defeat by Ira, she have the leftover work done at some point during the day when the boy would have to relinquish some cherished activity like art or sports. This plan worked well, and Ira did his homework with greater dispatch thereafter.

DR. P.: He is up at bat and swinging; and if he doesn't connect every time, that is not so bad.

MRS. H.: Apparently there has been some trouble on the bus lately. He had gotten hit by a couple of boys. So I said, "What did you do?" And he said he didn't do anything. So finally—maybe this isn't the right thing to tell him, but I told him to hit them back. I told him if he didn't stand up for his right, he'd be dead.

MISS M.: I have been telling the children in my group not to hit back. My feeling is that if you start that, the danger is the amount of activity on the bus. It's not the idea of not protecting yourself or anything like that; but if you are having a free-for-all on the bus, it is dangerous. So I have told the children, "If somebody hits you, do not hit back, but come and tell the teacher as soon as you get here so we can do something about it. And then the person who hit you is the one who is at fault, and you won't be in trouble."

DR. P.: Yes, I think you are right concerning the bus.

MRS. H.: Actually, he doesn't like to hit back, and his big brother is exactly the same way; they just don't want to fight. Instead, he will cry; he has come home crying several times in the past month. It disturbed me for a while, and then I finally said to hit them back.

DR. P.: It is difficult there because the only adult is quite seriously and completely occupied managing the bus; it's like a mother or father in a car with three or four kids scuffling in the back. It is a bad situation.

MRS. H.: Well, he hasn't complained lately.

DR. P.: Do you feel he is making pretty good educational progress?

MRS. H.: I think he is. Because as I say, when he was ill those few days, I would sit down and listen to him read. And of course his sister comes home with books, and she reads to me all the time; and of course what she does, he has to do also. Which is fine.

DR. P.: O.K. Mr. and Mrs. B., let's hear from you now.

MR. B.: The progress is phenomenal. Chester has been here only a couple of weeks. In the class at N———— School, he was totally unable to resist the stimuli of the rest of the kids. The arrangements here are absolutely ideal for him.

DR. P.: You mean he was always into a lot of mischievous play?

MR. B.: Oh, yes. With everything but the task at hand. No one has ever had any doubt what he could do if he'd pay attention long enough to get through one work, one example, or one sentence. The change is really quite remarkable. Mrs. B. has struggled with his reading over a period of time, and he has always read ahead of his class at home and behind his class at school. Now the two are at least equal. The last two weeks he has advanced a year in his reading.

MISS M.: Today I didn't permit him to read. He is in a reading group with two other boys. He began fooling around, and so I made him go back to his "office" and write the ABCs; and that really upset him because he wanted to read. He begged a half-dozen times, but I didn't let him do it because he didn't appreciate his opportunity. But I am glad to know he is that eager at home.

MR. B.: All these references to roughhousing have been making me wince a little bit. He is a very rough boy. Is he the guilty boy?

MISS M.: I find that he has met some past masters. I think he may have gotten away with a lot before when he was with children of his own age level; but now he is the smallest of the lot, and he gets thwarted every time he wants to start something. It is a little frustrating for him now, but I think he will get the idea soon.

MR. B.: He is having the time of his life. He absolutely loves it.

DR. P.: Let me throw in a word of caution here.

MR. B.: We realize we are going overboard on this.

DR. P.: No, we want you to feel proud and satisfied, but many times we get a kind of beginner's luck in some of these things. He may retreat after awhile. The novelty will have passed, and he may begin to raise some protest. So don't be surprised if you get a lessening of this brilliant performance.

MR. B.: We are ready for it.

DR. P.: That shouldn't mean anything different for you. Just hold the line. Mr. and Mrs. V.?

MRS. V.: Well, we too have been very satisfied. Of course Stanley slips from grace frequently, but it happens a lot more infrequently. However, you know last year we had a little trouble with dabbling with feminine garments. I thought I had that pretty well licked. But every once in a while I find something of mine in his room. I told him tonight that "of course I'll have to report this! I'll have to tell Miss M. that if this recurs I'll just simply bring the garment to school, and you may wear it the full week. Miss M. and I will get together on it, and we'll just have your playmates know that you like to do this, that you are a little boy and you like to wear something feminine." Sometimes it is shoes, sometimes it's a scarf; it is apt to be most anything. "We'll just see that you get to wear them if you have this secret desire. I think that your friends should share it," I said. He said, "Oh, you wouldn't do that," and I said, "Yes, I would." First he thought I was going to strike him, which I quite often have done when I found these things. I said, "No, I am not going to hit you, Stanley, but I am just going to take it to school." When I went upstairs, I found that my shoes had been replaced very carefully in my clothes closet, and I think Stanley is cured of this.

MR. V.: Is this proper technique?

DR. P.: I think this is pretty good. Because you are exposing him to a consideration that had not occurred to him and had apparently not occurred to you either before. It is a little bit like finding a kid smoking and making him go ahead and smoke the rest of the cigarette or cigar and get a little bit ill and learn his lesson that way. You can't do that just by scolding him. You have to introduce a social pressure, place this kind of behavior in a larger context. That could be more corrective than almost anything you can say.

MRS. V.: I went on to tell him that someday he would be a father, and that certainly fathers didn't go around in female attire, and that he would be ashamed to have this sort of thing known. He agreed. He would just die if one of his friends knew this.

MR. V.: I think that this may be partly due to—I am not intending to weaken this approach nor to minimize the seriousness of it, but Stanley, I think, is the kind of a youngster who likes to dress up. He is conscious of uniforms, headgear; he always loved to adorn himself with Indian headgear.

MRS. V.: But I don't object to that.

MR. V.: Oh, no. Some children, I suspect, are more inclined in this way.

DR. P.: He is just carrying it further?

Mrs. V.: He has used make-up, and I cured that with the same sort of treatment. I told him the next time I found lipstick around his face he would wear it to school, and I would see that it wasn't washed off. I would tell Miss M. that he was to wear make-up the entire week. Well, we've had no trouble along these lines; and tonight I thought I would just try the same with the garments.

Mrs. S.: Do you think that is really bad? One of my little children, when he was six or seven, went around the house with one of my brassières. He'd get in my drawer, get a clean one out, and put it on. He thought that was the most fun.

Dr. P.: Well, that's a little different, when he is five or six, from when he is ten or twelve. There is more elaboration, more fantasy, and more social connotation to it.

Miss M.: The other day someone in school came up to me and said something about fingernail polish, so we had a little discussion about it. They were talking about how, when they were little, they used to wear fingernail polish, and so we made a point that little children did that but big boys didn't. Stanley looked a little funny—I was watching him, and he looked very sheepish —and he said, "Yes, just little kids, and girls." He knows that things like that are not accepted at school. One day he had on three rings, and I told him to take off two of the rings. He said, "But they are boys' rings." I said I realized they were, but that he could wear one only. Whenever we can make reference to this sort of thing, we do.

Mrs. V.: I certainly appreciate that. Is he doing well in his reading now?

Miss M.: He is having so much trouble with his multiplication tables and long division that Mrs. W. and Mr. O. and I have worked with him on them a lot recently. But his effort and concentration are improving, so that's good, for now.

Dr. P.: How are other matters? How are other things progressing?

Mrs. V.: Everyone comments on the improvement in Stanley's behavior. His brother is a sophomore at college, and when he returns home he says it is now a pleasure to come and have Stanley around. Stanley's behavior has improved; my friends have commented on it too.

Dr. P.: All right. Fine. Mrs. G.?

MRS. G.: On behalf of my husband, who couldn't be here tonight, and myself—well, we are very pleased, all the way around. In fact, we can't get him to stop work.

DR. P.: You mean schoolwork?

MRS. G.: Yes. Mrs. W. gives him his arithmetic and reading, and he'll get so interested in it he doesn't want to stop.

MRS. W.: I wonder if he does it in sufficient time at home. My problem at school with him is that, if I am working with other children and I am not working with him individually, he will sit for an hour doing a few arithmetic problems, and most often he will copy the problems; and I will have to remind him every five minutes to get to work. I have gone over to him numerous times and said, "Mason, what are you thinking about?" He says he is thinking about nothing. It is a sort of daydreaming. I have found that I cannot use free time or anything like that as a method of motivating him to get his work done, because if we are having something in the afternoon, something special like the art teacher, and he hasn't finished his work, I ask him if he will hurry so that he will be finished in time, and even that doesn't motivate him. He'll still sit there. He doesn't object; he will just sit there and work while the other kids are having some activity that is more fun.

MRS. G.: He said to me today, "Mommy, I think my teacher got aggravated with me today." I asked him what he had done. "Well, while the others were playing, I was doing my work."

MRS. W.: I didn't get aggravated with him because he was doing his work. In fact, I think it is admirable that he wants to do it that badly. The thing that is disturbing me is why it should take him so long. Actually, an assignment like that he should have finished in about forty-five minutes at the very most. And he wouldn't have to do it continuously because I usually interrupt about halfway through by having him come up and read when his turn comes to read. So it isn't that I am keeping him at a continuous task for forty-five minutes. But instead of it taking him forty-five minutes, he will have spent three hours.

MRS. G.: At home the other night he had three pages, and he finished them in less than a half an hour; he had fifty some problems.

MRS. W.: That's funny because he only had one page assigned. I have never given him any more than that. Usually, the way the pages are set up, he isn't responsible for any of the written work on them. You see, he only does the actual problem, so it should only be about a half a page each night.

Mrs. G.: I know his daddy questioned him, "Mason, are you sure you have all this arithmetic work to do?" "Yes, I do, Daddy, and I got to get busy."

Mrs. W.: The only time he will ever have more than one page is when he hasn't done his work.

Dr. P.: He may be, judging from what you are saying, more conscientious than we realize and kind of spinning his wheels there in class. And if you chop it up in smaller bits of fifteen or twenty minutes, we might discuss that some more and see that he does a certain amount in fifteen or twenty minutes, and nail it down a little bit more. This might help to get him out of this sort of slump.

Mrs. W.: I have tried at times, for example, to show him how quickly one could write down problems. I have taken the arithmetic book and actually written out the problems for him so that all he had to do was do the answers, but this didn't speed him up. But I will take your advice and try that.

Dr. P.: Let's see what we can work out; let's give it some thought.

Mrs. G.: Are you very positive with him?

Mrs. W.: Well, I am afraid so.

Mrs. G.: Well, I am too, and when I tell him to do something, *he steps.*

Mrs. W.: He takes it very well; he doesn't get belligerent about it or give any back talk.

NINTH (AND LAST) MEETING, FIRST YEAR

Dr. P.: This is the ninth and last meeting of the parent discussion group, and this being our last meeting, we probably should get started. Mrs. H., will you begin since your name is first?

Mrs. H.: Well, I have nothing very terrific to report. I will say this: it has been a terrific struggle to get Ira to do his homework until the past few days. He has suddenly taken a terrific liking to multiplication and division, which pleased us all very much. He is now doing it without a struggle.

MISS M. (teacher): He asked me today if he could get some books to take home this summer. He said, "I might as well catch up and stop wasting time." I almost passed out!

MRS. H.: That could be apropos of the conversations I have been having with him lately, when I told him that he could progress much more rapidly than he had been if he would just do the work instead of horsing around. Every afternoon he has done himself out of play because I won't let him out until he has done his homework.

DR. P.: It shows that persistence pays off.

MRS. H.: Yes, except that he practically has ruined his whole spring. But it doesn't bother me any; I just devote the afternoon to being around. The only other thing I did, I discovered that— well, as I mentioned a long time ago, I get terribly impatient with him because I know that he knows what he is doing, and he just goads me on. And I know he does it. So I turned him over to his brother, who is in the ninth grade. Apparently the level of their getting together is much better than ours. I think he learns more from his brother than he was from me.

DR. P.: He takes more from him?

MRS. H.: Yes, he does. Not only, I think, because his brother was in school more recently than I, but because—well, he just figures that Morris knows what he is talking about. I often wonder if he thinks I don't know.

DR. P.: How has his behavior been otherwise?

MRS. H.: He is fine otherwise. I haven't any problems. He goes to bed on time, gets up on time. We have just gotten a dog, and that has helped. This morning, for the first time in a long time, he picked up everything that was on the floor; he felt the dog would get it.

DR. P.: You mean he picked up his room?

MRS. H.: Yes, his has been the messiest; but I discovered that this is about the age, it seems. The older boy went through the same thing of being horribly messy, and now he has straightened out and is very neat. Ira used to be very neat. I think he will go back to it; I'm not worried about it.

DR. P.: All right. Mrs. V.?

MRS. V.: I think that Stanley seems to be doing much better. I don't know how his teacher feels. (*Turns to teacher.*) Do you feel that he is?

MISS M.: Yes.

MRS. V.: His behavior, I think, has improved. As I wrote to his grandmother, for the first time in his life I'm really glad he is here. For a long time I really couldn't say that because it was a constant worry. But he really has been a very likable boy.

DR. P.: More tractable and also more fun?

MRS. V.: Yes. He spends a lot of time with me. His father travels a great deal, and we are alone; and I do find that when we are alone, he behaves better. Because he is not playing one against the other. Father is not a disciplinarian, and I am constantly having to spank both of them, practically. It is one of those things you can't make the father do. Well, when Stanley was little, you remember, he said, "All I have to do is say, 'Daddy, here I come,' and Daddy opens his arms." He knew that from the time he was a baby. It has helped a great deal, I think, to have Father away this spring.

DR. P.: Giving you a more clear-cut, unmitigated chance to operate?

MRS. V.: Yes, without interference. Then Stanley realizes that I have the authority to discipline him when his father isn't there, and he doesn't play one against the other.

DR. P.: Then when dad comes back, how does it seem?

MRS. V.: Well, of course, you remember the year before last, my telling my husband that he wanted to be an uncle and bring the gifts and do the nice things. Well, he tries awfully hard; he has improved greatly, but still likes to be the uncle.

DR. P.: There is a little too much of that still?

MRS. V.: Yes, a little too much, but I am sure he is working on it.

DR. P.: How about your son's school achievement? How do you feel about that?

MRS. V.: Well, I think perhaps he is doing better. I don't know how he is doing in his arithmetic now. I think he is doing well in all but spelling.

MISS M.: Yes, he has finished the arithmetic book, except that he has not covered long division by two numbers, which is required in fourth grade.

MRS. V.: Do you want me to work with him in it?

Miss M.: In a few days Larry will finish his book, and then I can take it up with both him and Stanley.

Mrs. V.: Do you think you'll have enough time this year?

Miss M.: Yes, Larry will be finished soon.

Mrs. V.: Then you'd rather I'd leave it alone for now?

Miss M.: Yes, please, and I'll take it up with him in class.

Dr. P.: Let's see, who is next? Mrs. S. is next.

Mrs. S.: Well, Alvin is, of course, still very new here, but I feel that his reading has begun to improve tremendously. He seems to be interested in reading slightly more than he was last month when we were here. (*Turns to the teacher.*) You weren't here last month, so I wasn't able to check, but I have checked since on his arithmetic. He hasn't been bringing in any homework. Is that all right?

Mrs. W. (teacher): He hasn't been bringing any home because I have been concentrating on his reading. He has a blanket assignment every night to prepare two stories. He has been doing better on his arithmetic in school; he has been sticking with it and doing it more accurately. He still is very, very slow, however. He is inclined to daydream a great deal of the time. He needs hundreds of reminders every day to get back onto his work.

Mrs. S.: How is his eating?

Mrs. W.: We've had quite a time with the eating. I tried your suggestion of telling him about the time every five minutes, but that didn't work. So finally I told him I was going to feed him whatever he had not finished by the time it was twelve thirty. He only took two mouthfuls before he was crying so hard that I couldn't get the spoon into his mouth. But he has been doing considerably better on eating ever since. Today I left him in the cafeteria to finish because he hadn't finished his dessert. I didn't want to take that away from him because it was good. He hurried with it, and he was two minutes later than the others in coming back.

Mrs. S.: Well, we have more or less licked it at home by saying, "If you are not through, it goes. That's all!"

Dr. P.: That is generally a good technique to use, where you can control it. It is a little easier for you to do that home than it is at school.

Mrs. S.: Yes, she has more children at her table than I do.

Mrs. W.: One of the things I feel is that Alvin is a very slightly built child and that he needs the food, and so I feel a sort of conflict. I want him to have the food, and yet I want him to eat it on time. You probably feel the same way.

Mrs. S.: Yes, but he is just slightly built. He eats quite well; he looks undernourished, but he is strong and wiry. I don't worry about it any more. And we don't have so much trouble at the table any more. His attitude at home, I think. There is much less friction. Although he has been escaping me these fine afternoons. He will come in, and if I happen to be upstairs, he'll leave his book on the hall table and scoot out. Then he'll call me from wherever he is and promise to be back at five. But he doesn't come back until six. So I have been having a little difficulty in checking on the homework.

Dr. P.: How about catching him some evening when he comes home and not letting him go back out because of his failure to hold to the line?

Mrs. S.: He doesn't go out after we have a late dinner.

Dr. P.: No, I mean when he comes in after school. Just nab him right there so that he can't get out.

Mrs. S.: Oh, yes, I can do that. I have found that I have to be a demon on consistency with him. That is why I raised my eyebrows at the dessert business. If you let him get away with anything that he knows he has to do, then that just opens the breach wide. I can't give in a millimeter to him. And yet, as I said, his behavior has been quite good. He has been affectionate and helpful. What do you think, Daddy?

Mr. S.: Well, yes, except for the streak a couple of weeks ago, when he reverted completely for a few days.

Mrs. S.: But he has been doing well with his room, keeping it neat. But this daydreaming! He has such big dreams, and he talks to me about them.

Dr. P.: What does he tell you in the way of daydreams, and what do you say?

Mrs. S.: He is planning airplanes. He is planning on selling cards so he can buy a bike, and various projects that he has in mind.

Dr. P.: Can some of these things be made concrete? Selling cards to buy a bike, for instance, as against planning airplanes, which is, of course, completely in fantasy realm right now.

Mrs. S.: Well, he builds model airplanes, and he has been doing better on that. Before, he used to start one and not finish it. But the selling of cards to buy a bike is something we tell him will have to wait until he finishes school because it would require a great deal of time. That is the current dream, I believe, and there are others. He says his head is so full of things.

Dr. P.: When he tells you about these dreams, you listen to him, and then you both talk about them concretely? Is that what happens?

Mrs. S.: Whenever I can. That is the difficulty. There is a conflict of demands. One person can't do it all.

Dr. P.: No, I realize that.

Mrs. S.: But whenever possible, we do talk about them.

Dr. P.: So that he begins to differentiate between what is really fantastic, on the one hand, and what is in some way practical and can be worked on.

Mrs. S.: I am hoping to do that. But it is pretty difficult with the wild imagination he has.

Dr. P.: You see, you can't get to his thinking or his implicit behavior except through some channel of doing, some action channel. If you can keep that in mind and try to nail down the things in the fantasies that you think in some way relate to something he can do, then that will help him to discriminate. Instead of just dismissing and pooh-poohing, or something like that.

Mrs. S.: Releasing it, you mean, and concentrating it in one line.

Dr. P.: Yes, nailing it down.

Mrs. S.: Well, we started to make up a bedtime story of one of his ideas of space travel. That petered out after a while because he got tired of it.

Dr. P.: You see, it is like any ideas that any of us have. If we objectify them and put them out and look at them and expose them to the light of day, then what is meritorious shows up, and what isn't can be discarded. But if you never expose them, then you go on fooling yourself. So you want to help him to take them and expose them. So encourage him to tell you what it is he's thinking of, and then say, "Well, what can we do about some of these ideas? What is practical here?" This doesn't imply any criticism; it simply applies the criterion of practicality.

MRS. W.: Now at school, when I ask him what he is thinking about, he says, "Nothing."

MRS. S.: He did that for quite a while, but recently he has been telling me.

MRS. W.: I think it is an encouraging sign if he will talk about it. I wish he would at school sometimes.

MRS. S.: He might be a little ashamed in front of the others.

DR. P.: Yes, this is the business of exposing ideas. You might say to him something like "Are you thinking about airplanes?" Use some cue that you think might fit, and draw him out that way. Especially if you can take him off to the side someplace.

MRS. S.: He does better with individuals than in a group.

MRS. W.: Well, I have never asked him in a public situation. It is usually when he is in his "office" and he hasn't been working. Rather than call out, "Get busy, Alvin," I have gone over and talked to him.

MRS. S.: Well, it may take time. It took a long time until I became friends with him.

DR. P.: Yes, this kind of thing you have to be persistent with too.

MRS. S.: Consistency and understanding—those are key words.

DR. P.: Let's see, he came in after Christmas?

MRS. S.: It has been about six or seven weeks.

DR. P.: I see, almost two months.

MRS. S.: Well, I am quite encouraged about the reading. I think that was the thing that got him way behind the eight ball. Last time I mentioned that he is volunteering to read things, like labels on packages and some of the coupons on things. He is trying to read comics and cartoons and headlines and things that interest him. And when he reads, I think he reads quite well.

DR. P.: His spontaneity in trying to read all these things is a very good sign.

MRS. W.: I have seen a big change in school. When he first came, he seemed to be overconfident. In arithmetic he'd say he knew how to do it; and of course, he'd get most of it wrong. Now I don't have any of these excuses from him. In fact, if he gets stuck, he will come up and ask me to help him; and I have found that in most cases it is just the small things he needs help with, like the table of fours.

MRS. S. *(turning to the father of the boy)*: Well, Father, what do you think about this arithmetic thing? You work with him on it.

MR. S.: His arithmetic is all right. When he applies his mind to it, he can do excellently. But he has a lovely tendency to retreat from everything; and then it doesn't go very fast, and he makes mistakes. I am not worried about his arithmetic. This, I don't think, is a basic problem.

DR. P.: As you deal with these fantasies and dreams more adequately and persistently and he stays on the ball with other things, I think this retreating will certainly diminish, and his power of concentration will, of course, correspondingly increase.

MR. S.: Yes, that should follow. Part of it, I think, is escapism.

DR. P.: Well, it's not wanting to be bothered with this kind of thing at this time. We all put things off.

MR. S.: It is human nature, I suppose. It is not nice to do things that are rough. It is much easier to do something that is fun, even in thought processes.

DR. P.: Thinking is a hard job.

MR. S.: I have tried to sell him on the idea that this is a job he is supposed to be working at, but this really hasn't paid off yet— maybe someday.

DR. P.: We have seen signs of it in all the kids, more or less.

MRS. S.: What they need is success. A feeling of being able to cope with it. They have to find their own way of digging their own ditches. We can't do it for them.

DR. P.: All right, Mrs. B.

MRS. B.: Well, I am not as happy about Chester as I was four weeks ago. I know he isn't at peace with himself now, as he was then. I think it is that he doesn't get along with the other children. I know he gets along well at home.

DR. P.: What does he say about school experiences?

MRS. B.: Well, it is not in school so much as it is after school.

DR. P.: You mean in the neighborhood?

MRS. B.: Yes,[2] I think Alvin told him that his father wouldn't let

---

[2] The beginning of a small controversy in the group, the only one of its kind during the entire first year of the group meetings.

Alvin play with Chester, and Larry's mother told Chester he couldn't come in the yard, and this has been the pattern of Chester's life. The children have never objected to Chester, but the parents don't want him around. And if you could please tell me why, I would like to know. This is the only way I can help Chester; it's to find out why. I don't think Chester's behavior, as far as I can observe, is any worse than the other boys'. But I wouldn't think of telling any of the boys that come into our yard that they can't come in, that they can't play with Chester. So I would like to know exactly. What does Chester do that makes the parents say that he can't play with their children?

Mrs. S.: I apologize. I tried to get hold of you, but I couldn't. It was because the homework has to be done first. That's the rule. And Alvin has been told that when he comes home he can have a little snack, then do his homework, and then go out to play. But he has been leaving his book and sneaking out, and he said he was going to play with Chester. I said he can't play with Chester until his homework is done. And that is what that is all about.

Dr. P.: It is not anything personal? It is just a matter of the homework?

Mrs. S.: No, it isn't anything against Chester.

Mrs. B.: Can you help me, Mrs. V.?

Mrs. V.: Well, I had the same experience, and I don't think Stanley would be in this school if the same thing hadn't occurred. Stanley was getting along beautifully with a boy in the neighborhood, and the child was all that Stanley wanted to be. Stanley helped him night after night after school to collect newspapers. And I happened to say to the mother one day, "It was such a wonderful thing that he found your Steve." I said that "he hadn't conformed as some of the children do, and finding your son has been the most marvelous thing that has ever happened to him." She immediately investigated and decided that if he didn't conform, she didn't want him. So she told her child he was no longer allowed to play with Stanley. The teacher said to me, "What on earth has happened to Stanley?" That feeling of rejection came over him and undid everything. You know, when we had those meetings he was coming out of it just as happy as he could be. I have often thought that before she leaves this area I would like to tell her, "I hope you don't break some other child's heart, because you have been the cruelest person."

MRS. B.: I know exactly what you mean. Everyone in our neighborhood, every parent, has told Chester they don't want him in their yard. In fact it has reached such a point that if we can possibly sell our house, we are going to move. I cannot understand it. I have had destruction in my yard; I have had bratty children in my yard; and I would call the parents, if necessary, and say, "Your child has done this, and I think you should take care of it." But to tell a child, "I don't want you," I don't understand it. But it has been done to Chester again and again. The last teacher he had at N_____ was, unfortunately, practically forced to say the same thing to Chester: "You are a pest in the class, and I can't stand you." And of course this has had a very bad effect on him. At home. I guess I told you the first time I talked with you, I cannot judge Chester outside. At home, he is a nuisance, but he has a good time. He conforms. I can get a great deal out of him. And I don't know why. I know he is obstreperous, but there is something more than this.

DR. P.: How long has he been here now?

MRS. B.: Here? Nine weeks. Oh, he has improved a great deal. But the other day when he called you and said we were going to the Y, as we passed your house he ducked. And I asked him what was the matter, and after some talk I found out he didn't say he was going to the Y with me; he said he was going to the Y with Larry's mother. I asked Stanley why he said that, and he said, because his father doesn't want him to play with Chester. So I took him back to his bicycle and told him to go home and tell his father that he was not allowed to come into this yard until his father calls me and says it is all right to come. I told him I cannot have him come in here if his father doesn't want him to come.

MRS. S.: He didn't tell us that.

MRS. B.: That was on Thursday, and I haven't seen Alvin since. Mr. B. was going to come here today, but he is ill and couldn't make it. But I told him I was going to bring this up, and I told him that I thought very rightly that Alvin hadn't said anything about it at home.

DR. P.: Do you think some of this is childhood exaggeration under pressures?

MRS. B.: I think a great deal of it is childhood exaggeration, but I know Chester doesn't say he isn't wanted someplace that he hasn't been told he isn't wanted. I have overheard some people telling him he isn't wanted in no uncertain terms. Chester is embarrassed by it. He has a very adult reaction to it. He comes home and he doesn't tell me, but he is ashamed that he has been spoken to in this way.

DR. P.: How has he improved? As you said a minute ago, you thought he had.

MRS. B.: His reading is improved for one thing. He never brings his book home, so he is reading the second half of the second-grade book at home.

MRS. W.: I wish he would bring his book home because he has an assignment every night to prepare three stories.

MRS. B.: Oh, he doesn't get out of it because he just has a harder book to read at home.

DR. P.: He doesn't get out of anything. Good!

MRS. W.: He is slowing up the group, however. Chester is one of three in a reading group. When he isn't prepared, it slows up the whole group; and I have tried to motivate him by telling him that he will have to stay behind while the others go ahead, but this hasn't worked. He gives me the answer that he has the same book at home.

MRS. B.: Well, it isn't the same one; it is the next one.

MRS. W.: I think too, that he becomes a little bit overconfident because he is reading a harder book at home. I was trying to encourage them today by saying we want to finish this book so that they will be on such and such a level for next fall. And Chester said, "Well, I'm already there." You see, he gets the idea that he is doing a harder book at home and that as soon as he is finished he is going to be on that level. That, of course, from our point of view, is not the instructional level. It is very important for him to stay where we are until he gets a firm foundation in that. Otherwise, do you see what will happen when he gets into this third-grade book? It won't be any thrill. It is just like the book that he is on now. There is no pleasure in it because he knows the outcome of the story. And I can tell them, "Let's see what happens to Johnny Jim," and Chester knows; so you can't motivate him, you see.

MRS. B.: Well actually, of course, last year he read those books. He finished the second-grade books last year. So he knows them.

MRS. W.: But somehow or other he either regressed or has lost a certain amount of his vocabulary because he is still having trouble with some of these words. I think that if we can work together at the same place, at the same level, maybe this will help. But I can see that he has made some improvement since he has been here, specifically in arithmetic.

MRS. B.: Oh, yes. He *has* improved. His *willingness* to do it is something. He reads faster and with more expression. He knows what he is reading. He isn't so apt to stop at the end of the line.

DR. P.: How is his behavior in school?

MRS. W.: He had a setback, and I think perhaps these activities outside of school carry over to his school behavior. But I think he has been so hyperactive and so talkative he just cannot keep quiet for two seconds. He has to talk out loud and get out of his seat. It has just been one big struggle to keep him still and keep him quiet. I haven't been very successful in taking care of it the way it should be taken care of.

DR. P. (*looking at the mother*): Has he said very much about the school here to you?

MRS. B.: This one day he asked me to write a note to the bus driver because he was going to be beaten up on the bus and he wanted to be sure that I would tell the bus driver not to let anyone beat him up. I wrote a note telling her what Chester said and that it would be just as well for her to know that this was in the offing. I didn't put too much stress on it. I felt that whatever one said on one afternoon probably wouldn't be carried over to the next morning. But he really was worried. He likes school; I know that.

DR. P.: There is no doubt that he sees these things the way he reports them to us. Do you think he is trying to get a more sympathetic response from you or any other adults?

Mrs. B.: He is the troublemaker. I know he is a troublemaker. I am not saying that Chester is an easy boy to have around or that people shouldn't say, "Go home. I can't stand you any more." I feel like saying it myself many times. But I don't know—his total activities are not the kind that would make me say to anyone, "I don't want you to play with my child." In other words, he seems to me to be a troublemaker but not a bad boy.

Dr. P.: Well, children learn how to get under our skins. They know which stops to use to get the best response in terms of what they want. And sometimes there is not a great deal of resemblance between what they say and what actually occurred. If they find that something can arouse an adult and get some response from him, then they will use this kind of thing. I think we have to have tongue in cheek a lot of times about what they report has gone on. I know it seems this way to them, but our role as adults is often fulfilled better if we can apply some correction and reduce these exaggerations. I just don't know how much of this sort of thing is going on here; I am raising a question.

Mrs. B.: Well, with Alvin, he told me that his father said he shouldn't play with Chester. That wasn't anything Chester said.

Mrs. S.: I know what that was about. Alvin came home and said that Chester was beating him up or something. His father said, "Well, you shouldn't play with Chester." That was all.

Mrs. B.: I told my husband this morning, Mr. S. probably said something weeks ago about "Don't play with him now," or "Get off my back," or something. But Alvin still goes on as though this is some restriction you have put on him. That is why I wanted to talk to you about it.

Mr. S.: Yes, I can recall—and you must realize that this comes to me when I come home in the evening—but I can recall a number of occasions that I have had to be real firm with Alvin about not goofing off, if I may use that phrase, about doing his homework in the afternoon. This has been a rather consistent struggle and I have said, if you are doing such and such in the afternoon, it has got to stop. There have been two or three occasions when Alvin has said, well, I am playing with so-and-so, and we were going to get in a fight or he threatened to beat me if I didn't do so-and-so. So I said, "Look, you are not going to fool around with people who are going to influence your behavior pattern. If you can't stand up to them because they are bigger than you, and the only thing you can do is to do the things that you shouldn't because you are going to get beat up, then you just quit fooling around with them." I don't want him to get the idea that he is going to be beaten or have to do things that people want him to do, otherwise he gets beat up.

MRS. B.: They came in one afternoon. I know. Earl brought Chester in about five forty-five, and they had been having a fight—Alvin and Chester. I was annoyed that Earl had interfered. At any rate, Earl brought the problem to me, and I couldn't ignore it. I told Chester to keep still and wanted Alvin to tell me everything that happened in the afternoon. So Alvin told me, and boy, I wouldn't spend five minutes with him from the story I got. And of course all this time I had to keep saying, "No, you keep still, Chester; it's Alvin's turn." So finally, when Alvin got all through, he ended up with this terrible fight for which Chester obviously was completely to blame, and I turned to Chester and said, "All right, now you tell me everything that happened." Well, Alvin was an awful boy. Everything that happened, including being tied to a bicycle, being poked with sticks, and all these awful things, and finally this fight for which Alvin was obviously to blame. So I said, "Well, it sounds to me as though you folks just don't enjoy each other at all, and I don't think you should play together any more. It is foolish to play with anybody you don't like any better than that." Oh, no, that wasn't the case at all. Everything was really just fun up until this last fight, and that was a *real* fight. "Well, it sounds to me as though you folks can get along very well for a couple of hours, and that's all you can play together," I said. So I said Chester should come in every afternoon at five. He could play with Alvin until five, and that would be just fine. So they kind of looked at each other and shook hands and said that would be all right. Then the next day was the day we went to the Y, and Alvin said his father told him he couldn't play with Chester. I thought we were off on a pretty good start. Obviously, if I listened to just either one of them that day, it sounded as though the other one was a terror.

DR. P.: Sure. But many of these things that a child hears a parent say could be interpreted, "You can't play with so-and-so if and when this type of behavior occurs." This doesn't mean that so-and-so is forever forbidden.

MRS. B.: Oh, yes, I knew that was what was meant. But Chester doesn't understand this.

MRS. S.: I think Alvin gets into trouble like that because he knows he has done something wrong to begin with, and he gets mad at himself, and he transfers it to someone else. I have seen that happen. He gets off on the wrong foot in the morning, and then he can't get along with anyone for the rest of the day until he can straighten himself out. And once he is straightened out, he is so happy with himself.

DR. P.: All right, Mrs. A.?

MRS. A.: Cecil has not been as good as he was at home, but I can see in the last week or so that he is improving a little. He got so, there, that everything you'd say to him he would pick an argument. Like one morning he got up and asked me if I had seen the apple blossoms on the tree in the back yard, and I said yes. And he said, "Well, you don't have to be so mean about it." And I said, "What did you want me to say?" It's just things like that.

DR. P.: Just had a chip on his shoulder?

MRS. A.: Yes, all the time.

DR. P.: Yes, he gets that way every once in a while.

MRS. A.: That's right. You don't know how to answer him. He picks everything apart.

DR. P.: Don't you think it would be better not to discuss unnecessary things with him? Don't give him any leeway.

MRS. A.: Well, he seems to be getting along better with the children in the neighborhood. He plays ball every evening. In fact, I can't get him in ever to do that reading. I was telling the teacher about that yesterday. When he comes home from school, he says he is too tired, and out he goes. Then after dinner he doesn't feel like doing it then; he'll do it after a while.

DR. P.: How about in the morning?

MRS. A.: Well, he did that a couple of days, and he made himself too late. Last night he did read. He had twenty pages, which was the full two stories. That is the first time he has ever done that. His bicycle was taken away yesterday and put in the basement because of something here at the school. He came home from school very angry about that. Boy, he was mad! He talked about things that happened six months ago. It was a nut school. Boy, was he mad!

DR. P.: How about today?

MRS. A.: No, today he was all right.

DR. P.: Did he read this afternoon?

MRS. A.: He didn't bring the book home.

MRS. W.: That was the last thing I told him. Oddly enough, he doesn't want me to know that his bicycle really was taken away. I asked him today very quietly about that, and he said he had ridden his bicycle to school. I said, "Now Cecil, you'd better be telling me the truth because this was an agreement between your mother and me. We both thought it should be done; and if you have ridden your bicycle to school, I am going to have to call her up." Then he finally admitted that he had his bicycle taken away.

MRS. A.: Well, let me tell you about that. Yesterday morning he said that he had a terrible cold in his leg, and he was limping. I didn't hear any more about it until he was ready to go to bed last evening. Then he said that the cold had gotten worse in his bones, and he wanted me to rub it with alcohol, and I did that. His daddy had taken his bicycle to the basement. We have no outside entrance, so he cannot get it out through the basement window by himself. This morning he couldn't walk at all. He was a total invalid, and finally at twenty minutes after nine he got ready to walk down the front steps, and he could not take a step. I would have to carry him down the steps if I expected him to go to school, he said.

DR. P.: He showed you how badly he needed that bicycle.

MRS. A.: So anyway, what wound up, I made a bargain. I took him two blocks in the car and put him out. Oh, the way he was limping, I didn't think he would ever get here by lunch time. I wanted so bad to go down the block and see if he was running, but I was afraid he would see me. Before he got out of the car, though, he said he would have to stay here all night if I didn't come and pick him up. So I wasn't home at one thirty when he got there; and when I came in, he was running around the back yard catching bees in a jar.

MRS. W.: He came in this morning and went directly up to the office to talk to Mr. O., which is an infringement of the rules, of course. He had some bruises, I suppose of previous fights, and he went up to show Mr. O. his badly bruised legs. He came down to the room limping and ailing. But, probably fortunately for the situation, I have a letter from another mother, who asked if I would please do something about Cecil because he was beating up her child. So I just looked him straight in the eye and told him it was good for him, that I thought he deserved every one of those bruises because he had bruised another child, and that I had no sympathy at all for him. And he soon forgot all his aches and pains. He was perfectly all right the rest of the day!

MRS. A.: I asked him how his legs were, and he said they felt much better. I mean he really puts on an act.

DR. P.: It shows you how skeptical you always have to be in taking a child's protests at face value.

DR. H.: It is also an indication of the extremes they will go to to get what they want. It doesn't seem humorous unless you know that you are really being conned into something or out of something.

MRS. S.: What to do about it? Alvin sometimes wants to be carried and babied. Well, I go along with it until I think he is just using me for something; then I just put a stop to it. It is awfully difficult sometimes. We need more techniques.

DR. P.: Well, that is true. You just don't know until you have been over the road a few times. And even then, you are not *perfectly* sure.

MRS. A.: Now he came home tonight and told me that he didn't have to read because he was further ahead, that he had read more last night than he was supposed to. Which he had not read, I know; he only read two stories.

MRS. W.: I think I know what he was referring to. There were three stories left to be read in that book, and he finished all those last night. Now he may be a little ahead of himself. But I don't want the parents or the children to relax on it because eventually we will catch up.

Mrs. A.: Well, he is still very anxious to come to school.

Dr. P.: Do you think you can say something to him about not coming to school if he hasn't done his reading or whatever it is that is deficient? Say, "Well, you can stay home and stay in your room today," or something like that. You were looking for something when you held the bicycle as a consequence. You might keep the school thing in mind, if you think it is strong enough.

Mrs. W.: I think this should wait until the bicycle restriction is over. He threatened. He said, "I won't come to school." I said that would be just fine.

Dr. H.: The school thing is one we can't back up over a sustained period of time.

Mrs. S.: I am afraid there might be too much enthusiasm over this kind of discipline.

Dr. H.: The only trouble with it is that if we were called upon to do so, we couldn't back it up.

Dr. P.: Mrs. G.?

Mrs. G.: We are still very well pleased with arithmetic and reading, and Mason indicates that he wants to bring his reader home every night so he can finish. He was all enthused this evening when I got home from work that he did go into third grade and that he would be with the group that he was supposed to be with.

Mrs. W.: I told him that I wanted him to complete his third-grade arithmetic and to complete all the first-grade reading, so that he would be prepared in the fall to do fourth-grade arithmetic and second-grade reading. That's what I told him.

Mrs. G.: He was all enthused. He wants to get back into dictionary work and—

Mrs. W.: Well, we had one showdown this week, the only showdown or display of real stubbornness that I have really had from him. You see, he was absent for several days, and then he was off on his vacation, and so he was about fifteen pages behind in arithmetic. But these pages happen to include review work in addition and subtraction, and some multiplication. The rest of the boys in his group were ready to have division explained to them, so I went ahead and included Mason in that group. I gave an assignment to all of them in division after I had explained it. Then after he finished that, I wanted him to go back and do half a page of the work he had missed when he was out. Well, he refused to do this because the other boys didn't have to do it. I explained to him why he had to do it, and he was determined he wasn't going to do it. So he said, "My mother told me that my problem was reading, and I want to get caught up on my reading." I said, "Your mother is absolutely right, your problem is reading; but you cannot get behind in arithmetic." I told him he would have to do it, but he just sat. This was from about ten thirty in the morning on. He refused to do it. I encouraged him about three times to get busy, but he wouldn't. So I finally said, at eleven thirty, "You can't possibly do these five rows by twelve, but if you haven't got three rows done by twelve, you can't go to lunch." So he didn't do it.

Mrs. G.: That's the day he didn't eat his lunch. He came home and went to the icebox. I asked him if he was hungry and he said, "No, but my stomach hurts. I guess I am."

Mrs. W.: Well, I wouldn't let him go to lunch. I thought this might motivate him. I said, "As soon as you finish, you may come to the cafeteria." Well, he fooled around all through the lunch period, and he went without his lunch. After lunch I sent him over to Miss M.'s room. I said, "If you don't want to work here, maybe you'll work next door." So he went over there, and he finally did something. He didn't finish, so I said he could not come back to school until he had the work finished. So he did it. I think he learned from that because I haven't had any trouble with him since. He is doing his back work now, as well as his current assignments. And that is why I had this talk with him today.

Mrs. G.: We are very well pleased. If he would just keep going.

Mrs. W.: He too has a problem of daydreaming. He could do a tremendous amount of work if he would just set his mind to it. Does he tell you what he dreams about?

Mrs. G.: Well, he loves models and trains, and he is all the time down there wiring something, blowing fuses. I feel, well, it's educational for him. He gets these charts out and fixes his trains.

DR. P.: Do you think he is planning or really daydreaming? Have you any way of assessing how much of this is one or the other?

MRS. G.: Well, he is figuring something out, and after awhile he he goes into something.

DR. P.: He goes into some action?

MRS. G.: Yes. He seems to figure things out first, and then he is fixing something or wiring something.

DR. P.: You don't see that in school because, of course, we don't have the tools, electrical equipment. He can't blow the fuses here.

MRS. W.: I don't know; sometimes I think he could blow them. He seems to be uninterested in everything at school. He will talk about this reading, for example, but he is uninterested. He seems sort of lethargic. He moves slowly even when he is playing. I have never seen Mason have any energy.

MRS. G.: No, he is more calm and relaxed, but he is constantly on the go. One thing he does miss, of course. When he was in the other school, he had recess. At lunch time they had a ball game, and he misses that.

MRS. W.: The thing that is so striking to me here at school is that even when we have physical education, he is just as lethargic about that.

MRS. G.: And yet he thoroughly enjoys it. He comes and talks about it.

DR. P.: It isn't that he doesn't enjoy it; it is just that he doesn't have the typical kind of reaction to it.

MRS. G.: I think it is because he is gaining weight. He feels self-conscious about it. He seems to go through those lazy spells. I notice it more when he gains weight.

DR. P.: Are there any other comments? Mrs. Van M., do you want to say anything?

MRS. VAN M. (principal): Well, they are pretty nice little children. I think they are most charming. I enjoy Chester very much. I know how impatient we must all feel at times; but I think if we all persist, we really have never lost a case.

MRS. H.: I don't know if this will help anyone, but we have a sort of unwritten law in the neighborhood that if a child comes into our yard and acts up, that child has to go home. Feeling that if my children, the three of them, can't have somewhere where they can play well, the way they want to play in their own yard, then it is too bad. We have had a couple of incidents, and I have simply told the neighborhood child, if they want to play nicely, I would be very happy to have them; if they won't play nicely, I wished they'd go home. The same thing applies all over the neighborhood. The result is that the children get along pretty well together. There are so many ages—from fourteen on down. But nobody is restricted to any particular child.

Mrs. Van M.: There is nothing personally directed to any individual child?

Mrs. H.: No. If my children act up in someone's yard, that parent has my absolute wish that they send my child home.

Mrs. Van M.: I was thinking, a while ago, about these two boys who have been fighting. Frequently, if parents set the same type of regulations for children that play together—if they both said, "Now you have to do your homework before you go out to play," maybe we wouldn't be pitting one against the other. Maybe you two might do that—and have the same regulations, including a rule that Chester cannot play until he has done his homework. Then we won't get into that situation of one feeling that the other has a privilege he doesn't have.

Mrs. B.: I didn't mean to overemphasize this thing and Mrs. S.'s part in it. Chester has been told by everybody in our neighborhood he is just a problem boy. It isn't that he is sent home because he misbehaves. The other children are not allowed to go into his yard. He is completely ostracized. I am not kidding myself; I am not taking Chester's word for this. This is an absolute fact. I have one close neighbor who has been my neighbor for eighteen or twenty years, and she puts up with Chester. She doesn't particularly want him there, but we have been so close so long that she wouldn't want to say for him to leave.

Dr. P.: Would it help for you to talk to these parents and know specifically what Chester has done on given occasions, as a corrective measure? Chat with them a little bit, tell them you know he has caused them this difficulty, and maybe this will help straighten it out.

MRS. B.: Since there are probably twenty children in the neighborhood and nineteen are getting along very well, they are not the least bit interested if Chester isn't getting along. What do you do? They don't care if he plays with their children or not. He is a troublemaker, so let him go home. One father was very kind and called us up and said that he had taken his son to the hospital to have several stitches taken in his head because Chester had thrown a rock at him, and this was typical. We were horrified but not surprised. We kept Chester in the house all that day. That evening Mr. B. called the father and asked how the boy was and offered any financial aid, and so forth. The father said, "I'm much calmer now than I was when I first talked to you this morning. Now that I have heard this whole story from several other children, I can't say that I blame Chester; but I do say that I wish you would keep him away from here." But this story that he told us at nine o'clock that night was the same story Chester told us at noontime.

FIFTH (AND LAST) GROUP MEETING, SECOND YEAR

DR. P.: Why don't you start, Mrs. K.?

MRS. K.: On conference day a week or two ago, I walked in and Larry was standing in the hallway. He had a tiff, I guess, with one of the boys in the class. And one time out of school last week, he went to a cub scout picnic. He was playing catch with a boy, and a third boy would kick the ball in the creek whenever they missed the ball. So Larry told him, "If you do that again, I'll hit you." So the boy did it again one or two times, and Larry hit him and then walked home. He just left; he figured he was in trouble, he might as well go home. But I haven't heard about that from any source but Larry.

DR. P.: How has he been otherwise?

MRS. K.: He has been pretty good.

DR. P.: It has been almost two months since we met. That was about the tenth or twelfth of March. How is he doing in responding to your discipline at home?

MRS. K.: He seems to be responding all right.

DR. P.: What about school?

MRS. K.: As far as I know, he is getting along all right. But I think there was some unfortunate incident today.

DR. P. (*speaking to the teacher*): Do you want to tell us what happened?

MISS M. (teacher): I am trying to think what brought it about. I believe it had something to do with language.

DR. P.: You mean language he used or language work?

MISS M.: Language work. I am afraid I can't remember.

DR. P.: Has he been doing schoolwork fairly well?

MISS M.: Yes, if he is sure he can do it, he will proceed. Of course, any time there is something he thinks is new, why then we hear that he can't do it. But he is trying. He'll venture into some of these activities. And when I have a chance to sit and talk to him about it or we check the work together, then he finds it isn't new work at all. He hasn't been able to see the relationship between what he has done and what he is doing.

MRS. K.: He is that way in everything. He gives up before he even tries. We have talked to him a good deal about that. For instance, the softball game Saturday. The first inning the other team was leading, and as far as Larry was concerned, the game was lost. It *was*, eventually, but not until the score reached thirteen or fourteen. But he is like that; if it seems too big for him, he gives up.

DR. P.: What do you say to him at those times?

MRS. K.: Oh, we try to talk him out of it. When he is playing games, we tell him that is not the way a good sport does and in order to play games with other children he has to be a good sport.

DR. P.: Do you let him get out, or do you keep him in the game?

MRS. K.: Oh, no, we keep him in the game.

DR. P.: What do you think would happen if you just sort of ignored this introductory complaint that you get from him and just didn't answer.

MRS. K.: Well, it depends on whether it is a case of his going on and doing it or whether he will just give up. It would be all right to ignore it, but I think he should continue to try, and prove to himself it can be done.

DR. P.: That is what I mean—neither let him quit nor respond very much to his complaint.

MISS M.: We have been doing just a little bit of that in the classroom. The way we work is that the children who are at their seats work on their own. If I am working with a child and someone is always jumping up and running over to ask questions, I have just gotten to the point that when that happens, we just gently turn our shoulders and continue with the reading rather than turn around and see what the question is. And one or two of them—Larry is one of them—may get a little disturbed, but less and less each time. He will go back to his seat and find that there is something else he can do if he can't go ahead with that one particular activity.

DR. P.: So here he is finding some recourse without complaining too much or bowing out.

MISS M.: Now today, he was concerned about his arithmetic—a particular problem with fractions. We hadn't done any subtracting of unlike fractions before; we have only added them. So as soon as he saw the words "Subtract unlike fractions" at the top of the paper, he was sure he couldn't do it. So I said we would talk about it later. I told him to go ahead with his science work; we would go over the arithmetic later. Then a few minutes later, I turned around and he was sitting in his "office" doing his arithmetic. He found he could do it.

DR. P.: So if you just don't hear him too clearly, he will go ahead.

MISS M.: Yes, but I don't want to do it all the time. He is older than the others in there, and I feel that I am working all the time in favor of the younger ones. But I try very hard to spend fifteen or so minutes with everyone each day in arithmetic, reading, and science.

DR. P.: Of course, it isn't so much that you are pushing him away as that you are pushing him into something else, giving him an alternative. Is that all? Do you have any more comments? All right then, shall we go to Mrs. O.? Do you want to tell us about your son? [3]

[3] Mr. and Mrs. O. were in attendance at the group meeting for the first time. Their son had been in the special class only a few weeks.

MRS. O.: I find that the greatest problem with my son is his getting along with the other children. He has a terrible time.

DR. P.: You mean before or now, here at the school?

MRS. O.: Well, he is still having some trouble, but I find it isn't as bad as it was. But there for a while I just had to watch him constantly. He would just hit another child for no reason at all.

DR. P.: He was aggressive and fighting all the time?

MRS. O.: Yes, very aggressive and a very poor loser. As long as he could be the boss, everything was all right. But the minute the other child wanted to have his way, well, then it was a different story.

MR. O.: That is when the trouble begins. He want to be the leader. But we have noticed that since he has been coming here, there has been some change.

DR. P.: What do you do at home when he is so demanding?

MRS. O.: Well, I have tried different things. I have tried—for one thing, I have limited his space to play in. And I find that has helped a lot. I tell him that when he gets along with the other children, he can go a little further away and play with them. But until I can depend on him, I can't let him go.

DR. P.: When he starts a fight or has difficulty, do you call him in?

MRS. O.: Yes.

DR. P.: Does he get by with very much?

MRS. O.: Well, not too much any more. He was getting away with an awful lot, but since November we have really tightened up on him.

DR. P.: What other situations have developed besides fighting with his peers?

MRS. O.: Well, he has so much trouble in school in not doing his work.

DR. P.: Before he came here, you mean?

MRS. O.: Yes, he would just refuse to do it. He would start his paper, do part of it, and the rest of it would be unfinished. He wouldn't stay in his seat. He would roam around the classroom, talking.

MISS M.: Quentin said one day, not long after he had been here, "Gee, this place is almost like a prison." One of his observations about what he could do and couldn't do. He is seeing the light now. He is recognizing the fact that the work is set out for him; he must accomplish, and it hasn't been easy. He hasn't really tried, lots of times. He'd say he couldn't do it or didn't know what to do. But gradually he is developing vocabulary and writing, and he can understand just what he is capable of doing. We have come to the point where he can do a little of the work independently.[4]

MISS M.: We used the "offices" very consistently for a couple of weeks. I introduced him to office No. 6, and that has become his private property for working. Either he himself would slip into it or, sometimes, I'd usher him in. Working in the office is more effective than looking around the room to see what the other children are doing. He was always interested in what the other children were up to. He still is, but he is using his own time. About his working with other youngsters, we have had no particular problem there.

MRS. O.: He doesn't have trouble as long as the child is his age or maybe a little older. But there are so many in our neighborhood who are so much younger than he is, and they will do anything he says. But at times if they refuse to do so, he doesn't like it.

DR. P.: What does he do then, sort of slap them around?

MRS. O.: Yes, or he'll take them by the hand with the intention of seeing that they will do it.

DR. P.: If you catch him on these things, and can bring him in and curtail his freedom at such a time, this may be a useful way to cope with it. Don't talk or lecture to him, but say, "If you act this way, then you are going to lose your free play time; if you can behave, then it will be restored."

MR. O.: As far as I can see, since he has started over here—of course I am not home in the daytime—there is a great improvement.

DR. P.: Well, let's keep our ear to the ground.
      Mrs. H.?

MRS. H.: I have nothing very profound to relate. Ira is no angel, but he is becoming a normal boy. We have a system of fines

---

[4] This comment clearly indicates what is meant by setting *requirements* of achievement—along with *limits* on behavior—around which the child learns to mobilize his efforts and develop a "success pattern."

in our house which goes for all three children. It seems to work beautifully. One day he'll leave a room that looks like a pigsty, but the next day he manages to clean it up because the fine has doubled. Occasionally, if he isn't down for breakfast on time, he loses dessert and television. Then he'll come down on time for the rest of the week. So you see, there is nothing very outstanding.

DR. P.: You are coping with the things that do arise, and nothing very serious has arisen.

MRS. H.: I have been terribly pleased to see that he has taken such an interest in a variety of things. He is eating up these scientific books that he brings home. I know he can't read them all, but he loves to look at them. And he and his brother have been making so many models, we'll have to get a bigger house. But that is all. He is taking a good, healthy interest in everything around him, which is a wonderful, wonderful thing to watch. He reads to us occasionally, too.

MR. H.: Tell them about the show.

MRS. H.: Oh, yes. One night he told us he had tickets for a show, at "Ira's Theater, Ira's room," such and such a time. We all had to sign our names on the tickets if we were coming. Naturally, we did. We went to his room and sat on the beds. He stood up in front of us, and he proceeded for one half hour to tell us what he is doing in school. Not only that, he did it very well, no stammering or hesitating; he knew exactly what he wanted to say. He told us all about his arithmetic— how far he has gotten along, exactly what the times table meant to him and why the nines were the hardest, and so forth; and what he was doing in reading, how far he was in relation to the other boys in class. He really gave us a very good insight into what he was doing in school, and talked practically for one half hour. Then I think he ended up by singing a song. But he really was very cute and did it very well.

DR. P.: He did himself, his teacher, and his class proud, didn't he?

MRS. H.: He really did. And he has told us that when school was over, he'd have another show for us. We told him we were so pleased we'd like to hear the end of the show.

DR. P. (*to the boy's teacher*): Do you have anything to add?

MISS M.: I have nothing special to add. Ira has really blossomed in all areas. He comes in in the morning and starts right in with his work. He knows exactly what to do. He will generally start with science; that is his first love. But he knows that he has much to accomplish during the day. That has always been one of his problems, getting everything done; he would slow down and dream. There are very, very few days when he does that now.

MRS. H.: Do you know what I say to him when he goes out the door in the morning? You see, I figure that all children are contrary, so my parting shot in the morning is, "Now, be sure you bring home lots of homework, so you can stay in all afternoon." It has worked like a charm. I know this may not be good psychology, but it works!

DR. P.: Mrs. B.?

MRS. B.: Well, Chester has developed something new. He seems to argue with me about everything I tell him to do. It may be because I was gone a great deal last week, and his father has been out of town, and Chester was left pretty much in charge. It has had one good effect; Earl and Chester got back on a friendly basis again.

DR. P.: What is the difference in their ages?

MRS. B.: Nine years. Earl is almost eighteen, and for years and years they were just very fond of each other. Then the last couple of years, well, most of the time they have been just fussing; Chester teased Earl too much. Earl just couldn't take it. He took it just as long as he could, and then he would tell Chester, "Oh, go away," and of course this hurt Chester very much. Anyway, as I said, last week I was away quite a lot, and Chester and Earl have gotten back on a very friendly basis. They are much at ease with each other again. This is all very well; but now that I have taken over the household again, I'll tell Chester to empty the garbage, and he answers, "I don't have to empty the garbage. Why do you want me to empty the garbage for?"

DR. P.: He has assumed a bit of independence.

MRS. B.: Well, maybe that's it, because this is brand-new; he has never done this before. So I tell him to write ten times, "I will not argue any more." But this is something new, and I hope it is transient; this has not been his habit. Other than that, he seems to be coming along very well.

Dr. P.: Has he been getting along, these past two months?

Mrs. B.: He is getting along with the other children in the neighborhood better than he has ever in his life. It really is wonderful; now he is just one of the boys.

Dr. P. (*turning to his teacher*): How is he doing in school?

Mr. W. (teacher): Well, as we discussed in our conference, it was not too long ago that he was not making too much progress. But after the last time he was sick, he came back and has been rolling right along. Actually, we finished up one book that he was reading in, and we are now in another one. He has made an awful lot of gain in arithmetic. I have been able to introduce many more new things to him.

Dr. P.: You mean he is more willing?

Mr. W.: Yes, he is really eager now for new ideas, and he is always asking me for the next step, even though he may not be ready for it. He is that eager to move ahead.

Dr. P.: No behavior problems, especially?

Mr. W.: The only behavior problem is that when anyone speaks up, he feels that this is his opening to do so also. I have been trying to curb that by just ignoring him and have asked the group to do so too. That has worked to an extent, but it still crops up every so often.

Dr. P.: But he will stop if you raise your hand or give him some signal that he doesn't have the floor. This is apparently part of his eagerness. Anything else, Mrs. B.?

Mrs. B.: No, except that I would be very happy to write to Mr. R.[5] if he is the one to write to. I would hate to see these classes discontinued. I think they are doing really remarkable work.

Mrs. Van M. (principal): Frankly, I don't think it would hurt, if you all feel this way, to show Mr. R. that you do. I myself, as a principal, wrote to him because I am so enthusiastic about what has happened to these children. So I feel that if you as parents express your feelings to him, it will certainly help. I think he needs to know.

[5] The county superintendent of schools.

Mrs. Z.: Is there a possibility that these classes may be discontinued?

Mrs. Van M.: No, we just want to encourage him in this program.

Dr. P.: This might encourage him to have *more* classes of this sort. So if you feel positive about them, make it known to him.

Mrs. Z.: What is the address?

Dr. P.: Mrs. Van M. will give you all the information at the end of the session.

Mrs. G., what have you to report?

Mrs. G.: First, I want to say that my husband was sorry he couldn't be here. We are still very well pleased with the boy's progress. As far as reading, he is trying to read everything he can get his hands on. He goes ahead on his own. The only time he comes to us is if there is a big word. He wants to know why the teacher won't give him another reader.

Mr. W.: This is a sequential development he has to know. He's on this level, and he will gradually move to the next level.

Mrs. G.: He read that other book in three nights, and he said, "Mommy, I am doing pretty good, and I have been asking him for a new reader for three days. He tells me he is going to get it, but when is he going to do it?"

Mr. W.: I am waiting for the time when he is capable of it. I don't feel that he is quite ready for the next one I have for him.

Mrs. G.: He is worried about that reader, and when he was sick, he said, "Mommy, I'm going to have an awful lot of catching up to do."

Mr. W.: I encourage him to get books from the library. Of course, the books that he wants are mainly connected with railroads, and the books on the railroads that we have here are few and limited, and he's covered them five or six times. But I still try to get him to make a choice from some of the books I put up for them in the library. There is adequate material around for him to read in this library; it's just getting him to do it.

Mrs. G.: He is getting into the *World Books* at home. He goes for the books with animals and machinery. That's what he is interested in.

Dr. P.: Anything else?

Mrs. G.: Just one thing. The teacher said at the conference that he acted as if he had something on his mind. Well, he was worried about his trophy. But then when he got it, well, that was it.

Dr. P.: His trophy? Can you tell us about it?

Mrs. G.: He is on the bowling team of the county recreation center. He was on one of the winning teams, and each one got a trophy.

Dr. P.: He was a little preoccupied with this for a while, was that it?

Mrs. G.: Yes, the week they were supposed to have gotten it, it rained, and it was postponed until the following week. He was afraid if it rained again, maybe he wasn't going to get it.

Dr. P.: He is a pretty good bowler?

Mrs. G.: Yes, he loves sports. He wants to make good grades because he wants to play football and baseball in high school. And I tell him that if he doesn't keep up his grades, he can't play on these teams.

Dr. P.: How is he doing at home?

Mrs. G.: We have no problem at home. He goes in and does his work. Just before he was taken sick, he had all that arithmetic and homework. He finished all his work and had it all right. We don't have any trouble at home. When he reads his spelling book, he says, "Mommy, I have had this before; this is baby stuff." That is what he thinks about most of his work. It's all coming back in his mind, what he evidently missed before. He just looks over the work and says, "I'm ready." I ask him, "Are you sure you studied it?" And when I hear him, he spells them right off.

Dr. P.: He is getting a little more efficient in his learning. (*Speaks to the teacher.*) Anything else about his school performance?

Mr. W.: I think that he has the idea sometimes that these things are very simple until we get down into them, and then he finds that learning them and making them stick, not memorizing them, is a little more difficult than he thought. In spelling, he'll memorize the words for the spelling test, but I try to get him to carry them over into his regular work. Then I notice, using spelling as an example, that the words were memorized for a particular occasion, and I try to get him to— The reason I go over them and over the words is to teach the children to sound them and use other techniques in learning them. So that when they come to them, they can recall them.

Mrs. G.: That is what I do at home. When I hear his spelling lesson, I go back two or three chapters. He'll stumble on some of them, and we go over them; then he gets them. Maybe in the group he feels conspicuous or something, afraid to speak out?

MR. W.: I thought so too, at first. But I don't believe that is true now.

MRS. G.: He wants to know when he is going upstairs with the boys and girls. He is tired of being in a class with all boys.

DR. P.: Mrs. S., what do you have to report?

MRS. S.: Well, we've been so encouraged about Alvin we don't know how to—to express it. He's reached a new plateau. He seems to accept things as they are, not kick against them. He is interested in reading—reading things voluntarily, digging things out of the library. We haven't found the nonsense books which you thought he shouldn't be reading. He mentioned that he would like to have *Treasure Island*; he wants to read that. He is interested in everything, and as far as I know, he hasn't been having trouble with his work.

MR. W.: Well, you know, today I had to keep him in because he had not completed his assignment.

MRS. S.: Oh, this isn't good, because he said he stayed in because you wanted him to help you.

MR. W.: Well, he did help me after he got through this work. I had a little job I was doing, and he asked if he could help. I said he might help after he did his work, that work came first.

DR. P.: It's just a matter of emphasis here.

MRS. S.: Oh, he's so clever.

DR. P.: You might ask him at these times if, besides helping the teacher, he did have to make up a little work, so that you get a fuller picture.

MR. W.: I would like to say that the time before when I kept him in, I stayed quite late. I kept him busy most of the time with the work he was weakest in, and then the next day he was the first one finished. Completed all of his work and was coming up asking if there was something else he could do.

MRS. S.: I keep telling him how good this is.

MR. W.: This is the first time since then.

DR. P.: About how long ago?

MR. W.: About three weeks.

MRS. S.: Since we say that he has reached a new plateau, maybe sometimes he feels the altitude. But we have been getting good reports about him on every side, even in Sunday school. The Sunday school teacher came over to me and said, "Alvin was so good today; he read the lesson." And he had been telling her he didn't read English too well but that he was fine in Portuguese. But he is being much more what he should be. He seems much freer, and has more confidence in himself. He is a doll, all right. (*Turns to husband.*) Ed, what do you want to add about him?

Mr. S.: Well, the main comment that I would have to add to all the glowing comments you have made is that he has a long way to go. To behave properly with his younger brother, I mean.

Dr. P.: What happens there?

Mr. S.: He has a tendency, when he is not watched, to bulldoze the baby, if I may use that expression.

Dr. P.: How old is the baby?

Mr. S.: Three.

Dr. P.: And Alvin is about twelve?

Mr. S.: Yes, and he wants to descend to the baby's level quite often when they are by themselves, not as much as he used to, but still more than he should. He wants to play with Calhoun on his level and run the games and call the shots, and this leads to quite substantial trouble sometimes.

Dr. P.: The little one just can't keep up.

Mr. S.: Oh, the little one resents it bitterly because he has a mind of his own, and we hear about it.

Mrs. S.: Oh, that is working out. During the day you don't see too much of it any more.

Mr. S.: Well, I see enough of it when I am around to know it is still a problem. This, I think, is one phase; if he can pass that, it will be a sign of maturity which he has not demonstrated so far.

Dr. P.: What do you do when he starts irritating the younger one?

Mr. S.: Well, I usually call him away and tell him if he doesn't grow up, we'll work him over, or—well, various and sundry devices. I usually try to impress him with the fact that he is too old to do this type of thing, that it is a childish thing that someone four or six years old would do, that a twelve-year-old shouldn't, he has to learn to be trusted, and so forth and so on.

Dr. P.: Can you think of something you can have him do to distract him from the situation?

MRS. S.: That is what I do.

MR. S.: Well, I haven't thought of that approach too well.

DR. P.: Rather than merely draw attention to what he is not doing correctly, move him on to something that you want him to do. Have him run an errand or—

MR. S.: I have sent him in to watch television, to get him out of the way. But I realize this is just a temporary expedient, not constructive at all.

DR. P.: Well, if you can move him a few times into something that is positive that he can do—bring you his homework, run an errand, or help his mother with dinner, or whatever—that's constructive.

MRS. S.: Feed the cats.

DR. P.: Yes, something that is a positive alternative for what he is doing. This might be more acceptable to him, and he might be moved quicker toward what you want to accomplish.

MR. S.: There are usually quite a number of chores, none of which he is too fond of, which are regarded as constructive in the family circumstances, that we can try out for size.

MRS. S.: But there are times when he does things that are inexcusable and I just have to lay it on him. He can't be permitted to get away with some of the things he does. They are dangerous. It is so much better now, but there was a time I didn't dare leave him alone with the baby. Now I can until I hear screeches on both sides. Then I descend and try to part them. If it is a bad situation, then Alvin must be punished; he must be taught that is not desirable. But if it is something that just arises as a result of the differences in their ages and understanding, then I try to get Alvin off somewhere or get Calhoun off somewhere and separate them. I don't believe you can talk too much.

DR. P.: No, you spoil your efforts if you do.

MR. S.: Of course, one more problem is that as Alvin gets better, Calhoun gets older, too, and gets more ideas of his own. This makes for some trouble.

MRS. S.: And he hasn't always learned too desirable things from Alvin. But he is a sweet boy and a good boy. They both are.

DR. P.: Let's keep them!

MRS. S.: Yes, I like them.

Dr. P.: Anybody else?

Mrs. Van M.: I am just enjoying the differences between the way we feel about our children now and the way we felt a year ago. That makes me very happy. It makes it all worthwhile, so much so that I will give that address to you right now.

APPENDIX B.
TEACHERS' OBSERVATIONS
AND COMMENTS

METHODS AND TECHNIQUES
APPLIED TO THE INSTRUCTION
OF EMOTIONALLY DISTURBED CHILDREN [1]

In keeping with the general philosophy of providing a well-structured classroom for the education of emotionally disturbed children, this teacher has tried, in this program, many methods and procedures gleaned from personal experience and from the experiences of others. Some of the ideas have worked most satisfactorily, while others have proved less useful. The spirit of experimentation has therefore proved important during the years of work with these children.

The success of a structured classroom program depends upon the rapport between teacher and pupil. The teacher sets limits and standards, and the child has to understand, accept, and work within these limits and standards. All limits must be set many, many times, until it is clear that they do not change (except for good reason) and no amount of protest will help. With an understanding of the firmness of the limits and standards

[1] This section was prepared by Miss Rebecca A. Mauzy, teacher of the younger group during the second and third years of the project described at length in this volume.

will come willing acceptance and honest approval of the "rules for living" involved. An atmosphere of cooperative effort will usually result. The consistency of this kind of classroom environment leads to the relaxing of tensions and to a recognition of the individual and his emotional and educational needs.

Classroom arrangement and daily assignments. Part of the furnishings of the classroom in this program has been a series of small "offices," or booths, along one wall. These were provided for the children to use at times when they felt a need to work alone or when the teacher felt that they could use the solitude to an advantage. Sure signs of growth have existed when a child either preferred the quietude of the booths in order to get his work done or wanted to do the work there and then return to the large-social-group atmosphere.

The use of the assignment book as a daily guide to seat work or work in the booth has proved very effective. It is as useful today as it was in the beginning of this program for emotionally disturbed children. The purposes of the assignment book have been the following:

1. To let the child see what his work for the day will be—what is expected of him

2. To limit the amount of oral explanation by the teacher

3. To permit greater simplification of all directions

4. To permit more consideration of individual differences and needs

In the beginning of the program the assignments were short enough to appeal to the child's short attention span, yet long enough to help sustain activity and allow each child to exercise his skills. As skills were developed and work was better done, the program expanded. Through the months and years, the youngsters have developed pride in checking off each item accomplished, and this has helped them to accept variety and scope in daily assignments as well as greater individual initiative and follow-through. The latter is shown in their having come to exercise greater care and deliberation in choosing and working on what comes first, second, third, and so on, in each day's work. The assignment book has become an anchor helpful in allowing a child to know at all times where he stands, where he's been, and where he is expected to go.

Knowing the child's level. The key to progress has been mastery of materials. With these children more than with average or normal children, it was essential to know their beginning levels in the various tool, or fundamental, subjects. When a gleam of interest appeared in a child's eyes, it was at least a provisional signal that the teacher was hitting the mark with a child, reaching the child's level of understanding and desire.

As a result of success in selecting and working from the child's initial level, progress in working toward higher levels of accomplishment has been made, as has been demonstrated in two ways:

1. The program has been expanded to include units in science and social studies; that is over and above the basic instruction in reading, writing, spelling, and arithmetic.

2. The program has progressed to a point where group activities may be profitable: discussion periods, films and discussions, map study, group reading, and book reports with discussion.

The interest of the children in these new areas of knowledge and the opportunity to share interest and knowledge have helped lead to the successes noted. These are, however, primarily based on the painstaking development of skills in the fundamentals, which were sorely lacking at the outset of the program.

Teaching a sense of responsibility. The children needed a sense of responsibility related to something other than themselves. Room duties will serve as an example. The children asked for such duties; a "room duties wheel" was set up. Each week the wheel turns a spoke, and a new duty comes up for each child. With the performance of duties have come specific requirements in behavior and self-discipline. It is these small acts of accomplishment that have done most both to reduce the tendency of the children to prod and tease and to replace unsocial acts with responsibility and praise for acceptable work.

Just as there are rules for living, there are rules for many activities. Games are made for building educational skill, with materials designed to show how vowels are used in words, to aid in combining sounds to form words and in doing simple mental arithmetic problems, to teach spelling, and so on. The rules of the educational games are laid down and must be followed.

Education games used in this program have included an "arithmo" game based on the four fundamental arithmetic processes of addition, subtraction, division, and multiplication. This game is a take-off on the common bingo game which most children know well. Also used has been a modified lotto game in which ten letters are given out to each child to see what words he can build with them. By adding letters to their supply, they can make more and better words. One group in the program has found "Fractions Are Easy as Pie" useful in developing the part concept of a fraction.

Less academically inclined games, but games that nonetheless teach the importance of sharing, taking turns, and following the rules, have been relished by the children: Chinese checkers, spin-the-bottle, and "Aunt Minnie Is Going to Minnesota." Informal, group-shared moments playing these games have provided important lessons in tolerance, patience, and forbearance.

Outdoor games, which allow more activity and physical contact, often further the same general purposes as the above-mentioned games, provided they are carried on under a general supervisory structure. This teacher's group of children, being younger than the group taught by Mr. Wysong (see page 295), have seemed somewhat less distracted and "tuned up" by physical activity than the older boys.

Signs of progress. Signs of progress, beyond a check mark in an assignment book, have proved important. Each day has been set up to allow some few minutes of free time to read, to work with arts or crafts, and this has provided signs of progress. Sometimes everyone has completed his work, allowing for a total-classroom, group-centered activity. At other times only one child or two have earned this privilege for the day.

If time has been misused during these free periods, the limits have been set tighter the next day. On the other hand, as the children have made better use of their time, it has been possible to give a great amount of selectivity to them for use as they have seen fit.

Yet another type of growth has been recorded through the use of charts. These concrete, visual means allow a child to know where he stands in his over-all reading progress. The reading of library books has been recorded on a chart called "On the Track in Reading," which is an incentive to better reading. A "reading thermometer" has also been used to show, by means of a vertical column that is shaded in as each new book is reported upon, the number of books the child has read. To stimulate progress in word recognition, each child has put a star on a crown when he has mastered the word list associated with a basic reading story. These concrete evidences of growth, so important to all the children, have created in them an interest in self-improvement and advancement, as well as an interest in keeping up with others. Such records serve both individual and social purposes.

The arts and crafts have a therapeutic value, too. Through the use of standard art media and craft projects which lend themselves to small-group cooperative work, the restless child learns to sit longer and to increase his attention span, as well as to bring work to a successful conclusion. In this program, media have been available for all the children: those who find pleasure in larger-scale activities like making the swinging and sweeping brush movements involved in painting on a canvas, as well as those who find quiet accomplishment in fashioning a small animal from clay.

Listening and concentrating. While there is time for activity, there needs to be time for listening. To fulfill this requirement, the teacher has read stories the group should know or played records of the standard classics composed by the world's great musicians. More recently, as the children's capacity for group sharing and listening has increased, oral book reports have been given by each child; each has selected the books he has most liked from his library reading to tell about. All of these activities have formed a common ground with the daily, "bread-and-butter" classroom activities.

Materials. The presentation of the above materials has, of course, been copied from tried and true educational procedures. Much work has been printed upon chart paper because of limited board space and because of the importance of individual initiative. The emphasis on skill building has entailed basic vocabulary development and the learning of number concepts based on concrete, as opposed to abstract, handling of numbers, with decided attention on the concrete. By the same token, specific information has received priority in the newer social studies and science parts of the curriculum. The cautious presentation of relationships is being included in a new program just now getting under way.

The use of workbooks has had a place in the reading program. The workbooks have been used to strengthen the areas in which some readers were weak, such as word recognition, vocabulary, comprehension, answering questions, and so on.

The final value of each of the many available techniques may never be known, and it is probably unessential that it be known. It is, rather, the collective results of many techniques, presented in versatile but clear and well-structured ways, that make for educational progress and good self-discipline. It is not day-by-day evidence of progress that is required either; weeks may go by before some signs of progress can be noted. Thus it is persistence, strong determination, and long-range confidence in the children that pay off.

The children who have been in the program are gradually beginning to take over for themselves; they are beginning to show clear signs of motivation and self-direction. The teacher is encouraged to hear these children ask: "May I read the next story when I finish my seat work?" "May I take some arithmetic home tonight?" "Can I show Bobby how to work those problems?"

SUMMARY OF METHODS AND
PROCEDURES USED IN TEACHING
THE EMOTIONALLY DISTURBED CLASSES [2]

The following methods and procedures have been used in teaching the emotionally disturbed children in this program. These methods are not unique. They are methods that most regular classroom teachers use to some extent; however, a greater adherence to routine and regulations has proved necessary in order to reach these children and sustain their application.

Methods and Procedures

The most successful way of making daily assignments was through the use of a daily assignment book for each child. This book, a 5- by 8-inch spiral notebook, was filled in by the teacher before class each day. The assignment had to be very clear and concise. The assignment had to be printed for some of the children; for others cursive handwriting could be used. After the book was first introduced, some time had to elapse before the children could or would use it independently. But when the children became familiar with the use of this book, it greatly reduced the occurrence of interruptions while the teacher was working with individuals. Another advantage of this procedure was that the child could see at the start of the day the work he was expected to complete. As each assignment was completed, it was checked off. Using this book also gave the teacher an excellent opportunity to make assignments according to individual needs.

In order for the teacher to work with the individual in this ungraded classroom, it was necessary to organize a schedule that

[2] This section was prepared by Mr. William Wysong, teacher in one of the classes during the second and third years of the project.

was consistent from day to day. The following plan was typical:

9:30–9:40   Opening exercises were held—Bible reading or story, Lord's Prayer, Pledge of Allegiance to the Flag, patriotic song, etc.[3] Children volunteered to lead the group, but were not forced to do so.

9:40–10:00   Necessary materials for work—paper, pencils, etc.— were gotten out. Assignments were gone over with each child. If group work was being assigned, instructions were given.

10:00–11:15 Teacher worked with individuals in reading, arithmetic, handwriting, language, and social studies. While teacher was working with individuals, others were doing their respective assignments. It took some time to determine just how much work to assign to each child since they were working on different grade levels.

11:15–11:30 Teacher checked with individuals on their work and got the group ready for lunch.

11:30–12:00 Lunch.

12:00–1:15   Work was finished. If a child had previously completed his assignments, there was an individual activity planned for him.

1:15–1:30   Day's work was evaluated; end-of-day preparations for homework and/or the next day's work were made.

The above sequence was planned and followed very closely, especially during the mornings. The afternoon program was handled more flexibly. A library period was available for one afternoon period of each week. Later in the year the helping teachers (art, music, physical education) visited the classroom for one instructional period every two weeks, on the average. These visits were scheduled from 12:00 M. to about 12:15 P.M. Because these children were not ready to receive instruction from many different individuals at the beginning of the school year, the helping teachers gave assistance then through conferencing with the classroom teacher.

---

[3] The nature of the opening exercises was left to the individual instructors; religious, patriotic, naturalistic, and other themes were used.

At the beginning of the year it was necessary to have individual reading and arithmetic instructional periods. Later, groups of two or three could be instructed in these areas, but some children were not ready for group work even by the end of the school year.

Instruction Based on Readiness Level

At the beginning of the year each child was placed on his instructional level in all areas. These levels were determined by standardized achievement tests, teacher-made inventory tests, teacher observations, and recommendations from former teachers. The coverage of material depended upon the progress of the individual child. New processes were not introduced until the earlier steps were mastered, as far as could be determined. In this way the child was relieved of as much pressure as possible in competing with others. He could begin to feel success on his own.

Remedial Teaching

These children had been exposed to much of the work in their regular classrooms, but because of the nature of their problems had not mastered the concepts involved or developed skills commensurate with their years in school. All the children were working below grade level; therefore all teaching was remedial in nature.

Reading. A reading text was chosen on the basis of the following criteria. Each book had to be (*a*) a book presenting new material on the child's instructional level; (*b*) a book based on sequential development of independent reading skills, with a teacher guide; (*c*) a book with a high interest level; (*d*) a book approved by the county board of education. It was difficult to find a book meeting all these criteria, especially on the child's interest level, as these children were usually several years retarded in reading.

In addition to following the manuals closely, the teacher needed to hold extra word recognition drills. Flash cards were used, individual word lists were kept by each child, and some phonetic games were used. The latter, however, did not prove successful, so were abandoned. The Lucille Schofield Phono-visual Charts were used successfully in presenting additional phonetic drill.

Other materials used were selected exercises from phonetic and the accompanying basal series workbooks. Each child did not have a workbook, and workbooks were not used as a daily means of instruction. On the average, each child received about fifteen to thirty minutes of reading instruction each day, but the exact amount varied from day to day.

Arithmetic. A basic series was used in the instruction of arithmetic. There was an advantage in this, as grouping could be done by allowing children to work with the same concept on various levels. Many concrete materials were used, such as beads, sticks, objects, number charts, and individual flash cards. Assignments were made on an individual basis. Drill work on an individual basis proved very successful for these children. Grouping for instruction in arithmetic became easier as time passed and was always more successful than group attempts to teach reading.

Handwriting. All the children but one were printing at the beginning of the school year. Even though the others had had cursive writing instruction, they were unable to use this as a means of expressing themselves. Their printing was also very poor. Therefore cursive writing was presented to the total group, letter by letter, with individual help as needed. After the alphabet was presented and they were writing in a legible hand, individual drill books were given to them. They used the drills from these books two or three times a week. After completion of a drill, an evaluation of progress was made by the pupil and teacher.

All language and writing activities were closely related to reading. In writing instruction periods the children wrote words taken from their reading vocabulary.

Social studies. No formal social studies program was introduced at the beginning of the year. For the most part all children lacked the independent reading abilities necessary to deal with the content areas. Their attention spans and interests were inadequate for this area of instruction. Also, their emotional instability would not permit any group activities at the beginning of the year. Later in the year a somewhat successful social studies activity was based on the study of maps. The children showed much interest in the study of maps; it was successful probably because it was so specific and pictorial. Some of the interests were developed around such activities as comparing the sizes of the continents and oceans, and finding the different mountain ranges, major rivers, largest lakes, and largest countries. The work periods had to be of short duration, and new material and concepts had to be introduced rapidly to hold attention.

Some of the more advanced children were later able to carry out an independently planned social studies program mainly consisting of simple research in the library.

Library. These children had access to the school library and had a library period once a week. Each child was helped in selecting books on his own reading level. These books were taken home to be read independently. To encourage the actual reading of these books, each child was expected to tell the class about the book he had chosen and read. It was necessary to have a routine for these book reviews. This proved very successful. The review period not only aroused interest in reading and reporting on one's own book but developed interest in books others had read. The plan was discontinued after the children showed interest in independent reading. It was reinstated, however, when they later showed signs of slackening in their interest in independent reading. They frequently drew pictures to illustrate parts of the books they liked best.

Another method that was used in motivating independent reading was for the teacher to read aloud the exciting parts in a book, then leave it up to the children to follow through.

Art. At the beginning of the school year a period was set

aside daily for some simple art activity. This practice had to be discontinued for a period of time because the children were such perfectionists that they became upset over their inability to complete the work or to be fully satisfied with results. Later in the year, as the children grew in attention span and motor skill, the art period was resumed with great success and satisfaction.

Common materials were used in the art activities—clay, paint, crayons, plasticine, papier-mâché, and paper. The following activities were most successfully employed: drawing, making animals, clay sculpturing of various figures, finger painting, paper sculpturing, weaving, and making presents.

Physical education. At the beginning of the school year a twenty- to twenty-five-minute physical education period was held at the end of each day. This proved to be unsuccessful, so the morning period was broken up with the physical activity. This too proved unsuccessful. These children seemed to have least emotional control during play. They would not, or could not, abide by the rules of even simple games. As a result, they were denied the privilege of participating whenever they did not abide by the standards set for them. This presented the problem of the teacher trying to supervise two groups, those trying to play the game and those eliminated from participation. The children were to have completed their daily work before being allowed to participate in play activities. As some did not complete their work on time, it was difficult to find a place for them to continue their work and still be under supervision.

On the basis of all these limitations, plus the fact that the children were in school a relatively short period of time each day, permission was received from the elementary level supervisor and the principal to discontinue daily physical education. One physical education period was given weekly, and every second week the helping physical education teacher worked with the group. This plan worked much better. The children learned to look forward to this period as a very special one, and their participation was on a higher level than it had previously been.

Control Techniques

Seating arrangement in the classroom. The children were seated at individual desks spaced as far as possible from each other. The most hyperactive children were placed on opposite sides of the room. Individual work booths were available but were used mainly on a voluntary basis; however, it was sometimes necessary to isolate a child who was having difficulty giving his attention to an assignment.

Walking in line. A chart was used to show the children who was to serve as line leader each day and to show the position of every other child in the line. Here again, those who had the most frequent personality clashes were separated in line.

Seating arrangement in cafeteria. A chart was posted in the room to show the seating arrangement for the children at the cafeteria table. The teacher ate at the table with the children during the entire year.

Leveling of consequences. For those who did not conform to the standards set for them the following control measures were used:

Withdrawal of privileges. The child was not allowed to participate in art activities, physical education, etc.

Extended school day. Unfinished work had to be completed before the child was allowed to go home. Parents were responsible for providing late transportation. The parents were notified by telephone whenever this step proved necessary.

Additional assignments. If a child had not used his free time wisely, he was not permitted free time, but had to continue with assigned work when he would otherwise have been free to do as he liked.

Time limits on assignments. Certain assignments were to be finished before the child was allowed to go to lunch. Adequate time was allowed for the work, but there were times when it was necessary for a child to eat a later lunch alone. This was a very effective corrective measure for the child who tended to waste his mornings.

Expediency. Expedient means and measures were more effective in correcting difficulties than delayed actions or threats or use of reasoning. It was sometimes necessary or desirable to firmly grasp a child by the shoulders and usher him into or out of activities, or give him a firm shake to "bring him to his senses" at a time he otherwise might have been out of control. Sometimes when the boys engaged in shin kicking at the table, the teacher applied the flat side of a yardstick or ruler to the shins of the offending boy or boys. When the boys understood that the teacher would give a controlled but firm swat in this manner for shin kicking, the activity was curbed in a matter of a few days. This method was arrived at, however, after all other methods failed. The importance of firmness and concrete action was again demonstrated.

The teacher made a great effort to administer all consequences of this type without any display of anger or exasperation. A friendly, helpful, but very firm relationship was maintained between teacher and pupils at all times.

APPENDIX C

DIRECTIONS

Please read over the following 26 items to be rated carefully. Rate each item on a 7-point scale, varying from an extreme negative degree at the left side of the continuum to the highest positive degree at the right. Think of the items as varying from a minus two (−2) through zero to a plus four (+4). Rate each child on each item in three ways (or from the standpoint of three settings):

1. With teacher in a controlled teaching situation (reading, arithmetic, other direct study activities)

2. Independent group activities (social-studies work groups; art, dramatics, organized physical education)

3. Teacher supervised but undirected activities (in free play, before and after school, free time in laboratory, etc.)

Try not to form a stereotype of the child. Rate him independently in each activity, for each item, as if he were a separate person. Let each rating be as independent of earlier or later ratings as possible. Try to think of *exact instances* for each rating rather than a general impression of the child.

PROPOSED RATING SCHEDULE FOR CLASSES OF EXCEPTIONAL CHILDREN, 1957–1958

1. Child's ability to stay with group activities and remain integral to them.

Impervious to group.	Hardly knows others are near.	Sees others but is indifferent to them.	Some response to others on occasion.	Takes others into consideration when he wants to.	Usually takes one or many others into regard.	Amenable to and ready to consider others at any time.

2. Child's ability to concentrate on and finish (follow through on) tasks given him.

Extremely flighty.	Flighty most of the time.	May or may not stay with task; not dependable.	Stays with task if supervised some.	Can stay with task on own to some extent.	Stays with tasks very well even against will.	Fine ability to concentrate and stick with requirements.

3. Child's ability to get along with peers.

Fights, or in conflict almost all the time.	In conflict often or most of the time.	Usually has too much conflict for his and others' welfare.	Conflicts coming under some control.	Makes an effort to control discord.	Gets along well nearly all the time; controls self well.	Little or no conflict at all; under good self-control.

4. Child's ability to comply with adult direction.

Defies adult at all turns.	Usually defiant and uncooperative.	Defiant and cooperative in random ways.	Some cooperation under some conditions.	Cooperative if he feels you mean business.	Usually cooperative and dependable.	Seldom or never uncooperative.

5. Child's ability to change to new activity under guidance or direction.

Won't change except under strong pressure.	Usually very reluctant to change; opposes it.	May or may not change; depends on "whim."	Changes with some effort; not willing.	Changes slowly but with some willingness.	Changes reasonably well and willingly in most cases.	Changes and complies well in all or nearly all instances.

6. Child's ability to meet and adjust to new situations.

Can't face or meet them.	Faces them with great difficulty.	Faces them only with specific adult help.	Meets and faces some new situations.	Can face and cope with several new situations.	Usually faces them well and readily.	Relishes new demands and copes readily and well.

7. Child's ability to act fairly and take his turn in appropriate settings.

Always wants to be first; demands it.	Rushes in to be first but can be stopped.	Will take turns if reminded in advance.	Goes first no more often than others.	Goes first only if asked or chosen.	Suggests taking turns; is cooperative and pliable usually.	Very mature; takes normal charge in fair-play terms; very reliable.

8. Child's pleasant and courteous attitude toward others.

Very rude and indifferent. Seems to do so with intention.	Usually rude and discourteous.	Rude or not in random, unpredictable ways and at unpredictable times.	Somewhat considerate of others.	Considerate if situation is clear to him.	Usually considerate; a dependable person in this way.	Very considerate, but not artificial or insincere.

9. Child's attitude toward those less capable, younger, or handicapped.

Very rude and indifferent; seems to intend it.	Usually rude and discourteous.	May or may not be rude; is unpredictable.	Considerate of others at times.	Considerate if he is in tune with the circumstances.	Usually considerate and dependable.	Very considerate; highly courteous without falseness.

10. Child's ability to share materials and equipment with others.

Wants all for himself always or nearly always.	Is hard to get him to share.	Shares only if cautioned in advance.	Shares in some ways or at some times.	Usually shares well.	Can be depended upon to share in nearly all instances.	Shares and takes responsibility for others readily and always.

11. Child's ability and willingness to help others.

Never helps others.	Helps others only under pressure.	Sometimes helps others.	Helps others if he likes them or what they are doing.	Helps others in many instances.	Usually readily helpful in attitude and action.	An excellent help to others; readily and cheerfully helpful always.

12. Child's care of school property.

Seems to destroy willfully and gleefully.	Usually destructive.	Destructive now and then, more by accident and carelessness.	Fairly careful in most ways.	Often careful and saving.	Quite careful and dependable.	Excellent carefulness; points out caution to others.

13. Child's ability to face own failures and shortcomings.

A very bad loser; always makes excuses.	Usually a bad loser and excuse maker.	Loses badly now and then; may face it well sometimes.	Usually a fairly good loser.	Faces losses and short-comings on most occasions.	A really good loser; faces shortcomings well.	Excellent loser but not indifferently; seeks correction of weaknesses.

14. Child's willingness to abide by general rules.

Breaks rules right and left.	Generally breaks rules.	Breaks rules and follows them in seemingly random ways.	Abides by rules if held up to him.	Can be depended upon in many ways to follow rules.	Generally follows rules well.	Excellent; very dependable and willing.

15. Child's ability to accept disagreement.

Can't accept disagreement ever.	Accepts disagreement badly.	May accept it on occasion.	Accepts disagreement if well presented.	Can accept it fairly well.	Accepts it readily.	Accepts it with openness; ready to improve or change.

16. Child's ability to accept constructive criticism.

Fights it bitterly.	Hates it but is passive.	Accepts it or not in inconsistent ways.	Accepts it under some circumstances.	Accepts it usually.	Takes it in good faith most of the time.	Accepts it readily; asks for it.

17. Child's concern for the welfare of the group as a whole.

Hostile to group and its welfare.	Often opposes and is hostile to group.	Unpredictably hostile and cooperative.	May accept group welfare, objectives at times.	Accepts group welfare on many occasions.	Takes group welfare as important.	Can be depended upon faithfully to do this.

18. Child's willingness to credit other members of group.

Hostile to credit given others.	Opposes credit to others.	May give credit or not.	Gives credit to others in some ways.	Willing to give credit to others.	Gives others credit most of the time.	Very fair and reliable this way.

19. Demonstrates self-confidence.

Utterly lacking.	Lacks it most of the time.	Shows it now and then; lacks it at random times.	Shows self-confidence in some ways.	Shows self-confidence in many ways.	Comfortably confident in most ways.	Very confident without bravado in all situations.

20. Child's acceptance of his share of responsibility.

Utterly irresponsible.	Very lacking in responsibility.	Shows it or not in unpredictable ways.	Accepts it in some ways.	Accepts it in many ways.	Very accepting.	A model of acceptance.

309

PROPOSED RATING SCHEDULE FOR CLASSES OF EXCEPTIONAL CHILDREN, 1957–1958 (*Continued*)

21. Child's refraining from violent temper outbursts.

In a temper all the time it seems.	Frequent temper displays.	Shows temper in unpredictable situations.	Controls temper on some occasions.	Usually hard to provoke.	Very fine self-control.	Never see temper; solves problems effectively.

22. Child's restraint from show-off behavior.

Shows off all the time.	A bit show-off usually.	Shows off and is restrained in random ways.	Avoids show-off behavior on some occasions.	Usually controls self pretty well.	Shows good control most of the time.	Always under healthy self-control.

23. Child's display of anxiety/apprehension.

Under constant anxiety.	Shows anxiety much of the time.	Is anxious now and then.	No anxiety on some occasions.	Anxious on a few occasions.	Rarely shows anxiety or apprehension.	No anxiety noticed at all.

24. Child's dependency on teacher for help/attention.

Always seeks help or attention.	Often seeks one or both.	Seeks both in random ways.	Able to get along on own on some occasions.	Gets along on own much of the time.	Very resourceful, usually on own.	Very independent and resourceful.

25. Child's popularity with other children.

Very unpopular.	Unpopular in most respects.	Popular—unpopular in hard-to-tell ways.	Popular with others in limited ways.	Fairly popular with others.	Very popular.	Probably most liked and popular.

26. Child's ascendency in meeting others, contacting others.

Most retiring and shy.	Usually retiring and shy.	Some ascendence in odd ways and times.	Somewhat ascendent at times.	Fairly ascendent and resourceful.	Very ascendent.	Most able and responsible here.

311

REFERENCES

1. Axline, Virginia: *Play Therapy,* Houghton Mifflin, Boston, 1947.

2. Beilin, Harry: "Teachers' and Children's Attitudes toward the Behavioral Problems of Children: A Reappraisal," *Child Develop.,* vol. 30, pp. 9–25, 1959.

3. Bettelheim, Bruno: *Love Is Not Enough,* Free Press, New York, 1949.

4. Cruickshank, William M., Frances A. Bentzen, Frederick H. Ratzeburg, and Marion T. Tannhauser: *Teaching Methodology for Brain Injured and Hyperactive Children,* Syracuse University Press, Syracuse, N.Y., 1961.

5. D'Evelyn, Katherine: *Meeting Children's Emotional Needs,* Prentice-Hall, Englewood Cliffs, N.J., 1957.

6. Devereux, George: *Therapeutic Education,* Harper, New York, 1956.

7. Freud, Anna: *Introduction to the Technic of Child Analysis,* Nervous and Mental Diseases Publishing, Washington, 1928.

8. Freud, Anna: *The Ego and the Mechanisms of Defense,* Hogarth, London, 1937.

9. Galanter, Eugene: *Automatic Teaching: The State of the Art,* Wiley, New York, 1959.

10. Goldberg, I.: "Use of Remedial Tutoring as a Method of Psychotherapy for Schizophrenic Children with Reading Disabilities," *Quart. J. Child Behavior,* vol. 4, pp. 273–280, 1952.

11. Haring, Norris G., George Stern, and William M. Cruickshank: *Attitudes of Educators toward Exceptional Children,* Syracuse University Press, Syracuse, N.Y., 1958.

12. Hay, L.: "A New School Channel for Helping the Troubled Child," *Am. J. Orthopsychiat.,* vol. 23, pp. 676–690, 1953.

13. Hayden, E. J.: "The Education of Detroit's Socially Maladjusted Children," *Action,* vol. 9, pp. 5–7, 1956.

14. Heil, Louis W., Marion Powell, and Irwin Feifer: *Characteristics of Teacher Behavior Related to the Achievement of Children in Several Elementary Grades,* Brooklyn College, Office of Testing and Research, Brooklyn, N.Y., 1960.

15. Hirshberg, J. Cotter: "The Role of Education in the Treatment of Emotionally Disturbed Children through Planned Ego Development," *Am. J. Orthopsychiat.,* vol. 23, pp. 684–690, 1953.

16. Hymes, James L., Jr.: *Teacher Listen: The Children Speak,* State Charities Aid Association, New York, 1949.

17. Hymes, James L., Jr.: *Behavior and Misbehavior,* Prentice-Hall, Englewood Cliffs, N.J., 1955.

18. Jacobson, Stanley, and Christopher Faegre: "Neutralization: A Tool for the Teacher of Disturbed Children," *Exceptional Children,* vol. 25, pp. 243–246, 1959.

19. Lippman, Hyman S.: *Treatment of the Child in Emotional Conflict,* McGraw-Hill, New York, 1956.

20. Medley, Donald M., and Harold E. Mitzel: "Some Behavioral Correlates of Teacher Effectiveness," *J. Educational Psychol.,* vol. 50, pp. 239–246, 1959.

21. Moustakas, Clark E.: *Children in Play Therapy,* McGraw-Hill, New York, 1953.

22. Moustakas, Clark E.: *The Teacher and the Child,* McGraw-Hill, New York, 1956.

23. Nass, Martin L.: "Characteristics of a Psychotherapeutically Oriented Group for Beginning Teachers," *Mental Hyg.,* vol. 43, pp. 562–567, 1959.

24. Neill, A. S.: *Summerhill: A Radical Approach to Child Rearing,* Hart Publishing, New York, 1960.

25. Newman, Ruth G.: "The Acting-out Boy," *Exceptional Children,* vol. 22, pp. 186–190, 204–216, 1956.

26. Pearson, Gerald H. J.: *Emotional Disorders of Children,* Norton, New York, 1949.

27. Pearson, Gerald H. J.: *Psychoanalysis and the Education of the Child,* Norton, New York, 1954.

28. Phillips, E. Lakin: "Cultural vs Intropsychic Factors in Childhood Behavior Problems," *J. Clin. Psychol.,* vol. 12, pp. 400–401, 1956.

29. Phillips, E. Lakin: *Psychotherapy: A Modern Theory and Practice,* Prentice-Hall, Englewood Cliffs, N.J., 1956.

30. Phillips, E. Lakin: "Contributions to a Learning Theory Account of Childhood Autism," *J. Psychol.,* vol. 43, pp. 117–124, 1957.

31. Phillips, E. Lakin: "Some Features of Child Guidance Clinic Practice in the U.S.A.," *J. Clin. Psychol.,* vol. 13, pp. 42–44, 1957.

32. Phillips, E. Lakin: "The Problem of Motivation: Some Neglected Aspects," *J. Rehabil.*, vol. 23, pp. 10–12, 1957.

33. Phillips, E. Lakin: "The Use of the Teacher as Adjunct Therapist in Child Guidance," *Psychiatry*, vol. 20, pp. 407–410, 1957.

34. Phillips, E. Lakin: "Experimental Results from Special Teaching Techniques for Emotionally Disturbed Children," paper presented to American Association for the Advancement of Science, Washington, Dec. 26, 1958.

35. Phillips, E. Lakin: "Newer Approaches," in Daniel Brower and L. E. Abt. (eds.), *Progress in Clinical Psychology*, vol. III, Grune and Stratton, New York, 1958, chap. 18.

36. Phillips, E. Lakin: "The Role of Structure in Psychotherapy," *Am. Psychologist*, vol. 14, p. 389, 1959. (Abstract.)

37. Phillips, E. Lakin: "Parent-Child Psychotherapy: A Follow-up Study Comparing Two Techniques," *J. Psychol.*, vol. 49, pp. 195–202, 1960.

38. Phillips, E. Lakin, and Norris G. Haring: "Results from Special Techniques for Teaching Emotionally Disturbed Children," *Exceptional Children*, vol. 26, pp. 64–67, 1959.

39. Phillips, E. Lakin, and M. H. S. Johnston: "Theory and Development of Parent-Child, Short-term Psychotherapy." *Psychiatry*, Vol. 17, pp. 267–275, 1954.

40. Phillips, E. Lakin, Daniel N. Wiener, and Norris G. Haring: *Discipline, Achievement and Mental Health*, Prentice-Hall, Englewood Cliffs, N.J., 1960.

41. Prescott, Daniel A.: *Emotions and the Educative Process*, American Council on Education, Washington, 1938.

42. Prescott, Daniel A.: *The Child in the Educative Process*, McGraw-Hill, New York, 1957.

43. Redl, Fritz, and William W. Wattenberg: *Mental Hygene in Teaching*, Harcourt, Brace, New York, 1951.

44. Redl, Fritz, and David Wineman: *Children Who Hate*, Free Press, New York, 1951.

45. Redl, Fritz, and David Wineman: *Controls from Within*, Free Press, New York, 1952.

46. Reid, Joseph H., and Helen R. Gagan: *Residential Treatment of Emotionally Disturbed Children*, Child Welfare League of America, New York, 1952.

47. Rogers, Carl R.: *Counseling and Psychotherapy*, Houghton Mifflin, Boston, 1942.

48. Rogers, Carl R.: *Client-centered Therapy*, Houghton Mifflin, Boston, 1951.

49. Sarason, Seymour B.: *Psychological Problems in Mental Deficiency*, Harper, New York, 1959.

50. Slavson, Samuel R.: *Re-educating the Delinquent through Group and Community Participation,* Harper, New York, 1954.

51. Strauss, Alfred A., and Laura E. Lehtinen: *Psychopathology and Education of the Brain-injured Child,* Grune and Stratton, New York, 1947.

INDEX